Violence in Buddhism

Violence in Buddhism

I.N. Singh

PRASHANT PUBLISHING HOUSE
DELHI-110094

Published by :
Prashant Publishing House
C-34, 28 Foota Road, Gali-3,
West Karwal Nagar, Delhi-110094
Phone : 011-22963970, Mob. : 9810396373
e-mail.: prashantpublishinghouse@gmail.com

Violence in Buddhism

First Published 2017

ISBN 978-93-80565-79-8

PRINTED IN INDIA
Published by Mr. R.K. Jha M/s Prashant Publishing House and Published at H.S. Offset House Press, Delhi.

Contents

	Preface	*(vii)*
1.	Buddhism and Violence	1
2.	Buddhism Violence in Myanmar	40
3.	Violence of Buddhism in Sri Lanka	81
4.	The Darker Side of Buddhism	108
5.	Buddhist Extremism and the Hypocrisy of 'Religious and Violence'	115
6.	Buddhist, Beliefs and Violence	157
7.	Myanmar's Buddhist and Terrorism	164
8.	Buddhist Violence in Burma	180
9.	Reasons for Buddhism's Attitude to Violence	190
10.	Philosophy of Buddhist	210
11.	Bhutanese Buddhist	257
	Bibliography	285
	Index	287

Preface

Violence in Buddhism refers to acts of violence and aggression committed by Buddhists with religious, political, and socio-cultural motivations. Buddhism is generally seen as among the religious traditions least associated with violence, but in the history of Buddhism there have been acts of violence directed, fomented or inspired by Buddhists.

A widespread stereotype in Western popular culture holds that Islam is a religion of violence while Buddhism is a religion of peace. Like most stereotypes, these claims belie the complex reality of the nature of human beings and religion. We noted in a previous column the problems with viewing Islam as either an inherently peaceful or inherently violent religion.

Now we will look at the issue from a different perspective — pacifist Buddhism could also be described as a violent religion. Buddhism is widely regarded in the West as a nonviolent faith, and there is ample justification for such a view. But throughout its history, Buddhism has also had its violent aspects, and scholars are now examining the history of violent Buddhism.

India was the homeland of Buddhism, and its most famous Buddhist king, Ashoka, is renowned for his conversion to Buddhism and renunciation of military conquest. Yet his edicts include notices that warfare, while inferior to "conquest by Dharma" (conversion), is still permitted, though it must be undertaken with restraint. In other words, he is describing a nascent Buddhist just-war theory.

Buddhism is just one of a number of causes and effects in current complex conflicts. The point is not to argue whether Buddhists are benevolent or violent people, but rather to accept that Buddhists are people, and therefore they share the same human spectrum of emotions, including depression, struggle, anger and violence. In this way we can acknowledge that however revered a tradition or culture may be, it is likely to have a darker side. Yet, if we want to explain that darker side, platitudes about human nature are not enough. Rather, we need to ask questions about specific configurations of Buddhist institutions with the state, minorities, and others, particularly at times of stress and change.

In Burma/Myanmar, Thailand, Tibet, and Sri Lanka the ways different lines of tension are configured will differ, given the various political and economic situations of these societies. One of the tasks for scholars is to analyze how Buddhists reconcile their doctrinal teachings of karma and non-violence with the sometimes active involvement of monks in acts of violence, when conflict involves real-world interests. All the matter is just compiled and edited in nature. Taken from the various sources which are in public domain.

This book will definitely prove to be a boon to teachers, students and research scholars.

—*Editor*

1

Buddhism and Violence

Violence in Buddhism implies exhibitions of severity and ill will deliberated by Buddhists with religious, political, and socio-social motivations. Buddhism is all around seen as among the religious traditions smallest associated with severity, however in the verifiable background of Buddhism there have been exhibitions of violence facilitated, actuated or excited by Buddhists.

LESSONS, EXPLANATIONS, AND PRACTICES

Buddhism wraps a grouping of traditions, feelings and significant practices, all things considered, in perspective of lessons attributed to Gautama Buddha. Ahimsa, a term implying 'not to damage', is a fundamental incredibleness in Buddhism.

Nirvana is the soonest and most consistent term used to portray the target of the Buddhist way and an authoritative devastation ofdukkha. Horrible exercises and insights, exercises which hurt and ruin others and contemplations which think about the same, frustrate supernatural advancement and the self-triumph which prompts the target of nearness and they are customarily regarded unskilled (akusala) and can't expeditious the goal of Nirvana. Buddha reproached butchering or harming living animals and upheld reflection or consideration (satipatthana) as right action (or conduct), along these lines "the rightness or deluding nature of a movement bases on whether the action itself would accomplish naughtiness to self and/or others". In the Ambalatthika-Rahulovada Sutta, the Buddha says toRahula:

In case you, Rahula, are jealous of doing a deed with the body, you should consider the deed with the body, therefore: That deed which I am rapacious of doing with the body is a deed of the body that may conduce to the naughtiness of self and that may conduce to the harm of others and that may conduce to the devilishness of both; this deed of body is awkward (akusala), its yield is anguish, its result is anguish.

The right action or right conduct (*samyak-karmânta / sammâ-kammanta*) is the fourth aspect of the Noble Eightfold Path and it said that the practitioner should train oneself to be morally upright in one's activities, not acting in ways that would be corrupt or bring harm to oneself or to others. In the Chinese and Pali Canon, it is explained as:

And what is right action? Abstaining from taking life, from stealing, and from illicit sex [or sexual misconduct]. This is called right action. — *Saccavibhanga Sutta*

For the lay follower, the *Cunda Kammaraputta Sutta* elaborates:

And how is one made pure in three ways by bodily action? There is the case where a certain person, abandoning the taking of life, abstains from the taking of life. He dwells with his... knife laid down, scrupulous, merciful, compassionate for the welfare of all living beings. Abandoning the taking of what is not given, he abstains from taking what is not given. He does not take, in the manner of a thief, things in a village or a wilderness that belong to others and have not been given by them.

Sarambha can be translated as "accompanied by violence." As the mind filled with lobha, dosa and moha (lust, hatred and delusion) is led to actions which are akusala. Indulging in violence is a form of self-harming. The eschewed of violence in society is recognized in buddhism as a prerequisite for the spiritual progress of society's members, because violence brings pain to beings with similar feelings to oneself. The Buddha is quoted in the Dhammapada as saying, "All are afraid of the stick, all hold their lives dear. Putting oneself in another's place, one should not beat or kill others". Metta (loving kindness), the development of mindstates of limitless good-will for all beings, and karuna, compassion that arises when you see someone suffering of the human being, are attitudes said to be excellent or sublime because they are the right or ideal way of conduct towards living beings (sattesu samma patipatti). The Sutta Nipata says "'As I am, so are these. As are these, so am I.' Drawing the parallel to yourself, neither kill nor get others to kill."

In Buddhism, to take refuge in the Dharma - one of the Three Jewels - one should not harm other sentient beings. The Nirvana Sutra states, "By taking refuge in the precious Dharma, One's minds should be free from hurting or harming others". One of the Five Precepts of Buddhist ethics or úîla states, "I undertake the training rule to abstain from killing." The Buddha reportedly stated, "Victory breeds hatred. The defeated live in pain. Happily the peaceful live giving up victory and defeat." These elements are used to indicate Buddhism is pacifistic and all violence done by Buddhists, even monks, is likely due to economic or political reasons.

The teaching of right speech (*samyag-vâc / sammâ-vâcâ*) in the Noble Eightfold Path, condemn all speech that is in any way harmful (malicious and harsh speech) and divisive, encouraging to speak in thoughtful and helpful ways. The Pali Canon explained:

And what is right speech? Abstaining from lying, from divisive speech, from abusive speech, and from idle chatter: This is called right speech.

Michael Jerryson, Associate Professor of Religious Studies at Ohio's Youngstown State University and co-editor of the book *Buddhist Warfare*, said that "Buddhism differs in that the act of killing is less the focus than the 'intention' behind the killing" and that all peoples have a "penchant for violence" and Buddhists are no different.

Gananath Obeyesekere, Emeritus Professor of Anthropology at Princeton University, said that "in the Buddhist doctrinal tradition... there is little evidence of intolerance, no justification for violence, no conception even of 'just wars' or 'holy wars.' ... one can make an assertion that Buddhist doctrine is impossible to reconcile logically with an ideology of violence and intolerance"

HISTORY OF BUDDHISM

The History of Buddhism spans from the 6th century BC to the present, starting with the birth of the Buddha Siddhartha Gautama. This makes it one of the oldest religions practised today. Throughout this period, the religion evolved as it encountered various countries and cultures, adding to its original Indian foundation Hellenistic as well as Central Asian, East Asian and Southeast Asian cultural elements. In the process, its geographical extent became considerable so as to affect at one time or another most of the Asian continent. The history of Buddhism is also characterized by the development of numerous movements and schisms, foremost among them the Theravada, Mahayana and Vajrayana traditions, punctuated by contrasting periods of expansion and retreat.

Life of the Buddha

According to the Buddhist tradition, the historical Buddha Siddhartha Gautama was born to the Shakya clan, at the beginning of the Magadha period (546-324 BC), in the plains of Lumbini, Southern Nepal. He is also known as the Shakyamuni (literally "The sage of the Shakya clan").

After an early life of luxury under the protection of his father, Suddhodana, the ruler of Kapilavastu (later to be incorporated into the state of Magadha), Siddhartha entered into contact with the realities of the world and concluded that real life was about inescapable suffering and sorrow. Siddhartha renounced his meaningless life of luxury to become an ascetic. He ultimately decided that asceticism was also meaningless and instead chose a middle way, a path of moderation away from the extremes of self-indulgence and self-mortification.

Under a fig tree, now known as the Bodhi tree, he vowed never to leave the position until he found Truth. At the age of 35, he attained Enlightenment. He was then known as Gautama Buddha, or simply "The Buddha", which means "the enlightened one".

For the remaining 45 years of his life, he travelled the Gangetic Plain of central India (region of the Ganges/Ganga river and its tributaries), teaching his doctrine and discipline to an extremely diverse range of people. The Buddha's reluctance to name a successor or to formalise his doctrine led to the emergence of many movements during the next 400 years: first the schools of Nikaya Buddhism, of which only Theravada remains today and then the formation of Mahayana, a pan-Buddhist movement based on the acceptance of new scriptures.

Early Buddhism

Before the royal sponsorship of Ashoka the Great in the 3rd century BC, Buddhism seems to have remained a relatively minor phenomenon and the historicity of its formative events is poorly established. Two formative councils are supposed to have taken place, although our knowledge of them is based on much later accounts. The councils tend to explain the formalization of the Buddhist doctrine and the various subsequent schisms inside the Buddhist movement.

Asian Expansion

In the areas east of the Indian subcontinent (today's Burma), Indian culture strongly influenced the Mons. The Mons are said to have been converted to Buddhism around 200 BC under the proselytizing of the Indian king Ashoka, before the fission between Mahayana and Hinayana Buddhism. Early Mon Buddhist temples, such as Peikthano in central Burma, have been dated between the 1st and the 5th century AD.

The Buddhist art of the Mons was especially influenced by the Indian art of the Gupta and post-Gupta periods and their mannerist style spread widely in South-East Asia following the expansion of the Mon kingdom between the 5th and 8th centuries. The Theravada faith expanded in the northern parts of Southeast Asia under Mon influence, until it was progressively displaced by Mahayana Buddhism from around the 6th century AD.

Sri Lanka was allegedly proselytized by Ashoka's son Mahinda and six companions during the 2nd century BC. They converted the king Devanampiya Tissa and many of the nobility. This is when the Mahavihara monastery, a centre of Sinhalese orthodoxy, was built. The Pali Canon was put in writing in Sri Lanka during the reign of king Vittagamani (r. 29-17 BC) and the Theravada tradition flourished there, harbouring some great commentators such as Buddhaghosa (4th-5th century). Although Mahayana Buddhism gained some influence at that time, Theravada ultimately prevailed and Sri Lanka turned out to be the last stronghold of Theravada Buddhism, from where it would expand again to South-East Asia from the 11th century.

There is also a legend, not directly validated by the edicts, that Ashoka sent a missionary to the north, through the Himalayas, to Khotan in the Tarim Basin, then the land of the Tocharians, speakers of an Indo-European language.

In the areas west of the Indian subcontinent, neighbouring Greek kingdoms had been in place in Bactria (today's northern Afghanistan) since the time of the conquests of Alexander the Great around 326 BC: first the Seleucids from around 323 BC, then the Greco-Bactrian kingdom from around 250 BC.

The Greco-Bactrian king Demetrius I invaded India in 180 BC as far as Pataliputra, establishing an Indo-Greek kingdom that was to last in various part of northern India until the end of the 1st century BC. Buddhism flourished under the Indo-Greek kings and it has been suggested that their invasion of India was intended to show their support for the Mauryan empire and to protect the Buddhist faith from the alleged religious persecutions of the Sungas (185-73 BC), accounts which are disputed by historians.

One of the most famous Indo-Greek kings is Menander (reigned c. 160-135 BC). He apparently converted to Buddhism and is presented in the Mahayana tradition as one of the great benefactors of the faith, on a par with king Ashoka or the later Kushan king Kanishka. Menander's coins bear the mention "Saviour king" in Greek and sometimes designs of the eight-spoked wheel. Direct cultural exchange is also suggested by the dialogue of the Milinda Panha between Menander and the monk Nagasena around 160 BC. Upon his death, the honour of sharing his remains was claimed by the cities under his rule and they were enshrined in stupas, in a parallel with the historic Buddha (Plutarch, Praec. reip. ger. 28, 6). Several of Menander's Indo-Greek successors inscribed the mention "Follower of the Dharma" in the Kharoshthi script on their coins and depicted themselves or their divinities forming the vitarka mudra.

The interaction between Greek and Buddhist cultures may have had some influence on the evolution of Mahayana, as the faith developed its sophisticated philosophical approach and a man-god treatment of the Buddha somewhat reminiscent of Hellenic gods. It is also around that time that the first anthropomorphic representations of the Buddha are found, often in realistic Greco-Buddhist style: "One might regard the classical influence as including the general idea of representing a man-god in this purely human form, which was of course well familiar in the West and it is very likely that the example of westerner's treatment of their gods was indeed an important factor in the innovation" (Boardman, "The Diffusion of Classical Art in Antiquity").

Rise of Mahayana (1st c.BC-2nd c.AD)

The rise of Mahayana Buddhism from the 1st century BC was accompanied by complex political changes in northwestern India. The Indo-Greek kingdoms were gradually overwhelmed and their culture assimilated by the Indo-Scythians and then the Yuezhi, who founded the Kushan Empire from around 12 BC.

The Kushans were supportive of Buddhism and a fourth Buddhist council was convened by the Kushan emperor Kanishka, around 100 AD at Jalandhar or in Kashmir and is usually associated with the formal rise of Mahayana Buddhism and its secession from Theravada Buddhism. Theravada Buddhism does not recognize the authenticity of this council and it is sometimes called the "council of heretical monks".

It is said that Kanishka gathered 500 bhikkhus in Kashmir, headed by Vasumitra, to edit the Tripitaka and make references and remarks. Allegedly, during the council there were all together three hundred thousand verses and over nine million statements compiled and it took twelve years to complete. This council did not rely on the original Pali canon (the Tipitaka). Instead, a set of new scriptures was approved, as well as fundamental principles of Mahayana doctrine. The new scriptures, usually in the Gandhari vernacular and the Kharosthi script, were rewritten in the classical language of Sanskrit, to many scholars a turning point in the propagation of Buddhist thought.

The new form of Buddhism was characterized by an almost God-like treatment of the Buddha, by the idea that all beings have a Buddha-nature and should aspire to Buddhahood and by a syncretism due to the various cultural influences within northwestern India and the Kushan Empire.

Mahayana Expansion (1st c.AD-10th c.AD)

From that point on and in the space of a few centuries, Mahayana was to flourish and spread in the East from India to South-East Asia and towards the north to Central Asia, China, Korea and finally to Japan in 538 AD.

India

After the end of the Kushans, Buddhism flourished in India during the dynasty of the Guptas (4th-6th century). Mahayana centres of learning were established, especially at Nalanda in northeastern India, which was to become the largest and most influential Buddhist university for many centuries, with famous teachers such as Nagarjuna. The Gupta style of Buddhist art became very influential from South-East Asia to China as the faith was spreading there.

Indian Buddhism had weakened in the 6th century following the White Hun invasions and Mihirkulas persecution.

Xuanzang reports in his travels across India during the 7th century of Buddhism being popular in Andhra, Dhanyakataka and Dravida which today roughly correspond to the modern day Indian states of Andhra Pradesh and Tamil Nadu. While reporting many deserted stupas in the area around modern day Nepal and the persecution of Buddhists by Sanka in the Kingdom of Gouda. (In modern day West Bengal.) Xuanzang compliments the patronage of Harshavardana during the same period. After Harshavardanas kingdom, the rise of many small kingdoms that lead to the rise of the Rajputs across the gangetic plains and marked the end of Buddhist ruling clans along with a sharp decline in royal patronage until a revival under the Pala Empire in the Bengal region. Here Mahayana Buddhism flourished and spread to Bhutan and Sikkim between the 8th and the 12th century before the Palas collapsed under the assault of the Hindu Sena dynasty. The Palas created many temples and a distinctive school of Buddhist art. Xuanzang noted in his travels that in various regions Buddhism was giving way to Jainism and Hinduism. By the 10th century Buddhism had experienced a sharp decline beyond the Pala realms in Bengal under a resurgent Hinduism and the incorporation in Vaishnavite Hinduism of Buddha as the 9th incarnation of Vishnu.

A milestone in the decline of Indian Buddhism in the North occurred in 1193 when Turkic Islamic raiders under Muhammad Khilji burnt Nalanda. By the end of the 12th century, following the Islamic conquest of the Buddhist strongholds in Bihar and the loss of political support coupled with social and caste pressures, the practice of Buddhism retreated to the Himalayan foothills in the North and Sri Lanka in the south. Additionally, the influence of Buddhism also waned due to Hinduism's revival movements such as Advaita, the rise of the bhakti movement and the missionary work of Sufis.

Central and Northern Asia

Central Asia: Central Asia had been influenced by Buddhism probably almost since the time of the Buddha. According to a legend preserved in Pali, the language of the Theravada canon, two merchant brothers from Bacteria, named Tapassu and Bhallika, visited the Buddha and became his disciples. They then returned to Bacteria and built temples to the Buddha (Foltz).

Central Asia long played the role of a meeting place between China, India and Persia. During the 2nd century BC, the expansion of the Former Han to the west brought them into contact with the Hellenistic civilizations of Asia, especially the Greco-Bactrian Kingdoms. Thereafter, the expansion of Buddhism to the north led to the formation of Buddhist communities and even Buddhist kingdoms in the oases of Central Asia. Some Silk Road cities consisted almost entirely of Buddhist stupas and monasteries and it seems that one of their main objectives was to welcome and service travellers between east and west.

The Hinayana traditions first spread among the Turkic tribes before combining with the Mahayana forms during the 2nd and 3rd centuries BC to cover modern-day Pakistan, Kashmir, Afghanistan, eastern and coastal Iran, Uzbekistan, Turkmenistan and Tajikistan. These were the ancient states of Gandhara, Bacteria, Parthia and Sogdia from where it spread to China. Among the first of these Turkic tribes to adopt Buddhism was the Turki-Shahi who adopted Buddhism as early as the 3rd century BC. It was not, however, the exclusive faith of this region. There were also Zoroastrians, Hindus, Nestorian Christians, Jews, Manichaeans and followers of shamanism, Tengrism and other indigenous, nonorganized systems of belief.

Various Nikaya schools persisted in Central Asia and China until around the 7th century AD. Mahayana started to become dominant during the period, but since the faith had not developed a Nikaya approach, Sarvastivadin and Dharmaguptakas remained the Vinayas of choice in Central Asian monasteries. Various Buddhism kingdoms rose and prospered in both the Central Asian region and downwards into the Indian sub-continent such as Kushan Empire prior to the White Hun invasion in the 5th century where under the King Mihirkula they were heavily persecuted.

Buddhism in Central Asia started to decline with the expansion of Islam and the destruction of many stupas in war from the 7th century. The Muslims accorded them the status of dhimmis as "people of the Book", such as Christianity or Judaism and Al-Biruni wrote of Buddha as prophet "burxan".

Buddhism saw a surge during the reign of Mongols following the invasion of Genghis Khan and the establishment of the II Khanate and the Chagatai Khanate who brought their Buddhist influence with them during the 13th century, however within a 100 years the Mongols would convert to Islam and spread Islam across all the regions across central Asia.

Parthia: Buddhism expanded westward into Arsacid Parthia, at least to the area of Merv, in ancient Margiana, today's territory of Turkmenistan. Soviet archeological teams have excavated in

Giaur Kala, near Merv, a Buddhist chapel, a gigantic Buddha statue, as well as a monastery. Parthians were directly involved in the propagation of Buddhism: An Shigao (c. 148 AD), a Parthian prince, went to China and is the first known translator of Buddhist scriptures into Chinese.

Tarim Basin: The eastern part of central Asia (Chinese Turkestan, Tarim Basin, Xinjiang) has revealed extremely rich Buddhist works of art (wall paintings and reliefs in numerous caves, portable paintings on canvas, sculpture, ritual objects), displaying multiple influences from Indian and Hellenistic cultures. Serindian art is highly reminiscent of the Gandharan style and scriptures in the Gandhari script Kharosthi have been found.

Central Asians seem to have played a key role in the transmission of Buddhism to the East. The first translators of Buddhists scriptures into Chinese were either Parthian (Ch: Anxi) like An Shigao (c. 148 AD) or An Hsuan, Kushan of Yuezhi ethnicity like Lokaksema (c. 178 AD), Zhi Qian and Zhi Yao, or Sogdians like Kang Sengkai. Thirty-seven early translators of Buddhist texts are known and the majority of them have been identified as Central Asians.

Central Asian and East Asian Buddhist monks appear to have maintained strong exchanges until around the 10th century, as shown by frescoes from the Tarim Basin.

These influences were rapidly absorbed however by the vigorous Chinese culture and a strongly Chinese particularism develops from that point.

China

Buddhism probably arrived in China around the 1st century AD from Central Asia (although there are some traditions about a monk visiting China during Ashoka's reign) and through to the 8th century it became an extremely active centre of Buddhism.

The year 67 AD saw Buddhism's official introduction to China with the coming of the two monks Moton and Chufarlan. In 68 AD, under imperial patronage, they established the White Horse Temple, which still exists today, close to the imperial capital at Luoyang. By the end of the second century, a prosperous community had been settled at Pengcheng (modern Xuzhou, Jiangsu).

The first known Mahayana scriptural texts are translations made into Chinese by the Kushan monk Lokaksema in Luoyang, between 178 and 189 AD. Some of the earliest known Buddhist artifacts found in China are small statues on "money trees", dated circa 200 AD, in typical Gandharan style (drawing): "That the imported images accompanying the newly arrived doctrine came from Gandhara is strongly suggested by such early Gandhara characteristics on this "money tree" Buddha as the high ushnisha, vertical arrangement of the hair, moustache, symmetrically looped robe and parallel incisions for the folds of the arms." ("Crossroads of Asia" p209)

Buddhism flourished during the beginning of the Tang Dynasty (618-907). The dynasty was initially characterized by a strong openness to foreign influences and renewed exchanges with Indian culture due to the numerous travels of Chinese Buddhist monks to India from the 4th to the 11th century. The Tang capital of Chang'an (today's Xi'an) became an important centre for Buddhist thought. From there Buddhism spread to Korea and Japanese embassies of Kentoshi helped gain footholds in Japan.

However foreign influences came to be negatively perceived towards the end of the Tang Dynasty. In the year 845, the Tang emperor Wu-Tsung outlawed all "foreign" religions (including Christian Nestorianism, Zoroastrianism and Buddhism) in order to support the indigenous Taoism. Throughout his territory, he confiscated Buddhist possessions, destroyed monasteries and temples and executed Buddhist monks, ending Buddhism's cultural and intellectual dominance.

Pure Land and Chan Buddhism, however, continued to prosper for some centuries, the latter giving rise to Japanese Zen. In China, Chan flourished particularly under the Song dynasty (1127-1279), when its monasteries were great centres of culture and learning.

Today, China boasts one of the richest collections of Buddhist arts and heritages in the world. UNESCO World Heritage Sites such as the Mogao Caves near Dunhuang in Gansu province, the

Longmen Grottoes near Luoyang in Henan province, the Yungang Grottoes near Datong in Shanxi province and the Dazu Rock Carvings near Chongqing are among the most important and renowned Buddhist sculptural sites. The Leshan Giant Buddha, carved out of a hillside in the 8th century during Tang Dynasty and looking down on the confluence of three rivers, is still the largest stone Buddha statue in the world.

Korea

Buddhism was introduced around 372 AD, when Chinese ambassadors visited the Korean kingdom of Goguryeo, bringing scriptures and images. Buddhism prospered in Korea and in particular Seon (Zen) Buddhism from the 7th century onward. However, with the beginning of the Confucean Yi Dynasty of the Joseon period in 1392, Buddhism was strongly discriminated against until it was almost completely eradicated, except for a remaining Seon movement.

Japan

Japan discovered Buddhism in the 6th century when Korean monks travelled to the islands together with numerous scriptures and works of art. The Buddhist religion was adopted by the state in the following century.

Being geographically at the end of the Silk Road, Japan was able to preserve many aspects of Buddhism at the very time it was disappearing in India and being suppressed in Central Asia and China.

From 710 AD numerous temples and monasteries were built in the capital city of Nara, such as the five-story pagoda and Golden Hall of the Horyuji, or the Kofuku-ji temple. Countless paintings and sculptures were made, often under governmental sponsorship. The creation of Japanese Buddhist art was especially rich between the 8th and 13th century during the periods of Nara, Heian and Kamakura.

From the 12th and 13th, a further development was Zen art, following the introduction of the faith by Dogen and Eisai upon their return from China. Zen art is mainly characterized by original paintings (such as sumi-e and the Enso) and poetry (especially haikus), striving to express the true essence of the world through impressionistic and unadorned "non-dualistic" representations. The search for enlightenment "in the moment" also led to the development of other important derivative arts such as the Chanoyu tea ceremony or the Ikebana art of flower arrangement. This evolution went as far as considering almost any human activity as an art with a strong spiritual and aesthetic content, first and foremost in those activities related to combat techniques (martial arts).

Buddhism remains very active in Japan to this day. Around 80,000 Buddhist temples are preserved and regularly restored.

South-East Asia

During the 1st century AD, the trade on the overland Silk Road tended to be restricted by the rise in the Middle-East of the Parthian empire, an unvanquished enemy of Rome, just as Romans were becoming extremely wealthy and their demand for Asian luxury was rising. This demand revived the sea connections between the Mediterranean and China, with India as the intermediary of choice. From that time, through trade connection, commercial settlements and even political interventions, India started to strongly influence Southeast Asian countries. Trade routes linked India with southern Burma, central and southern Siam, lower Cambodia and southern Vietnam and numerous urbanized coastal settlements were established there.

For more than a thousand years, Indian influence was therefore the major factor that brought a certain level of cultural unity to the various countries of the region. The Pali and Sanskrit languages and the Indian script, together with Theravada and Mahayana Buddhism, Brahmanism and Hinduism, were transmitted from direct contact and through sacred texts and Indian literature such as the Ramayana and the Mahabharata.

From the 5th to the 13th century, South-East Asia had very powerful empires and became extremely active in Buddhist architectural and artistic creation. The main Buddhist influence now came directly by sea from the Indian subcontinent, so that these empires essentially followed the Mahayana faith. The Sri Vijaya Empire to the south and the Khmer Empire to the north competed for influence and their art expressed the rich Mahayana pantheon of the Bodhisattvas.

Vietnam

Srivijayan empire (5th-15th century): Srivijaya, a maritime empire centred at Palembang on the island of Sumatra in Indonesia, adopted Mahayana and Vajrayana Buddhism under a line of rulers named the Sailendras. Yijing described Palembang as a great centre of Buddhist learning where the emperor supported over a thousand monks at his court. Atisha studied there before travelling to Tibet as a missionary.

Sriviijaya spread Buddhist art during its expansion in Southeast Asia. Numerous statues of Bodhisattvas from this period are characterized by a very strong refinement and technical sophistication and are found throughout the region. Extremely rich architectural remains are visible at the temple of Borobudur (the largest Buddhist structure in the world, built from around 780 AD), in Java, which has 505 images of the seated Buddha. Srivijaya declined due to conflicts with the Chola rulers of India, before being destabilized by the Islamic expansion from the 13th century.

Khmer Empire (9th-13th century): Later, from the 9th to the 13th century, the Mahayana Buddhist and Hindu Khmer Empire dominated much of the South-East Asian peninsula. Under the Khmer, more than 900 temples were built in Cambodia and in neighbouring Thailand. Angkor was at the centre of this development, with a temple complex and urban organization able to support around one million urban dwellers. One of the greatest Khmer kings, Jayavarman VII (1181-1219), built large Mahayana Buddhist structures at Bayon and Angkor Thom.

Following the destruction of Buddhism in mainland India during the 11th century, Mahayana Buddhism declined in Southeast Asia, to be replaced by the introduction of Theravada Buddhism from Sri Lanka.

Emergence of the Vajrayana (5th Century): Vajrayana Buddhism, also called Tantric Buddhism, first emerged in eastern

India between the 5th and 7th centuries AD. It is sometimes considered a sub-school of Mahayana and sometimes a third major "vehicle" (Yana) of Buddhism in its own right. The Vajrayana is an extension of Mahayana Buddhism in that it does not offer new philosophical perspectives, but rather introduces additional techniques (upaya, or 'skilful means'), including the use of visualizations and other yogic practices. Many of the practices of Tantric Buddhism are also derived from Hinduism (the usage of mantras, yoga, or the burning of sacrificial offerings). This school of thought was founded by the Brahmin Padmasambhava.

Early Vajrayana practitioners were forest-dwelling mahasiddas who lived on the margins of society, but by the 9th century Vajrayana had won acceptance at major Mahayana monastic universities such as Nalanda and Vikramshila. Along with much of the rest of Indian Buddhism, the Vajrayana was eclipsed in the wake of the late 12th century Muslim invasions. It has persisted in Tibet, where it was wholly transplanted from the 7th to 12th centuries and became the dominant form of Buddhism to the present day and on a limited basis in Japan as well where it evolved into Shingon Buddhism.

Theravada Renaissance (11th Century AD): From the 11th century, the destruction of Buddhism in the Indian mainland by Islamic invasions led to the decline of the Mahayana faith in South-East Asia. Continental routes through the Indian subcontinent being compromised, direct sea routes between the Middle-East through Sri Lanka and to China developed, leading to the adoption of the Theravada Buddhism of the Pali canon, introduced to the region around the 11th century AD from Sri Lanka.

King Anawrahta (1044-1077); the historical founder of the Burmese empire, unified the country and adopted the Theravada Buddhist faith. This initiated the creation of thousands of Buddhist temples at Pagan, the capital, between the 11th and 13th century. Around 2,000 of them are still standing. The power of the Burmese waned with the rise of the Thai and with the seizure of the capital Pagan by the Mongols in 1287, but Theravada Buddhism remained the main Burmese faith to this day. The Theravada faith was also adopted by the newly founded ethnic Thai kingdom of Sukhothai around 1260. Theravada Buddhism was further reinforced during the Ayutthaya period (14th-18th century), becoming an integral part of the Thai society.

In the continental areas, Theravada Buddhism continued to expand into Laos and Cambodia in the 13th century. However, from the 14th century, on the coastal fringes and in the islands of South-East Asia, the influence of Islam proved stronger, expanding into Malaysia, Indonesia and most of the islands as far as the southern Philippines.

However, since 1966 with Soeharto's rise of power in the aftermath of the bloody events after the so called "September 30th, 1965 murders", allegedly executed by the Communists Party, there has been a remarkable renaissance of Buddhism in Indonesia. This is partly due to the Soeharto's New Order's requirements for the people of Indonesia to adopt one of the five official religions: Islam, Protestantism, Catholicism, Hinduism or Buddhism. Today it is estimated there are some 10 millions Buddhists in Indonesia. A large part of them are people of Chinese ancestry.

Expansion of Buddhism to the West: After the Classical encounters between Buddhism and the West recorded in Greco-Buddhist art, information and legends about Buddhism seem to have reached the West sporadically. During the 8th century, Buddhist Jataka stories were translated into Syriac and Arabic as Kalilag and Damnag. An account of Buddha's life was translated in to Greek by John of Damascus and widely circulated to Christians as the story of Barlaam and Josaphat. By the 1300s this story of Josaphat had become so popular that he was made a Catholic saint.

The next direct encounter between Europeans and Buddhism happened in Medieval times when the Franciscan friar William of Rubruck was sent on an embassy to the Mongol court of Mongke by the French king Saint Louis in 1253. The contact happened in Cailac (today's Qayaliq in Kazakhstan) and William originally thought they were wayward Christians (Foltz, "Religions of the Silk Road").

Major interest for Buddhism emerged during colonial times, when Western powers were in a position to witness the faith and its artistic manifestations in detail. European philosophy was strongly influenced by the study of oriental religions during that period.

The opening of Japan in 1853 also created a considerable interest for the arts and culture of Japan and provided access to one of the most thriving Buddhist cultures in the world. Buddhism started to enjoy a strong interest from the general population in the West during the 20th century, following the perceived failure of social utopias, from Fascism to Marxism. After the Second World War, the focus of progress tended to shift to personal self-realization, on the material as well as spiritual plane.

In this context, Buddhism has been displaying a strong power of attraction, due to its tolerance, its lack of deist authority and determinism and its focus on understanding reality through self inquiry. According to the latest census it is now the fastest growing religion in Britain.

Theravada Buddhist Council in 1871 (5th Buddhist Council)

Another Buddhist Council, this time presided by Theravada monks took place in Mandalay Burma now known as Myanmar in 1871 in the reign of King Mindon. The chief objective of this meeting was to recite all the teachings of the Buddha and examine them in minute detail to see if any of them had been altered, distorted or dropped. It was presided over by three Elders, the Venerable Mahathera Jagarabhivamsa, the Venerable Narindabhidhaja and the Venerable Mahathera Sumangalasami in the company of some two thousand four hundred monks (2,400). Their joint Dhamma recitation lasted for five months. It was also the work of this council to cause the entire Tripitaka to be inscribed for posterity on seven hundred and twenty-nine marble slabs in the Myanmar script after its recitation had been completed and unanimously approved. This monumental task was done by some two thousand four hundred (2,400) erudite monks and many skilled craftsmen who upon completion of each slab had them housed in beautiful miniature 'pitaka' pagodas on a special site in the grounds of King Mindon's Kuthodaw Pagoda at the foot of Mandalay Hill where it and the so called 'largest book in the world', stands to this day.

REGIONAL EXAMPLES

South-East Asia

Thailand

In Southeast Asia, Thailand has had several prominent virulent Buddhist monastic calls for violence. In the 1970s, nationalist Buddhist monks like Phra Kittiwuttho argued that killing Communists did not violate any of the Buddhist precepts. The militant side of Thai Buddhism became prominent again in 2004 when a Malay Muslim insurgency renewed in Thailand's deep south. At first Buddhist monks ignored the conflict as they viewed it as political and not religious but eventually they adopted an "identity-formation," as practical realities require deviations from religious ideals.

Myanmar

In 1930s Rangoon, nationalist monks stabbed four Europeans. In recent years the State Peace and Development Council (SPDC), the military regime of Burma from 1988 to 2011, had strongly encouraged the conversion of ethnic minorities, often by force, as part of its campaign of assimilation. The regimen promoted a vision of Burmese Buddhist nationalism as a cultural and a political ideology to legitimise its contested rule, trying to bring a religious syncretism between Buddhism and its totalitarian ideology.

The Saffron Revolution, a series of economic and political protests and demonstrations that took place during 2007, were led by students, political activists, including women, and Buddhist monks and took the form of a campaign of nonviolent resistance, sometimes also called civil resistance.

In response to the protests dozens of protesters were arrested or detained. Starting in September 2007 the protests were led by thousands of Buddhist monks, and those protests were allowed to proceed until a renewed government crackdown in late September 2007. At least 184 protesters were shot and killed and many were tortured. Under the SPDC, the Burmese army engaged in military offensives against ethnic minority populations, committing acts that violated international humanitarian law.

Myanmar had become a stronghold of Buddhist aggression and such acts are spurred by hardline nationalistic monks. The oldest militant organisation active in the region is Democratic Karen Buddhist Army (DKBA), headed by a Buddhist monk U Thuzana, since 1992. In the recent years the monks, and the terrorist acts, are associated with the nationalist 969 Movement particularly in Myanmar and neighboring nations. The violence reached prominence in June 2012 when more than 200 people were killed and around 100,000 were displaced. As of 2012, the "969" movement by monks (the prominent among whom is Wirathu) had helped create anti-Islamicnationalist movements in the region, and have urged Myanmar Buddhists to boycott Muslim services and trades, resulting in persecution of Muslims in Burma by Buddhist-led mobs. However, not all of the culprits were Buddhists and the motives were as much economic as religious. According to the Human Rights Watch report, the Burmese government and local authorities played a key role in the forcible displacement of more than 125,000 Rohingya people and other Muslims in the region. The report further specifies the coordinated attacks of October 2012 that were carried out in different cities by Burmese officials, community leaders and Buddhist monks to terrorize and forcibly relocate the population. The violence of Meiktila, Lashio (2013) and Mandalay (2014) are the latest Buddhist violence in Burma.

Michael Jerryson, author of several books heavily critical of Buddhism's traditional peaceful perceptions, stated that, "The Burmese Buddhist monks may not have initiated the violence but they rode the wave and began to incite more. While the ideals of Buddhist canonical texts promote peace and pacifism, discrepancies between reality and precepts easily flourish in times of social, political and economic insecurity, such as Myanmar's current transition to democracy." However several Buddhist leaders including Thích Nh¥t H¡nh, Bhikkhu Bodhi, Shodo Harada and the Dalai Lama among others condemned the violence against Muslims in Myanmar and called for peace, supporting the practice of the fundamental Buddhist principles of non-harming, mutual respect and compassion. The Dalai Lama said "Buddha always teaches us about forgiveness, tolerance, compassion. If from one corner of your mind, some emotion makes you want to hit, or want to kill, then please remember Buddha's faith. We are followers of Buddha." He said that "All problems must be solved through dialogue, through talk. The use of violence is outdated, and never solves problems." Maung Zarni, a Burmese democracy advocate, human rights campaigner, and a research fellow at the London School of Economics who has written on the violence in Myanmar and Sri Lanka, states that there is no room for fundamentalism in Buddhism. "No Buddhist can be nationalistic," said Zarni, "There is no country for Buddhists. I mean, no such thing as 'me,' 'my' community, 'my' country, 'my' race or even 'my' faith."

South Asia

India

Ashokavadana states that there was a mass killing of Jains for disrespecting buddha by King Ashoka in which around 18,000 followers of Jainism were killed. However this incident is controversial. According to K.T.S. Sarao and Benimadhab Barua, stories of persecutions of rival sects by Ashoka appear to be a clear fabrication arising out of sectarian propaganda.

Sri Lanka

Buddhism in Sri Lanka has a unique history and has played an important role in the shaping of Sinhalese nationalist identity. Consequently, politicized Buddhism has contributed to ethnic tension in the island between the majority Sinhalese Buddhist population and other minorities, especially the Tamils.

Mytho-historical roots

The mytho-historical accounts in the Sinhalese Buddhist national chronicle Mahavamsa ('Great Chronicle'), a non-canonical text written in the sixth century CE by Buddhist monks to glorify Buddhism in Sri Lanka, have been influential in the creation of Sinhalese Buddhist nationalism and militant Buddhism. The Mahavamsa states that Lord Buddha made three visits to Sri Lanka in which he rids the island of forces inimical to Buddhism and instructs deities to protect the ancestors of the Sinhalese (Prince Vijaya and his followers from North India) to enable the establishment and flourishing of Buddhism in Sri Lanka. This myth has led to the widely held Sinhalese Buddhist belief that the country is Sihadipa (island of the Sinhalese) and Dhammadipa (the island ennobled to preserve and propagate Buddhism). In other words, Sinhalese Buddhist nationalists maintain that they are the Buddha's chosen people, and that the island of Sri Lanka is the Buddhist promised land. The Mahavamsa also describes an account of the Buddhist warrior king Dutthagamani, his army, and 500 Buddhist monks battling and defeating the Tamil king Elara, who had come from South India and usurped power in Anuradhapura (the island's capital at the time). When Duthagamani laments over the thousands he has killed, the eight arhats (Buddha's enlightened disciples) who come to console him reply that no real sin has been committed by him because he has only killed Tamil unbelievers who are no better than beasts and go onto say: "thou wilt bring glory to the doctrine of the Buddha in manifold ways; therefore cast away care from the heart, O ruler of men."

The Dutthagamani's campaign against king Elara was not to defeat injustice, as the Mahavamsa describes Elara as a good ruler, but to restore Buddhism through a united Sri Lanka under a Buddhist monarch, even by the use of violence. The Mahavamsa story about Buddha's visit to Sri Lanka where he (referred to as the "Conqueror") subdues forces inimical to Buddhism, the Yakkhas (depicted as the non-human inhabitants of the island), by striking "terror to their hearts" and driving them from their homeland, so that his doctrine should eventually "shine in glory", has been described as providing the warrant for the use of violence for the sake of Buddhism and as an account that is in keeping with the general message of the author that the political unity of Sri Lanka under Buddhism requires the removal of uncooperative groups.

According to Neil DeVotta (an Associate Professor of Political Science), the mytho-history described in the Mahavamsa "justifies dehumanizing non-Sinhalese, if doing so is necessary to preserve, protect, and propagate the dhamma (Buddhist doctrine). Furthermore, it legitimizes a just war doctrine, provided that war is waged to protect Buddhism. Together with the Vijaya myth, it introduces the bases for the Sinhalese Buddhist belief that Lord Buddha designated the island of Sri Lanka as a repository for Theravada Buddhism. It claims the Sinhalese were the first humans to inhabit the island (as those who predated the Sinhalese were subhuman) and are thus the true "sons of the soil." Additionally, it institutes the belief that the island's kings were beholden to protect and foster Buddhism. All of these legacies have had ramifications for the trajectory of political Buddhism and Sinhalese Buddhist nationalism."

Rise of modern Sinhalese-Buddhist nationalism

With the rise of modern Sinhalese Buddhist nationalism in the late nineteenth and early twentieth centuries as a reaction to the changes brought under the British colonialism,the old religious mytho-history of the Mahavamsa (especially the emphasis on the Sinhalese and Tamil ethnicities of Duthagamani and Elara, respectively) was revitalized and consequently would prove to be detrimental to the intergroup harmony in the island. As Heather Selma Gregg writes: "Modern-day Sinhalese nationalism, rooted in local myths of being a religiously chosen people and of special progeny, demonstrates that even a religion perceived as inherently peaceful can help fuel violence and hatred in its name."

Buddhist revivalism took place among the Sinhalese to counter Christian missionary influence. The British commissioned the Sinhala translation of the Mahavamsa (which was originally written in Pali), thereby making it accessible to the wider Sinhalese population. During this time the first riot in modern Sri Lankan history broke out in 1883, between Buddhists and Catholics, highlighting the "growing religious divide between the two communities". The central figure in the formation of modern Sinhalese Buddhist nationalism was the Buddhist revivalist

Anagarika Dharmapala (1864–1933), who has been described as "the father of modern Sinhalese Buddhist nationalism". Dharmapala was hostile to all things un-Sinhalese and non-Buddhist. He was a racist who insisted that the Sinhalese were racially pure and superior Aryans while the Dravidian Tamils were inferior. He popularized the impression that Tamils and Sinhalese had been deadly enemies in Sri Lanka for nearly 2,000 years by quoting the Mahavamsa passages that depicted Tamils as pagan invaders. He characterized the Tamils as "fiercely antagonistic to Buddhism". He also expressed intolerance toward the island's Muslim minorities and other religions in general. Dharmapala also fostered Sinhalese Buddhist nationalism in the spirit of the King Dutthagamani who "rescued Buddhism and our nationalism from oblivion" and stated explicitly that the Island belongs to the Sinhalese Buddhists. Dharmapala has been blamed for laying the groundwork for subsequent Sinhalese Buddhists nationalists to create an ethnocentric state and for hostility to be directed against minorities unwilling to accept such a state.

Politicized Buddhism, the formation of ethnocracy and the civil war

Upon independence Sinhalese Buddhist elites instituted discriminatory policies based on the Buddhist ethno-nationalist ideology of the Mahavamsa that privileges Sinhalese Buddhist hegemony in the island as Buddha's chosen people for whom the island is a promised land and justifies subjugation of minorities. Sinhalese Buddhist officials saw that decreasing Tamil influence was a necessary part of fostering Buddhist cultural renaissance. The Dutthagamani myth was also used to institute Sinhalese Buddhist domination with some politicians even identifying with such a mytho-historic hero and activist monks looked to Dutthagamani as an example to imitate. This principal hero of Mahavamsa became widely regarded as exemplary by the 20th century Sinhalese Buddhist nationalists because of his defense of Buddhism and the unification of Sri Lanka that journalists started talking about "the Mahavamsa mentality".

D. S. Senanayake, who would become Sri Lanka's first prime minister in 1947, reaffirmed in 1939 the common Mahavamsa-based assumption of the Sinhalese Buddhist responsibility for the island's destiny by proclaiming that the Sinhalese Buddhists "are one blood and one nation. We are a chosen people. Buddha said that his religion would last for 5,500 [sic] years. That means that we, as the custodians of that religion, shall last as long." Buddhists monks became increasingly involved in post-independence politics, promoting Sinhalese Buddhist interests, at the expense of minorities. Walpola Rahula, Sri Lanka's foremost Buddhist monk scholar and one of the leading proponents of Sinhalese Buddhist nationalism, played a major role in advocating for the involvement of monks in politics, using Buddhist king Dutthagamani's relationship with the sangha to bolster his position. Rahula also argued for a just war doctrine to protect Buddhism by using the example of wars waged by Dutthagamani to restore Buddhism. Rahula maintained that "the entire Sinhalese race was united under the banner of the young Gamini [Dutthagamani]. This was the beginning of nationalism among the Sinhalese. It was a new race with healthy young blood, organized under the new order of Buddhism. A kind of religionationalism, which almost amounted to fanaticism, roused the whole Sinhalese people. A non-Buddhist was not regarded as a human being. Evidently all Sinhalese without exception were Buddhists." In reflecting on Rahula's works, anthropologist H.L. Seneviratne writes that, "it suits Rahula to be an advocate of a Buddhism that glorifies social intercourse with lay society . . . the receipt of salaries and other forms of material remuneration; ethnic exclusivism and Sinhala Buddhist hegemony; militancy in politics; and violence, war and the spilling of blood in the name of "preserving the religion"."

In 1956, the All Ceylon Buddhist Congress (ACBC) released a report titled, "The Betrayal of Buddhism", inquiring into the status of Buddhism in the island. The report argued that Buddhism had been weakened by external threats such as the Tamil invaders mentioned in the Mahavamsa and later Western colonial powers. It also demanded the state to restore and foster Buddhism and to give preferential treatment to Buddhist schools. The same year, S. W. R. D. Bandaranaike capitalized on the ACBC report and its recommendations as the foundation for his election campaign, using it as the 'blueprint for a broad spectrum of policy', which included introducing Sinhala as the sole official language of the state. With the help of significant number of Buddhist monks and various Sinhalese Buddhist organizations, Bandaranaike became prime minister after winning the 1956 elections. Bandaranaike had also campaigned on the basis of Sinhalese Buddhist nationalism, drawing influences from the writings of Dharmapala and the Mahavamsa, arguing that it was the duty of the government to preserve the Sinhalese Buddhist nature of the island's destiny. Once in power, Bandaranaike implemented the 1956 Sinhala Only Act, which would make Sinhala the country's official language and hence all official state transactions would be conducted in Sinhala. This put non-Sinhala speakers at a disadvantage for employment and educational opportunities. As a result, Tamils protested the policy by staging sit-ins, which in turn prompted counterdemonstrations by Buddhist monks, later degenerating into anti-Tamil riots in which more than one hundred people were injured and Tamil businesses were looted. Riots then spread throughout the country killing hundreds of people. Bandaranaike tried to mitigate tensions over the language policy by proposing a compromise with the Tamil leaders, resulting in a 1957 pact that would allow the use of Tamil as an in administrative language along with Sinhala and greater political autonomy for Tamils. Buddhist monks and other Sinhalese nationalists opposed this pact by staging mass demonstrations and hunger strikes. In an editorial in the same year, a monk asks Bandaranaike to read Mahavamsa and to heed its lessons: "[Dutthagamani] conquered by the sword and united the land [Sri Lanka] without dividing it among our enemies [i.e. the Tamils] and established Sinhala and Buddhism as the state language and religion." In the late 1950s, it had become common for politicians and monks to exploit the Mahavamsa narrative of Dutthagamani to oppose any concession to the Tamil minorities.

With Buddhist monks playing a major role in exerting pressure to abrogate the pact, Bandaranaike acceded to their demands in April 9, 1958 by tearing up "a copy of the pact in front of the assembled monks who clapped in joy." Soon after the pact was abrogated, another series of anti-Tamil riots spread throughout the country, which left hundreds dead and thousands displaced.

Preceding the 1958 riots, rhetoric of monks contributed to the perception of Tamils being the enemies of the country and of Buddhism. Both Buddhist monks and laity laid the foundation for the justifiable use of force against Tamils in response to their demand for greater autonomy by arguing that the whole of Sri Lanka was a promised land of the Sinhalese Buddhists and it was the role of the monks to defend a united Sri Lanka. Tamils were also portrayed as threatening interlopers, compared to the Mahavamsa account of the usurper Tamil king Elara. Monks and politicians invoked the story of the Buddhist warrior king Dutthagamani to urge the Sinhalese to fight against Tamils and their claims to the island, thereby providing justification for violence against Tamils. As Tessa J. Bartholomeusz explains: "Tamil claims to a homeland were met with an ideology, linked to a Buddhist story, that legitimated war with just cause: the protection of Sri Lanka for the Sinhala-Buddhist people." In order to appease Tamils amidst the ethnic tension, Bandaranaike modified the Sinhala Only Act to allow Tamil to be used in education and government in Tamil areas and as a result a Buddhist monk assassinated him on September 26, 1959. The monk claimed he carried out the assassination "for the greater good of his country, race and religion." It has also been suggested that the monk was guided in part by reading of the Mahavamsa.

Successive governments after Bandaranaike implemented similar Sinhalese Buddhist nationalist agenda, at the expense of minorities. In 1972, the government rewrote its constitution and gave Buddhism "the foremost place [in the Republic of Sri Lanka]" and making it "the duty of the state to protect and foster Buddhism." With another pact in 1965 that sought to establish greater regional autonomy for Tamils being abrogated (some members of the Buddhist clergy were at the forefront in opposing the pact) and the implementation of discriminatory quota system in 1974 that severely restricted Tamil entrance to universities, Tamil youth became radicalized, calling for an independent homeland to be established in the Tamil-dominated northeastern region of the island. In 1977, anti-Tamil riots spread throughout the country, killing hundreds of Tamils and leaving thousands homeless. A leading monk claimed that one of the reasons for the anti-Tamil riots of 1977 was the Tamil demonization of the Sinhalese Buddhist epic hero Dutthagamani which resulted in a justified retaliation. Another anti-Tamil riot erupted in 1981 in Jaffna, where Sinhalese police and paramilitaries destroyed statues of Tamil cultural and religious figures; looted and torched a Hindu temple and Tamil-owned shops and homes; killed four Tamils; and torched the Jaffna Public Library which was of great cultural significance to Tamils. In response to the militant separatist Tamil group LTTE killing 13 Sinhalese soldiers, the largest anti-Tamil pogrom occurred in 1983, leaving between 2,000 and 3,000 of Tamils killed and forcing from 70,000 to 100,000 Tamils into refugee camps, eventually propelling the country into a civil war between the LTTE and the predominately Sinhalese Buddhist Sri Lankan government. In the 1983 anti-Tamil pogrom, Buddhist monks lead rioters in some instance.

Cyril Mathew, a Senior Minister in President Jayawardene's Cabinet and a Sinhalese Buddhist nationalist who in the year preceding the pogrom reaffirmed the special relationship between Buddhism and Sinhalese and the Buddhist nature of the country, was also responsible for the pogrom. In the months following the anti-Tamil pogrom, authorizations for violence against Tamils began to appear in the press, with Tamils being depicted as interlopers on Dhammadipa.

The Mahavamsa narrative of Dutthagamani and Elara was also invoked to justify violence against Tamils. The aftermath of the pogrom spawned debates over the rights to the island with the "sons of the soil" ideology being called into prominence. A government agent declared that Sri Lanka's manifest destiny "was to uphold the pristine doctrine of Theravada Buddhism." This implied that Sinhalese Buddhists had a sacred claim to Sri Lanka, while the Tamils did not, a claim which might call for violence. The Sinhalese Buddhists, including the Sri Lankan government, resisted the Tamil claim to a separate homeland of their own as the Sinhalese Buddhists maintained that the entire country belonged to them. Another government agent linked the then Prime Minister Jayewardene's attempts to thwart the emergence of a Tamil homeland to Dutthagamani's victory over Elara and went on to say, "[w]e will never allow the country to be divided," thereby justifying violence against Tamils.

In the context of increasing Tamil militant struggle for separatism, militant Buddhist monks founded the Mavbima Surakime Vyaparaya (MSV) or "Movement for the Protection of the Motherland" in 1986 which sought to work with political parties "to maintain territorial unity of Sri Lanka and Sinhalese Buddhist sovereignty over the island". The MSV used the Mahavamsa to justify its goals, which included the usage of force to fight against the Tamil threat and defend the Buddhist state. In 1987, along with the MSV, the JVP (a militant Sinhalese nationalist group which included monks) took up arms to protest the signing of the Indo-Sri Lanka Accord which sought to establish peace in Sri Lanka by requiring the Sri Lankan government to make a number of concessions to Tamil demands, including devolution of power to Tamil provinces. The JVP, with the support of the Sangha, launched a campaign of violent insurrection against the government to oppose the accord as the Sinhalese nationalists believed it would compromise the sovereignty of Sri Lanka.

From the beginning of the civil war in 1983 to the end of it in 2009, Buddhist monks were involved in politics and opposed negotiations, ceasefire agreements, or any devolution of power to Tamil minorities, and most supported military solution to the conflict. This has led to Asanga Tilakaratne, head of the Department of Buddhist Philosophy in the Postgraduate Institute of Pali and Buddhist Studies in Colombo, to remark that "the Sinhala Buddhist nationalists are ... opposed to any attempt to solve the ethnic problem by peaceful means; and they call for a 'holy war' against Tamils." It has been argued that the absence of opportunities for power sharing among the different ethnic groups in the island "has been one of the primary factors behind the intensification of the conflict." Numerous Buddhist religious leaders and Buddhist organizations since the country's independence have played a role in mobilizing against the devolution of power to the Tamils. Leading Buddhist monks opposed devolution of power that would grant regional autonomy to Tamils on the basis of Mahavamsa worldview that the entire country is a Buddhist promised land which belongs to the Sinhalese Buddhist people, along with the fear that devolution would eventually lead to separate country.

The two major contemporary political parties to advocate for Sinhalese Buddhist nationalism are The Janatha Vimukthi Peramuna (JVP) and the Jathika Hela Urumaya (JHU) or "National Heritage Party", the latter of which is composed solely of Buddhist monks. According to A. R. M. Imtiyaz, these groups share common goals: "to uphold Buddhism and establish a link between the state and religion, and to advocate a violent solution to the Tamil question and oppose all form of devolution to the minorities, particularly the Tamils." The JHU, in shunning non-violent solutions to the ethnic conflict, urged young Sinhalese Buddhists to sign up for the army, with as many as 30,000 Sinhalese young men doing just that. One JHU leader even declared that NGOs and certain government servants were traitors and they should be set on fire and burnt due to their opposition to a military solution to the civil war. The international community encouraged a federal structure for Sri Lanka as a peaceful solution to the civil war but any form of Tamil self-determination, even the more limited measure of autonomy, was strongly opposed by hard-line Sinhalese Buddhist nationalist groups such as the JVP and JHU, who pushed for the military solution. These groups in their hard-line support for a military solution to the conflict, without any regard for the plight of innocent Tamil civilians, have opposed negotiated settlement, ceasefire agreement, demanded that the Norwegians be removed as peace facilitators, demanded the war to be prosecuted more forcefully and exerted influence in the Rajapaksa government (which they helped to elect), resulting in the brutal military defeat of the LTTE with heavy civilian casualties. The nationalist monks' support of the government's military offense against the LTTE gave "religious legitimacy to the state's claim of protecting the island for the Sinhalese Buddhist majority." President Rajapaksa, in his war against the LTTE, has been compared to the Buddhist king Dutthagamani by the Sinhalese Buddhist nationalists.

Violence against religious minorities

Other minority groups have also come under attack by Sinhalese Buddhist nationalists. Fear of country's Buddhist hegemony being challenged by Christian proselytism has driven Buddhist monks and organizations to demonize Christian organizations with one popular monk comparing missionary activity to terrorism; as a result, Sinhalese Buddhist nationalists, including the JVP and JHU, who oppose attempts to convert Buddhists to another religion, support or conduct anti-Christian violence. Number of attacks against Christian churches rose from 14 in 2000 to 146 or over 200 in 2003 and 2004, with extremist Buddhist clergy leading the violence in some areas. Anti-Christian violence has included "beatings, arson, acts of sacrilege, death threats, violent disruption of worship, stoning, abuse, unlawful restraint, and even interference with funerals". It has been noted that the strongest anti-West sentiments accompany the anti-Christian violence since the Sinhalese Buddhist nationalists identify Christianity with the West which they think is conspiring to undermine Buddhism.

In the postwar Sri Lanka, ethnic and religious minorities continue face threat from Sinhalese Buddhist nationalism. There have been continued sporadic attacks on Christian churches by Buddhist extremists who allege Christians of conducting unethical or forced conversion. The Pew Research Center has listed Sri Lanka among the countries with very high religious hostilities in 2012 due to the violence committed by Buddhist monks against Muslim and Christian places of worship. Extremist Buddhist leaders justify their attacks on the places of worship of minorities by arguing that Sri Lanka is the promised land of the Sinhalese Buddhists to safeguard Buddhism. The recently formed Buddhist extremist group, the Bodu Bala Sena (BBS), or Buddhist Power Force, founded by Buddhist monks in 2012, has been accused of inciting the anti-Muslim riots that killed 4 Muslims and injured 80 in 2014. The leader of the BBS, in linking the government's military victory over the LTTE to the ancient Buddhist king conquest of Tamil king Elara, said that Tamils have been taught a lesson twice and warned other minorities of the same fate if they tried to challenge Sinhalese Buddhist culture. The BBS has been compared to the Taliban, accused of spreading extremism and communal hatred against Muslims and has been described as an "ethno-religious fascist movement". Buddhist monks have also protested against UN Human Rights Council resolution that called for an inquiry into humanitarian abuses and possible war crimes during the civil war. The BBS has received criticism and oppostition from other Buddhist clergy and politicians. Mangala Samaraweera, a Sri LankanTheravada Buddhist politician who has served as Minister of Foreign Affairs since 2015, has accused the BBS of being "a representation of 'Taliban' terrorism'" and of spreading extremism and communal hatred against Muslims. Samaraweera has also alleged that the BBS is secretly funded by the Ministry of Defence. Anunayake Bellanwila Wimalaratana, deputy incumbent of Bellanwila Rajamaha Viharaya and President of the Bellanwila Community Development Foundation, has stated that "The views of the Bodu Bala Sena are not the views of the entire Sangha community" and that "We don't use our fists to solve problems, we use our brains". Wataraka Vijitha Thero, a buddhist monk who condemns violence against Muslims and heavily criticized the BBS and the government, has been attacked and tortured for his stances.

Buddhist opposition to Sinhala Buddhist nationalism

Sinhala Buddhist Nationalism is opposed to Sarvodaya, although they share many of the same influences like Dharmapâla's teachings by example, by having a focus upon Sinhalese culture and ethnicity sanctioning the use of violence in defence of dhamma, while Sarvodaya has emphasized the application of Buddhist values in order to transform society and campaigning for peace.

These Buddhist nationalists have been opposed by the Sarvodaya Shramadana Movement, a self-governance movement led by the Buddhist Dr. A. T. Ariyaratne and based in Buddhist ideals, who condemn the use of violence and the denial of Human rights to Tamils and other non-Buddhists. Ariyaratne calls for non-violent action and he has been actively working for peace in Sri Lanka for many decades, and has stated that the only way to peace is through "the dispelling of the view of 'I and mine' or the shedding of 'self' and the realization of the true doctrines of the interconnection between all animal species and the unity of all humanity," thus advocating social action in Buddhist terms. He stated in one of his lectures, "When we work towards the welfare of all the means we use have to be based on Truth, Non-violence and Selflessness in conformity with Awakening of All.". What Ariyaratne advocates is losing the self in the service of others and attempting to bring others to awakening. Ariyaratne has stated, "I cannot awaken myself unless I help awaken others.".

East Asia

Japan

The beginning of "Buddhist violence" in Japan relates to a long history of feuds among Buddhists. The sôhei or "warrior monks" appeared during the Heian period, although the seeming contradiction in being a Buddhist "warrior monk" caused controversy even at the time. More directly linked is that the Ikkô-shû movement was considered an inspiration to Buddhists in the Ikkô-ikkirebellion. In Osaka they defended their temple with the slogan "The mercy of Buddha should be recompensed even by pounding flesh to pieces. One's obligation to the Teacher should be recompensed even by smashing bones to bits!"

During World War II, Japanese Buddhist literature from that time, as part of its support of the Japanese war effort, stated "In order to establish eternal peace in East Asia, arousing the great benevolence and compassion of Buddhism, we are sometimes accepting and sometimes forceful. We now have no choice but to exercise the benevolent forcefulness of 'killing one in order that many may live' (issatsu tashô). This is something which Mahayana Buddhism approves of only with the greatest of seriousness..." Almost allJapanese Buddhists temples strongly supported Japan's militarization. These were heavily criticized by theChinese Buddhists of the era who disputed the validity of the statements made by those Japanese Buddhists supporters of the war. In response the Japanese Pan-Buddhist Society (Myowa Kai) rejected the criticism and stated that "We now have no choice but to exercise the benevolent forcefulness of 'killing one in order that many may live' (issatsu tashô)" and that the war was absolutely necessary to implement the dharma in Asia. The society re-examined more than 70 text written by Nichiren and re-edited his writings, making changes in 208 places, cutting all the statements that disagreed with the state Shinto. In contrast, a few Japanese Buddhists such as Ichikawa Haku and Seno'o Girô opposed this and were targeted.

During the 1940s, "leaders of the Honmon Hokkeshu and Soka Kyoiku Gakkai were imprisoned for their defiance of wartime government religious policy, which mandated display of reverence for the state Shinto." Brian Daizen Victoria, a Buddhist priest in the Sôtô Zen sect, documented in his book *Zen at War* how Buddhist institutions justified Japanese militarism in official publications and cooperated with the Imperial Japanese Army in the Russo-Japanese War and World War II. In response to the book, several sects issued an apology for their wartime support of the government.

In more modern times instances of Buddhist-inspired terrorism or militarism have occurred in Japan, such as the assassinations of the League of Blood Incident led by Nissho Inoue, a Nichirenist or fascist-nationalist who preached a self-styled Nichiren Buddhism.

Aum Shinrikyo, the Japanese new religion and doomsday cult that was the cause of the Tokyo subway sarin attack that killed thirteen people and injured fifty, drew upon asyncretic view of idiosyncratic interpretations of elements of early Indian Buddhism, Tibetan Buddhism and Hinduism, taking Shiva as the main image of worship, Christianmillennialist ideas from the Book of Revelation, Yoga and the writings of Nostradamus.

Its founder, Chizuo Matsumoto, claimed that he sought to restore "original Buddhism" and declared himself "Christ", Japan's only fully enlightened master and identified with the "Lamb of God". His purported mission was to take upon himself the sins of the world, and he claimed he could transfer to his followers spiritual power and ultimately take away their sins and bad deeds. While many discount Aum Shinrikyo's Buddhist characteristics and affiliation to Buddhism, scholars often refer to it as an offshoot of Japanese Buddhism, and this was how the movement generally defined and saw itself.

IS BUDDHIST MILITANCY THE NEXT WAVE OF GLOBAL TERRORISM?

Is anyone paying attention to this? Buddhist militancy appears to be the next wave of terrorism in Asia—and it could go global. It's been happening recurrently in Sri Lanka since the end of the ethnic civil war in 2009, with Buddhist monks attacking minority Muslims (as well as Christians). Similarly, in Myanmar since 2012, Buddhist monks have been openly attacking minority Muslim groups, including the Rohingya.

But now, extremist monks in both countries have formally linked up to form a global anti-Islamist pact. In September 2014, Buddhist monks in Myanmar, including Ashin Wirathu who once referred to himself as the "Burmese bin Laden," flew over to Sri Lanka to officially launch the global Buddhist alliance against Islamist militants. We haven't seen any follow-up on what this alliance means exactly. But at the time, they said the goal was to get more Buddhist groups to join their cause against Islamist militants—partly as they felt their governments would fail to tackle this perceived threat.

Yes, public figures like the Dalai Lama have "urged" the Buddhist militants in these countries to stop their apparent crusade. US President Barack Obama expressed the same rhetoric in his November visit to Myanmar. Even former US President Bill Clinton has frequently remarked how such Buddhist-led violence "sickens the world." And yet we don't see specific strategies being offered for how such militancy should be stopped, nor do we see local governments fully acknowledging the problem exists.

So, what can be done to derail this form of militancy to prevent its expansion from a regional threat to a global one? Strategies to tackle Islamist militancy include drone strikes, foreign intervention and militant rehabilitation camps. But none of these make sense for tackling Buddhist militancy at this early stage. Here are three preemptive steps for the world to consider in 2015.

UNDERSTANDING BUDDHIST MILITANCY

First, in order to determine how to stop Buddhist militancy, we need to be clear on *why* it has spread. Historians have explained it as a phenomenon rooted in an ancient narrative of the Mahavamsa in Sri Lanka, while in Myanmar it was a response to British colonialism. But what about today? Foreign governments, universities and/or international organizations need to commission studies on why such hatred has now surfaced in such a significant way, especially if local governments are not yet in a position to fully acknowledge the problem. Let's put some academic experts and ambitious PhD students to work.

Second, we need to consider *where* else Buddhist militancy might spread. Members of the new anti-Islamist pact have said their goal is to build "networks" with more Buddhist societies globally. Where might this happen? Besides Myanmar and Sri Lanka, historically there are accounts of Buddhist violence in Thailand, Japan and Tibet. Other countries with a notable Buddhist population (though not necessarily representing the same branch of Buddhism) are Cambodia, Bhutan, Laos and Vietnam—could these all be potential recruitment pools for the extremist Buddhist alliance?

And, outside of Asia, are there particular Buddhist centers in Europe or the United States that might be targeted by these militant monks? For the moment, we don't yet see this Buddhist alliance having a global reach through social media or other avenues, but it's likely part of their game plan and needs to be monitored by tech experts.

Third, *who* might financially support this Buddhist alliance against Islamist militants? If part of the goal of this anti-Islamist pact is to create an "international Buddhist force" and "pool resources to fight for the faith," this would logically require some form of fundraising effort. We know the funding strategies of Islamist extremist groups like al-Qaeda (which favors ransoms) and the Islamic State (which profits from oil). But who will fund this growing Buddhist alliance globally? Intelligence agencies need to start investigating possible donors or funding strategies.

If we look the other way now, Buddhist militancy will continue to gain ground in Asia and beyond in 2015. Yes, it is not as serious a global threat as Islamist militant groups like the Islamic State, the Taliban or al-Qaeda.

But let's note that the war of extremist words has begun. Islamist extremist groups have acknowledged public plans to avenge their "Muslim brothers" who've been killed by Buddhist extremists. If we don't launch a preemptive strike now, we may be witnessing a bloody battle between religious extremists—Buddhist vs Islamist—posing a new threat to global stability in the coming years.

HAMBLIN & PETERSON: BUDDHISM AND VIOLENCE

A widespread stereotype in Western popular culture holds that Islam is a religion of violence while Buddhism is a religion of peace. Like most stereotypes, these claims belie the complex reality of the nature of human beings and religion. We noted in a previous column the problems with viewing Islam as either an inherently peaceful or inherently violent religion.

Now we will look at the issue from a different perspective — pacifist Buddhism could also be described as a violent religion. Buddhism is widely regarded in the West as a nonviolent faith, and there is ample justification for such a view. But throughout its history, Buddhism has also had its violent aspects, and scholars are now examining the history of violent Buddhism.

India was the homeland of Buddhism, and its most famous Buddhist king, Ashoka, is renowned for his conversion to Buddhism and renunciation of military conquest. Yet his edicts include notices that warfare, while inferior to "conquest by Dharma" (conversion), is still permitted, though it must be undertaken with restraint. In other words, he is describing a nascent Buddhist just-war theory.

Notably, however, Ashoka also ordered the massacre of 18,000 Jains for blaspheming the Buddha. And the numerous Buddhist kings of medieval India were indistinguishable from contemporary non-Buddhist kings in their military activities. The Pala kings, for example, while noted for their patronage of Buddhist temples, monasteries and universities, also conquered most of northern India in the ninth century.

Asian martial arts, as popularized in the West, are said to have originated in China at the Shaolin Chan (Zen) Buddhist monastery, which trained its monks in both armed and unarmed forms of combat as part of their spiritual exercises. (They are also the background to the militant Jedi monastic order in Star Wars, with the Chinese "chi" converted into the Star Wars' Force.) Shaolin warrior monks helped establish the Tang dynasty in China in the seventh century. From China, Buddhist militant monastic orders spread to Korea (Bool Kyo Mu Sool), Tibet (Lama Pai) and, most importantly, Japan.

Paradoxically, Japanese Zen Buddhism, which is often viewed as one of the most pacifistic forms of Buddhism, was militarized by the Japanese warrior aristocracy. Bushido, the Japanese samurai warrior code, is in many ways the martial expression of Zen Buddhism. Japanese Buddhism also produced warrior monks ("sohei"), of Tendai Buddhism. These monks played crucial roles in numerous conflicts in medieval Japan, fighting against rival Buddhist temples, rioting and supporting samurai political factions.

The Dalai Lama of Tibet is rightly seen today as one of the premiere advocates of nonviolence in the modern world, well deserving his Nobel Peace Prize. But many of his predecessors ascended to their positions as rulers of Tibet through coups, exiles and murders — most notably the fifth Dalai Lama. The Dalai Lamas rose to power in Tibet largely because of their ideological support for the militant claims of the Buddhist Dzungar Mongols.

In modern times, too, there are many examples of Buddhist militant ideology and terrorism. Over the past few decades, for instance, Buddhist monks were at the forefront of violent extremism in southern Myanmar (Burma), most notably that of the "Democratic Karen Buddhist Army" and the "969 Movement," which has engaged in anti-Muslim riots and terrorism. In Thailand, some anti-communist monks declared that killing communists did not violate Buddhist commandments.

In the Sri Lankan civil war (1983-2009), some Buddhists engaged in fighting and terrorism based on explicitly Buddhist holy-war ideology. In modern Japan, many Buddhists supported Japan's aggression in the Second World War, declaring that "We now have no choice but to exercise the benevolent forcefulness of 'killing one in order that many may live.'" Modern radical militant Japanese Buddhist sects such as Nichiren and the apocalyptic Aum Shinrikyo have been involved in violence and terror attacks.

Now, we need to re-emphasize that we are not attempting to demonize Buddhism or claim that it is an inherently violent religion. Violent and pacifist qualities can be found in all religions. More importantly, violent people will often use religion as a rationalization for their violence. By focusing only on the violent characteristics of Buddhism — as with any other religion, for that matter — one could argue Buddhism to be violent. And Buddhist violence can indeed be found throughout the world and in all periods. But that, of course, would grossly misrepresent the impact and history of Buddhism.

2

Buddhism Violence in Myanmar

Buddhism in Myanmar is prevalently of the Theravada custom, rehearsed by 89% of the nation's populace It is the most religious Buddhist nation as far as the extent of ministers in the populace and extent of pay spent on religion.Adherents are undoubtedly found among the predominant Bamar individuals, Shan, Rakhine, Mon, Karen, Zo, and Chinese who are very much coordinated into Burmese society. Friars, all things considered known as the sangha, are revered individuals from Burmese society. Among numerous ethnic gatherings in Myanmar, including the Bamar and Shan, Theravada Buddhism is drilled in conjunction with nat revere, which includes the pacification of spirits who can mediate in common undertakings.

As to the day by day schedules of Buddhists in Myanmar, there are two most famous practices: merit-production and vipassanâ. Theweizza way is the slightest well known; it is an obscure shape fairly connected to Buddhist goal that includes the mysterious. Merit-production is the most widely recognized way embraced by Burmese Buddhists. This way includes the recognition of the Five Precepts and amassing of good legitimacy through philanthropy and great deeds (dana) to get an ideal resurrection. The vipassana way, which has made strides since the mid 1900s, is a type of knowledge contemplation accepted to prompt illumination. The weizza way, is an elusive arrangement of mysterious practices, (for example, recitation of spells, samatha and speculative chemistry) and accepted to prompt life as a weizza (likewise spelt weikza), a semi-everlasting and extraordinary being who anticipates the presence without bounds Buddha, Maitreya (Arimeitaya).

HISTORY

The historical backdrop of Buddhism in Myanmar likely expands more than two thousand years. The Sâsana VaCsa (Burmese Thathana Win), composed by Pinyasami in 1834, outlines a great part of the historical backdrop of Buddhism in Myanmar. As indicated by the Mahavamsa, a Pali annal of fifth century Sri Lanka, Ashoka sent two bhikkhus, Sona and Uttara, to Suvarnabhumi around 228 BC with different friars and consecrated writings, including books.

An Andhra Ikshvaku engraving from about the third century alludes to the transformation of the Kiratas to Buddhism, why should thought have beenTibeto-Burman-talking people groups of Myanmar. Early Chinese writings of about the same date talk about a "Kingdom of Liu-Yang," where all individuals worshiped the Buddha and there were a few thousand samaGas. This kingdom has been related to a district some place in focal Burma. A progression of epigraphic records in Pali, Sanskrit, Pyu and Mon datable to the sixth and seventh hundreds of years, has been recouped from Central and Lower Burma (Pyay and Yangon). From the eleventh to thirteenth hundreds of years, the Bamar lords and rulers of the Pagan Kingdom manufactured endless stupas and sanctuaries.

The Ari Buddhism time incorporated the love of bodhisattvas and nâgas. Theravada Buddhism was embedded at Bagan surprisingly as ahead of schedule as the eleventh century by the Bamar lord Anawrahta (1044-1077). In year 1057, Anawratha sent an armed force to overcome the Mon city of Thaton to acquire theTipimâka of the Pâli Canon. He was changed over by a Mon bhikkhu,Shin Arahan, to Theravada Buddhism. Shin Arahan's recommendation prompted obtaining thirty arrangements of Pali sacred texts from the Mon lord Manuhal by power. Mon society, starting there, came to be to a great extent acclimatized into the

Bamar society situated in Bagan. In spite of endeavors at change, certain components of Ari Buddhism and conventional nat love proceeded, for example, adoration for the bodhisattvaAvalokiteœvara (Lawka nat). Successive kings of Bagan continued to build large numbers of monuments, temples, and pagodas in honour of Buddhism, and there is inscriptional evidence of a Theravadin vihara for bhikkhunis from 1279.

Burmese rule at Bagan continued until the first Mongol invasion of Burma in 1287. Towards the end of the 13th century, Buddhism declined due to the invading Tatars. In the 14th century, another lineage was imported from Sri Lanka to Ayutthaya, the capital of the ThaiAyutthaya Kingdom. A new ordination line, that of the Thai Forest Tradition, thus entered Myanmar.

The Shan, meanwhile, established themselves as rulers throughout the region now known as Myanmar. Thihathu, a Shan king, established rule in Bagan by patronising and building many monasteries and pagodas.

The Mon kingdoms, often ruled by Shan chieftains, fostered Theravada Buddhism in the 14th century. Wareru, who became king of Mottama, patronised Buddhism, and established a code of law, the *Dhammasattha*, compiled by Buddhist monastics. King Dhammazedi, formerly a Mon bhikkhu, established rule in the late 15th century at Inwa and unified the sangha in Mon territories. He also standardised ordination of monks set out in the Kalyani Inscriptions. Dhammazedi moved the capital back to Hanthawaddy (Bago). His mother-in-law, Queen Shin Sawbu, was also a great patron of Buddhism. She is credited for expanding and gilding the Shwedagon Pagoda, giving her own weight in gold.

The Bamars, who had fled to Taungoo before the invading Shan, established a kingdom there under the reigns of Tabinshwehti and Bayinnaung, who conquered and unified most of modern Myanmar. These monarchs also embraced Mon culture and patronised Theravada Buddhism.

In the reigns of succeeding kings, the Taungoo Dynasty became increasingly volatile and was overthrown by the Mon. In the mid-18th century, King Alaungpaya defeated the Mon, expanded the

Bamar kingdoms, and established the Konbaung Dynasty. Under the rule ofBodawpaya, a son of Alaungpaya, a unified sect of monks ("Thudhamma") was created within the kingdom. Bodawpaya restored ties with Sri Lanka, allowing for mutual influence in religious affairs. During the reigns of the Konbaung kings that followed, both secular and religious literary works were created. King Mindon Min moved his capital to Mandalay.

After Lower Burma had been conquered by the British, Christianity began to gain acceptance. Many monks from Lower Burma had resettled in Mandalay, but by decree of Mindon Min, they returned to serve the Buddhist laypeople. Schisms arose in the sangha; they were resolved during the Fifth Buddhist Synod, held in Mandalay in 1871.

The Fifth Council was convened at Mandalay in Myanmar on the first waning day of Tazaungmone, 1232 Myanmar Era, 2415 B.E (November 1871). The scriptures inscribed on palm-leaves could not last for a long time. Besides there might be many variations in rewriting the scriptures from copy to copy. Therefore, the scriptures were inscribed on marble slabs to dispel these disadvantages.

Two thousand and four hundred bhikkhus led by Venerable Jagarabhivamsa Thera (Tipitakadhara Mahadhammaraja-dhirajaguru) of Dakkhinarama Monastery, Mandalay, convened, to recite and approve the scriptures. King Mindon initiated and supported the Fifth Great Council to the end. The scriptures were first inscribed on seven hundred and twenty-nine marble slabs) in the precinct of Lokamarajina Pagoda at the foot of Mandalay Hill. From 1860 to 1868, the Tipitaka was engraved on 729 marble slabs and assembled in the Kuthodaw Pagoda. It took seven years, six months and fourteen days to finish this work. Then the bhikkhus recited to approve the inscriptions for five months and three days. In 1871, a new *hti* (the gold umbrella that crowns a stupa) encrusted with jewels from the crown was also donated by Mindon Min for the Shwedagon now in British Burma. After the Fifth Great Council. the Pali Texts were translated into Myanmar language, and the Doctrinal Order was promulgated to the whole country for purpose of purification and propagation of the Buddha's Teachings.

During the British administration of Lower and Upper Burma, also known as *Burma Proper*, government policies were secular which meant monks were not protected by law. Nor was Buddhism patronised by the colonial government. This resulted in tensions between the colonised Buddhists and their European rulers. There was much opposition (including by the Irish monk U Dhammaloka) to the efforts by Christian missionaries to convert the Burmese people, Bamar, Shan, Mon, Rakhine and plains Karen, with one exception - the hill tribes. Today, Christianity is most commonly practised by the Kuki, Kachin, and the Kayin. Notwithstanding traditional avoidance of political activity, monks often participated in politics and in the struggle for independence.

Since 1948 when the country gained its independence from Great Britain, both civil and military governments have supported Theravada Buddhism. The 1947 Constitution states, "The State recognizes the special position of Buddhism as the faith professed by the great majority of the citizens of the Union." The Ministry of Religious Affairs, created in 1948, was responsible for administering Buddhist affairs in Myanmar. In 1954, the prime minister, U Nu, convened the Sixth Buddhist Synod at Kaba Aye Pagoda in Rangoon (Yangon), which was attended by 2,500 monks, and established the World Buddhist University.

During the military rule of Ne Win (1962–1988), he attempted to reform Myanmar under the Burmese Way to Socialism which contained elements of Buddhism. In the 8888 Uprising, many monks participated and were killed by Tatmadaw soldiers. The succeeding military regime, the State Peace and Development Council (SPDC) patronised Buddhism, although persecution of Buddhists contrary to the regime, as well as persons of other religions, namely Islam and Christianity, continues.

TRADITIONS

The culture of Myanmar is deemed synonymous with its Buddhism. There are many Burmese festivals all through the year, most of them related to Buddhism. The Burmese New Year, *Thingyan*, also known as the Water Festival, has its origins in Hinduism but it is also a time when many Burmese boys celebrate *shinbyu*, a special rite of passage by which a boy enters the kyaung for a short time as asâmaGerî.

Veneration

A Burmese Buddhist household contains an altar or shrine to the Buddha, with at least one dedicated image of the Gautama Buddha. The Buddha image is commonly placed on a "throne" called a *gaw pallin*.

Before a Buddha statue is used for veneration at home, it must be formally consecrated, in a ritual called *anay gaza tin* . This consecration, led by a Buddhist monk, who recites*aneka jâti saCsâraC* (translated as 'through the round of many births I roamed'), the 153rd verse of the Dhammapada (found in the 11th chapter).

The consecration rite, which can last a few hours, is held in the morning and consists of four primary parts:

1. Offerings (candles, flowers, incense, flags) made to the Buddha
2. Chanting of *paritta* (typically Mangala Sutta, Metta Sutta, Ratana Sutta, Pubbhana Sutta)
3. Recitation of *aneku jâti saCsâraC*
4. Recitation of the Twelve Nidânas

The consecration rituals are believed to imbue the Buddha image with a sacred quality that can protect the home and surroundings from misfortune and symbolically embody the powers of the Buddha.

Shinbyu

It is the most important duty of all Burmese parents to make sure their sons are admitted to the Buddhist *Sangha* by performing a shinbyu ceremony once they have reached the age of seven or older. A symbolic procession and ceremony of exchanging princely attire with that of an ascetic follows the example of Gautama Buddha. He was born a royal prince named Siddartha Gautama, but left his palace on horseback followed by his loyal attendant Chanda after he found out that life is made up of suffering (dukkha) and the notion of self is merely an illusion (anatta) when one day he saw the "Four Great Signs" - the old, the sick, the dead, and the ascetic - in the royal gardens. All Buddhists are required to keep the basic Five Precepts , and novices are expected to keep the Ten Precepts . Parents expect them to stay at the kyaung immersed in the teachings of the Buddha as members of the Sangha for three months or longer. They will have another opportunity to join the Sangha at the age of 20, taking the upasampada ordination, to become a fully ordained bhikkhu, keeping the 227 precepts of the full monastic rules or Pâtimokkha and perhaps remain a monk for life.

Buddhist holidays

Thingyan usually falls in mid-April and tops the list of Public holidays in Myanmar. Vesak, the full moon in May, is the most sacred of all as the Buddha was born, became enlightened, and entered parinibbana (died) on the same day. It is celebrated by watering the Bodhi Tree.

Pagoda festivals held throughout the country also usually fall on full moon days and most of them will be on the full moon of Tabaung (February/March) including the Shwedagon Pagoda. They attract not only crowds of pilgrims from near and far, often in caravans of bullock carts, but they also double as great market fairs where both local and itinerant traders set up their stalls and shops among food stalls, restaurants, and free open-air stage performances as well as theatre halls.

Vassa

The three monsoon months from mid-July to mid-October is Vassa, a time when people are busy tilling their land and planting the rice paddies and bhikkhus remain in kyaungs. New robes are offered to bhikkhus at the beginning of Vassa, the end of which is marked by the Thadingyut Festival.

After the harvest, robes are again offered at Kathina, usually held during October or November.Uposatha days are observed by keeping the Eight Precepts by laypersons during Thingyan and Vassa and by devout Buddhists all the year round.

Parents and elders also receive obeisance from younger members of the family at the beginning as well as the end of lent, after the tradition established by the Buddha himself. It was during Vassa that he ascended to the TâvatiCsa Heaven to preach a sermon, as an act of gratitude, to his mother who had become a deva, and he was welcomed back to earth with a great festival of lights. Teachers receive the same obeisance, a tradition started by National Schools founded in defiance of the colonial administration and continued after independence by state schools.

Wedding ceremonies - nothing to do with religion and not conducted by the Sangha - are not held during the three months of Vassa, a custom which has resulted in a spate of weddings after Thadingyut or *Wa-kyut*, awaited impatiently by couples wanting to tie the knot.

Buddhist education

Theravadins send their children to kyaungs to receive a Buddhist education, learning the Pâli Canon, the life story of Gautama Buddha, the 550 Jataka tales - most importantly the Ten Great Incarnations and the 38 Buddhist Beatitudes - as soon as they have a good grounding of the three Rs. Monks were the traditional teachers of the young and old alike until secular and missionary schools came into being during the British colonial administration.

There has been a revival of monastic schools since the 1990s with the deepening economic crisis. Children from poor families that can ill afford fees, uniforms and books have renewed the demand for a free monastic education, and minority groups such as the Shan, Pa'O,Palaung, Lahu and Wa are benefitting from this revival.

MONASTICISM

Buddhist monks, who are venerated throughout Burmese society, are approximately 500,000 strong. Nuns form an additional 75,000. Monks belong to one of two primary monastic orders: Thudhamma Nikaya (88% of Buddhist monks) and the more orthodox Shwegyin Nikaya (7% of Buddhist monks).

Burmese monastic orders do not differ in doctrine but in monastic practice, lineage and organisation structure. Other minor monastic orders include the Dwara Nikaya in Lower Burma, and Hngettwin Nikaya in Mandalay, both of which have a few thousand member monks. There are nine legally recognised monastic orders in Burma today, under the 1990 Law Concerning Sangha Organizations. There are also esoteric Buddhist sects or *weizza* not recognised by any authority that incorporate non-Buddhist elements like alchemy, magic and occultism.

The overwhelming majority of Burmese monks wear maroon robes, while others wear ochre, unlike in neighbouring Theravada countries like Thailand, Laos and Sri Lanka, where monks commonly wear saffron robes.

Women

The full bhikkhuni (nuns) lineage of Theravada Buddhism died out, and for various technical and social reasons was therefore permanently absent. The governing council of Buddhism in Myanmar has ruled that there can be no valid ordination of women in modern times, though some Burmese monks disagree. However, as in many other Theravadin countries, women have created a niche for themselves as renunciants not recognised by the state-empowered Sangharaja or even the Sangha in general. In Myanmar, these women are called thilashin. A thilashin is a female lay renunciant whose vows are the same as those of sâmaGerîs "novitiate nuns". Like the maechi of neighbouring Thailand and the dasa sil mata of Sri Lanka, thilashin occupy a position somewhere between that of an ordinary lay follower and an ordained monastic. However, they are treated more favourably than most maechi, being able to receive training, practice meditation and sit for the same qualification examinations as the monks.

Thilashins observe the ten precepts and can be recognised by their pink robes, shaven head, orange or brown shawl and metal alms bowl. Thilashins go out on alms rounds on uposatha and receive uncooked rice or money.

Thilashins are addressed with the honorifics *sayale* and *daw*. These are used as honorifics to the Buddhist name given.

Thilashins often reside in either separate quarters or in segregated kyaung (temple-monasteries). They do not have to look after the monks, but may help cook if required. Although ranked lower than the monks, they are not subservient to them.

There have been efforts by some thilashins to reinstate the bhikkhuni lineage, although there are reservations from the government and general populace. A new Theravada bhikkhuni sangha was first convened in 1996, and since then many more have taken the full vows. However, within Myanmar, thilashins remain the only monastic option for women at this time. In 2003, Saccavadi and Gunasari were ordained as bhikkhunis in Sri Lanka, thus becoming the first female Myanmarese novices in modern times to receive higher ordination in Sri Lanka.

POLITICS

Buddhism made major contributions in the development of Burmese politics. Burmese nationalism first began with the formation of theYoung Men's Buddhist Associations (YMBA) - modelled on the YMCA - which started to appear all over the country at the start of the 20th century. Buddhist monks along with students had been in the forefront of the struggle for independence and later for democracy, the best known leaders in history being U Ottama and U Seinda in Rakhine State, and U Wisara who died after a protracted hunger strike inYangon prison. A major thoroughfare in Yangon is named after U Wisara. The League of Young Monks based in Mandalay is a well known activist organisation. The Burmese word for boycott is *thabeik hmauk* , which literally means to turn the monk's alms bowl upside down - declining to accept alms in protest.

Civilian governments, after the country gained independence, patronised Buddhism, donating large sums to fund the upkeep and building of Buddhist monuments. In addition, leaders of political parties and parliamentarians, in particular U Nu, passed legislation influenced by Buddhism. He declared Buddhism the state religion which alienated minority groups, especially the Kachin. This added yet another group to the growing number of ethnic insurgencies. The present military government has been so keen to be seen as patrons of Buddhism that it has become a joke- "Burmese TV has only two colours, green and yellow" - describing the military green uniforms and monk's yellow robes or golden pagodas which dominate the screen.

Shwedagon Pagoda has been an important venue for large public meetings where both Aung San and his daughter Aung San Suu Kyihad made their famous speeches. During the second university strike in history of 1936, the students camped out on the Shwedagon terraces.

Aung San Suu Kyi returned from London to lead the National League for Democracy which was founded during the 1988 popular uprising, but was placed under house arrest in 1989; since she is a devout Buddhist and leader of the opposition, she is considered a socially engaged Buddhist.

Saffron Revolution

In September 2007, Buddhists again took to the streets in the Saffron Revolution, a mass protest against the military government. Thousand of junta military and police forces poured into Yangon to try to control the situation, which rapidly deteriorated. A curfew was imposed and on 25 September troops surrounded Sule Pagoda. The protest continued to grow with regular citizens joining to support and defend the Buddhists. Overnight, junta forces invaded all the kyaungs in the country and imprisoned thousands of monks. It was reported that Nobel prize winning human rights activist and Buddhist Aung San Suu Kyiwas removed from her home where she languished under house arrest and moved to the infamous Insein Prison. Mass protests erupted over this and junta troops began firing on monks, civilians, and demonstrators in the largest clash since 1988, which left thousands injured and hundreds dead. Images of the brutality were aired worldwide. Leaders around the world condemned the junta's actions and many nations imposed economic sanctions on Myanmar in protest. The President of the United States, George W. Bush, addressed the United Nations, stating, "Every civilized nation has a responsibility to stand up for people suffering under a brutal military regime like the one that has ruled Burma for so long." The Burmese junta responded by trying to control media coverage, curtail travel, censor news stories, and shut down access to the Internet.

In November 2008, U Gambira, a leader of the All Burma Monks' Alliance, was sentenced to 68 years in prison, at least 12 years of which will be hard labour; other charges against him are still pending. In early 2009, his sentence was reduced to 63 years. His sentence was protested by Human Rights Watch, and Amnesty Internationalconsiders him a prisoner of conscience. Both groups called for his immediate release. Gambira was released during a mass pardon of prisoners on 13 January 2012 as part of the 2011–2012 Burmese political reforms. He ceased to be a monk in April 2012, stating that he had been unable to find a monastery to join due to his status as a former prisoner. He was re-arrested at least three times in 2012, and as of 11 December 2012, was released on bail.

CULTURE OF MYANMAR

The culture of Myanmar (also known as Burma) has been heavily influenced by Buddhism and the Mon people. Burmese culture has also been influenced by its neighbours India, Thailand and China. In more recent times, British colonial rule and westernisation have influenced aspects of Burmese culture, including language andeducation.

ARTS

Historically, Burmese art was based on Buddhist or Hindu cosmology and myths. There are several regional styles of Buddha images, each with certain distinctive characteristics. For example, the Mandalay style, which developed in the late 1800s, consists of an oval-shaped Buddha with realistic features, including naturally curved eyebrows, smaller but still prominent ears, and a draping robe. There are 10 traditional arts, called *pan sè myo* , listed as follows:

1. Blacksmith
2. Woodcarving
3. Goldsmith
4. Stucco relief
5. Masonry

6. Stone carving
7. Turnery
8. Painting
9. Lacquerware
10. Bronze casting

In addition to the traditional arts are silk weaving, pottery, tapestry making, gemstone engraving, and gold leaf making. Temple architecture is typically of brick and stucco, and pagodas are often covered with layers of gold leaf while monasteries tend to be built of wood (although monasteries in cities are more likely to be built of modern materials). A very common roofing style in Burmese architecture is called *pyatthat* , which is a multi-tiered and spired roof.

Literature

Burmese literature has been greatly influenced by Buddhism, notably the Jataka Tales. Since orthodox Buddhism prohibited fiction, many historical works are nonfiction. However, British colonisation introduced many genres of fiction, which have become extremely popular today. Poetry features prominently, and there are several forms of poetry unique to Burmese literature. By 1976, only 411 titles were published annually, compared to 1882, when 445 titles were published. Various factors, especially the lengthened bureaucratic process to obtain printing permits, censorship, and increasing economic hardship of consumers because of the socialist economic schemes, contributed to the decline of Burmese literary output.

Popular novels have similar themes to Western novels, often involving adventure, espionage, detective work, and romance. Many writers also translate Western novels, especially those of Arthur Hailey and Harold Robbins. The flourishing translation sector is the result of the Burmese government, which did not sign the Universal Copyright Convention Agreement, which would have forced Burmese writers to pay royalties to the original writers.

Short stories, often published in magazines, also enjoy tremendous popularity. They often deal with everyday life and have political messages (such as subtle criticisms of the capitalist system), partly because unlike novels, short stories are not censored by the Press Scrutiny Board. Poetry is also a popular genre today, as it was during the monarchical times, but unlike novels and other works, which use literary Burmese, poetry uses vernacular rather than literary Burmese. This reform movement is led by left-leaning writers who believe laymen's language (the vernacular and colloquial form of Burmese) ought to be used instead of formal Burmese in literature.

One of the greatest female writers of the Post-colonial period is journalist Kyaw Ma Ma Lay. Khin Myo Chit was another important writer, who wrote, among her works, The 13-Carat Diamond (1955), which was translated into many languages. The journalist Ludu U Hla was the author of numerous volumes of ethnic minority folklore, novels about inmates in U Nu-era jails, and biographies of people working in different occupations. The Prime Minister U Nu himself wrote several politically oriented plays and novels. Other prolific writers of the post-colonial era include Thein Pe Myint (and his The Ocean Traveller and the Pearl Queen, considered a Burmese classic), Mya Than Tint (known for his translations of Western classics like War and Peace), Thawda Swe and Myat Htun. Distinguished women writers, who have also been an ever-present force in Burmese literary history, include Kyi Aye, Khin Hnin Yu, and San San Nweh. Burmese Historians: Ba Shin, Than Tun, Thant Myint-U, Htin Aung, Sao Saimong, Myoma Myint Kywe, and San C. Po were famous in Burma.

Dance

Dance in Burma can be divided into dramatic, folk and village, and nat dances, each having distinct characteristics. Although Burmese dance has been influenced by the dance traditions of its neighbours, in particular Thailand (*yodaya aka*), it retains unique qualities that distinguish it from other regional styles, including angular, fast-paced and energetic movements and emphasis on pose, not movement.

Music

Various types of Burmese music use an array of traditional musical instruments, assembled in an orchestra known as *hsaing* *waing*which the Burmese *saing saya* Kyaw Kyaw Naing has made more widely known in the West. Traditional folk music is atypical in Southeast Asian music, as it is characterised by sudden shifts in rhythm and melody as well as change in texture and timbre. An instrument unique to Burma is the *saung-gauk*, an arched harp that can be traced to pre-Hittite times.

Classical traditions of Burmese music are found in the*Mahagita*, an extensive collection of classical songs and are typically divided into indoor and outdoor ensembles. These songs tend to be about various legends in Pali and subsequently in Burmese intermingled with Pali, related to religion or the power and glory of monarchs, and then the natural beauty of the land, forests and the seasons, eventually feminine beauty, love, passion and longing, in addition to folk music sung in the paddy fields. Pop music, both adopted and homegrown, however, dominates the music of Burma today.

CUSTOMS

The "traditional" Burmese greeting is *mingalaba* ; this is, however, a comparatively recent form of greeting, originating in the 1960s as a replacement in schools for the English language greeting "Good morning/afternoon, teacher" in the newly nationalised missionary schools. Greetings such as "Have you eaten?" and "How are you?" are still common. "Hello" is also a popular greeting nowadays, whereas it used to be confined to answering the phone.

Dress

The typical garment of the Burmese is the Indian lungi or *longyi*, a sarong worn by both men and women. This replaced the traditional paso for men and tamein for women by the 20th century. For business and formal occasions, Bamar men wear a Manchu Chinese jacket over an English collar shirt (sometimes donning a turban called *gaung baung*), while Bamar women wear a blouse buttoned at the front, called *yinzi* or to the side, called *yinbon* , and a shawl. In urban areas, skirts and pants are becoming more common, particularly among the young. During the British colonial era, Burmese nationalists associated traditional clothing, in particular *Yaw longyi* , a type of longyifrom the Yaw region, and *pinni taikpon* , a fawn-coloured collarless jacket, with anti-colonialism and nationalist sentiment, because of a clampdown in the 1920s over increasing dissent. Wearing "traditional" clothing was seen as a mode of passive resistance among the Burmese. British rule nonetheless influenced hair fashion and clothing. Cropped short hair, called *bo ke* replaced long hair as the norm among Burmese men.

Similarly, women began wearing hairstyles like *amauk* , consisting of crested bangs curled at the top, with the traditional hair bun . The female sarong (*htamein*) became shorter, no longer extending to the feet, but to the ankles, and the length of the sarong's top decreased to reveal more waistline. This period also saw the introduction of a sheer muslin blouse for women, revealing a corset-like lace bodice called *za bawli* .

Speech

The Burmese language is very age-oriented. The use of honorifics before personal names is the norm, and it is considered rude to call a person just by their name without the honorific unless they are known from childhood or youth or in the case of a younger underling. Young males are addressed as *Maung* or *Ko* (lit. brother), and older or senior men as *U* (lit. uncle). Likewise, young females are addressed as *Ma* (lit. sister), and older or senior women as *Daw* (lit. aunt), regardless of their marital status. 'Aunty' or 'Uncle' is commonly used as well today. The first and second person pronouns vary depending on whom one is speaking to and are age-dependent. Elders are spoken to in a more respectful manner and a special vocabulary exists for speaking to Buddhist monks.

Manners

Burmese society operates on *ana* , a characteristic or feeling that has no English equivalent. It is characterised by a hesitation, reluctance or avoidance, to perform an action based on the fear that it will offend someone or cause someone to lose face, or become embarrassed. Also, there is the concept of *hpon* , which translates to "power". It is used as an explanation for the varying degrees of ethnic, socioeconomic, and gender differences between people in a society. *Hpon*refers to the cumulative result of past deeds, an idea that power or social position comes from merit earned in previous lives. This idea is used to justify the prevalent view that women are less equal than men, who are considered to have more *hpon*.

Age is still considered synonymous with experience and wisdom, hence venerated. Parents and teachers are second only to the Three Jewels , together making up the Five Boundless Beneficence, and are paid obeisance (called gadaw) at special times of the year such as*Thingyan*, beginning and end of Buddhist Lent, and usually parents before one leaves on a journey. Elders are served first at meals, and in their absence a spoonful of rice is put aside first in the pot as a token of respect before serving the meal. Young people would avoid sitting on a higher level than the elders or passing in front of them unless unavoidable, and then only treading softly with a slight bow. Things would be passed to the elders using both hands together. Men may cross their legs sitting on a chair or a mat but women generally would not.

Children are taught from young 'to venerate one's elders, to respect one's peers, and to be kind to the young and weak'. Parents are believed to be solely responsible for their children's behaviour as reflected by the expressions: *mi ma hsonma, hpa ma hsonma* and *ami youk tau hnoukkyan, ahpa youk tau ko amu-aya kyan* (bad language from bad mother, bad body-language from bad father). Saying "thank you" however is not Burmese custom between friends and within the family.

It is considered rude to touch a person's head, because it is the "highest" point of the body. It is also considered taboo to touch another's feet, but worse still to point with the foot or sit with feet pointing at someone older, because the feet are considered the lowest. Also, pointing a finger at Buddha images is considered blasphemous, although this custom has slowly eroded. Shoes are always taken off upon entering homes, monasteries and pagoda compounds. A custom of the Burmese is to perambulate clockwise around a pagoda, not counterclockwise.

Physical demonstrations of affection in public are common between friends of the same gender or between members of the family, but seldom seen between lovers. It is thus common to see friends walking together holding hands or with arms round each other, but couples rarely do so, except in major cities.

CUISINE

Burmese cuisine has been influenced by Indian, Chinese and Thai cuisines as well as domestic ethnic cuisines. It is not widely known throughout the world and can be characterised as having a mildly spicy taste, with a limited use of spices. A typical Burmese meal consists of several meat curries, a soup, steamed rice and fermented sauce of preserved fish, along with vegetables for dipping. Condiments like balachaung, Indian-style pickles and pickled vegetables are commonly served alongside the dishes. Althoughfish sauce and shrimp paste are commonly used ingredients, as in other Southeast Asian cuisines, Burmese cuisine also makes extensive use of chickpeas, lentils and tamarind, which is used to add a sour flavour rather than the lime juice or vinegar used in other cuisines.

Ethnic cuisines, in particular Shan cuisine, are also prominently found throughout Burma, as are Indian and Chinese dishes, particularly in urban areas. The de facto national dish is mohinga , rice noodles in a rich fish soup. Salads, especially laphet thoke, which is a salad of pickled tea leaves, are also popular dishes. The Burmese traditionally eat with their fingers, although the usage of Western utensils and chopsticks have become more widespread, especially in towns and cities. Indian breads like paratha and naan or rice noodles are also commonly eaten with dishes, in addition to rice.

WEDDINGS

Traditional Burmese folklore considers love to be destiny, as the Hindu god Brahma writes one's destiny in love on a child's brow when he or she is six days old, called *na hpuza* . A Burmese wedding can be religious or secular and extravagant or simple. Traditionally, a marriage is recognised with or without a ceremony when the man's longyi (sarong) is seen hanging from a rail of the house or if the couple eats from the same plate. Dowries are typically unheard of, and arranged marriage is not a custom of the Burmese.

Weddings are traditionally avoided during the Buddhist lent, which lasts three months from July to October. Generally speaking, Buddhist monks are not present to conduct the wedding and solemnise the marriage, as they are forbidden to officiate a marriage, which is considered a worldly affair (*lokiya*). However, they may be invited to bless the newly wed couple and recite a protective *paritta*. Typically, the bride and groom arrange an almsgiving feast to monks the morning of the wedding to gain merit.

A more extravagant wedding requires months of preparation, including consultation with an astrologer in choosing the most auspicious time and setting of the event. Also, a master of ceremonies, typically a brahmin, is hired to preside over the ceremony. The bride and groom sit on cushions next to each other. At the beginning of the wedding, the Brahmin blows a conch shell to commence the ceremony and joins the palms of the couple, wraps them in white cloth, and dips the joined palms in a silver bowl. The Burmese word "to marry" is *let htat* , which literally means "to join palms together". After chanting a few Sanskrit mantras, the brahmin takes the couple's joined palms out of the bowl and blows the conch shell to end the ceremony. Afterward, entertainers perform, and the wedding is ended with a speech by a guest of higher social standing. Wedding receptions at a hotel, serving tea and ice cream, are common in urban areas.

FUNERALS

Burmese funerals typically last a week, with the body traditionally buried or cremated on the third day. Burial is common, but cremation, more common in the cities, is also practised by orthodox Buddhists and monks in Burma. A coin, called *Ku-Doe-ga* is placed in the mouth of the deceased person, to pay a "ferry toll" for crossing death. Before the actual interment of the body, an offering of turmeric-coated rice is given to appease the*bhummazo* , the guardian deity of the earth. During the actual funeral, gifts in the form of paper fans containing the deceased person's name, as well as Buddhist scriptures relating to theimpermanence of life (anicca) and samsara are distributed to all attendees.

In urban areas, flower wreaths and florals are typically given at a funeral, as well as money, for less well-to-do families. However, in villages, more practical gifts such as food items are given to the grieving family. For seven days, the windows and doors of the house in which the person died may be left open, to let the deceased person's consciousness or "spirit", called *leippya* leave the home, and a vigil may be kept at nighttime. On the seventh day, called *yet le* , a meal is offered to monks, who in turn recite blessings, protective parittas and transfer merit to the deceased, concluded with a Buddhist water libation ceremony.

RELIGION

Burma is a predominantly Theravada Buddhist country. Buddhism reached Burma around the beginning of the Christian era, mingling with Hinduism (also imported from India) and indigenous animism. The Pyu and Mon kingdoms of the first millennium were Buddhist, but the early Bamar peoples were animists. According to traditional history, King Anawrahta of Bagan adopted Buddhism in 1056 and went to war with the Mon kingdom of Thaton in the south of the country to obtain the Buddhist Canon and learned monks. The religious tradition created at this time, and which continues to the present day, is a syncretalist mix of what might be termed 'pure' Buddhism (of the Theravada school) with deep-rooted elements of the original animism or nat worship and even strands of Hinduism and the Mahayana tradition of northern India.

Islam reached Burma at approximately the same time, but never gained a foothold outside the geographically isolated seaboard running from modern-day Bangladesh southward to Irrawaddy Delta (modern Rakhine State, formerly Arakan, an independent kingdom until the eighteenth century). The colonial period saw a huge influx of Muslim (and Hindu) Indians into Yangon and other cities, and the majority of Yangon's many mosques and temples owe their origins to these immigrants.

Christianity was brought to Burma by European missionaries in the 1800s. It made little if any headway among Buddhists, but has been widely adopted by non-Buddhists such as the Chin, Karen, and Kachin. The Roman Catholic Church, Myanmar Baptist Convention and the Assemblies of God of Burma are the largest Christian denominations in Burma. Burma is home to the second largest population of Baptists in the world, after the United States, the result of American missionary work.

The Chinese contribution to Burma's religious mix has been slight, but several traditional Chinese temples were established in Yangon and other large cities in the nineteenth century when large-scale Chinese migration was encouraged by the British. Since approximately 1990 this migration has resumed in huge numbers, but the modern Chinese immigrants seem to have little interest in religion. Some more isolated indigenous peoples in the more inaccessible parts of the country still follow traditional animism.

Burma has nominal guarantees of freedom of religious expression, although religious minorities (Christians and Muslims), particularly those in the countryside are subject to discrimination. Sporadic riots between Burmese Buddhists and Burmese Muslims are not uncommon, and tensions between the two religious groups are high, particularly in major cities. In 2001, after the Taliban's destruction of the Buddhas of Bamiyan, religiously motivated riots broke out between Buddhists and Muslims across major cities in Burma, includingSittwe, Pyay, Taungoo and Bago. The current regime's nationalistic policy of *Bama san-gyin,* which considers Buddhism a key element of Burmese-ness, does provide a systemic bias in favour of Buddhists in terms of preferment in the armed forces and other State structures.

Pagodas and monasteries

Aspects of Burmese culture are most apparent in religious sites. The country has been called the "Land of Pagodas" as the landscape is dominated by Buddhist pagodas or stupas. The four most important Burmese Buddhist pilgrimage sites are Shwedagon Pagoda inYangon, Mahamuni Buddha in Mandalay, Kyaiktiyo Pagoda in Mon State, and Bagan, an ancient capital by the Ayeyarwaddy River where thousands of stupas and temples have stood for nearly a millennium in various states of repair .

Pagodas are known by their Pali terms *zedi* or *pahto* , but are also commonly called *hpaya* which is synonymous with "Buddha". Monasteries are known as *hpongyi kyaung* , hpongyi meaning monk, and since they have traditionally been places of learning where village children are taught how to read and write including and more importantly Pali, the language of the Buddhist scriptures, school also came to be called *kyaung* in the Burmese language.

TRADITIONAL FESTIVALS

There are twelve months in the traditional Burmese calendar and twelve corresponding festivals. Most of the festivals are related to Burmese Buddhism and in any town or village the local *paya pwè* (the pagoda festival) is the most important one.

The most well-known festival is Thingyan, a four-day celebration of the coming lunar new year. This festival is held prior to the Burmese New Year, the first day of Tagu which falls in mid-April. Similar to other Southeast Asian new year festivals (e.g. Songkran), people splash water on one another. However, Thingyan has religious significance, marking the days in which Buddhists are expected to observe the Eight Precepts of Buddhism.

Sports

Football is the most popular sport in Burma. Chinlone is an indigenous sport that utilises a rattan ball and is played using mainly the feet and the knees, but the head and also the arms may be used except the hands. Burmese kickboxing called *Lethwei* is popular and tournaments may be seen at pagoda festivals. A form of Burmese martial arts derived from the Shan called*thaing*, divided into *bando* (unarmed combat) and *banshay* (armed combat), rather similar to Chinese Kung fu, is also practised. Of the twelve seasonal festivals, regattas are held in the month of *Tawthalin* (August/ September), and equestrian events were held by the royal army in the time of the Burmese kings in the month of *Pyatho* (December/ January). During British rule, the game of cricket was played by the ruling British, with the Burma national cricket team playing a number of first-class matches. The team exists today, although no longer of first-class quality and is an affiliate member of the International Cricket Council. Burma also has a basketball team, which qualified for the Asian Games in the past.

BUDDHIST MONASTICISM

Buddhist monasticism is one of the earliest surviving forms of organized monasticism in the history of religion. It is also one of the most fundamental institutions of Buddhism. Monks and nuns are considered to be responsible for the preservation and dissemination of the Buddha's teaching and the guidance of Buddhist lay people.

History and development

Although empirically unproven, traditional stories in some Buddhist schools assert (based on the Pâli Canon) that the order ofBuddhist monks and nuns was founded by Gautama Buddha during his lifetime over 2500 years ago. The Buddhist monastic lifestyle grew out of the lifestyle of earlier sects of wandering ascetics, some of whom the Buddha had studied under. It was not really isolationist or eremetic: the sangha was dependent on the lay community for basic provisions of food and clothing, and in return sangha members helped guide lay followers on the path of Dharma. Individuals or small groups of monks – a teacher and his students, or several monks who were friends – traveled together, living on the outskirts of local communities and practicing meditation in the forests. Monks and nuns were expected to live with a minimum of possessions, which were to be voluntarily provided by the lay community. Lay followers also provided the daily food that monks required, and provided shelter for monks when they were needed. Some Buddhist schools assert that during the Buddha's time, many retreats and gardens were donated by wealthy citizens for monks and nuns to stay in during the rainy season (although there is as yet no archaeological evidence to support this claim - evidence only exists for such monastic enclosures at a much later date). Out of this tradition grew two kinds of living arrangements for monastics, as detailed in the Mahavagga section of the Vinaya and Varsavastu texts:

1. avâsâ: a temporary house for monastics called a vihara. Generally more than one monk stayed in each house with each monk in his own cell, called a *parivena*.
2. ârâma: a more permanent and more comfortable arrangement than the avasa. This property was generally donated and maintained by a wealthy citizen. This was more lavish (as suggested by the name – *Araama* means both *pleasant* and *park*). It generally consisted of residences within orchards or parks.

One of the more famous Arama is Anathapindika's, known as *Anathapindikassa arame*, built on Prince Jeta's grove. It had buildings worth 1.8 million gold pieces built in a beautiful grove, with the total gift worth 5.4 million gold pieces.

After the parinirvana of the Buddha, the Buddhist monastic order developed into a primarily cenobitic movement. The practice of living communally during the rainy vassaseason, prescribed by the Buddha, gradually grew to encompass a settled monastic life centered on life in a community of practitioners. Most of the modern disciplinary rules followed by monks and nuns—the Patimokkha—relate to such an existing, prescribing in great detail proper methods for living and relating in a community of monks or nuns. The number of rules observed varies with the order; Theravada monks follow around 227 rules. There are a larger number of rules specified for bhikkhunis.

Monastic life

Buddhism has no central authority, and therefore many different varieties of practice and philosophy have developed over its history, including among monastic communities, sometimes leading to schisms in the sangha. The information presented here, unless otherwise noted, characterises only certain Buddhist monks who follow the most strict regulations of the 'Southern Schools' tradition. The oldest existing set of texts concerning a Buddhist form of life are those of the Pâli Canon. Although no copy of these texts comes from the time of the Buddha, because of its relative age the Pâli Canon is used by some monastic communities to define their conduct and identity. In some schools of Buddhism, notably those lineages in South East Asia (Sri Lanka, Thailand, etc.) that compose Theravada, the Buddhist monastic community is theoretically divided into two assemblies, the male bhikkhu (Pali, Skt. bhikshu) assembly, and the female bhikkhuni (Skt. bhikshuni) assembly. According to some stories, although his followers initially consisted only of men, the Buddha recognized women as followers after his stepmother, Mahaprajapati, asked for and received permission to live as an ordained practitioner. Also the Buddha's disciple Ananda strongly insisted on including female order. Female monastic communities in the bhikkhuni lineage were never established in the Vajrayanacommunities of Tibet and Nepal; Theravada communities formerly existed, but died out between the 11th and 14th century. Ordination in the bhikkhuni lineage continues to exist among East Asian communities, and attempts have been made at a revival in Southeast Asia and Sri Lanka. Such divisions are more rarely made in the Northern schools, or in the West.

Monks and nuns are expected to fulfill a variety of roles in the Buddhist community. First and foremost, they are expected to preserve the doctrine and discipline now known as Buddhism. They are also expected to provide a living example for the laity, and to serve as a "field of merit" for lay followers, providing laymen and women with the opportunity to earn merit by giving gifts and support to the monks. In return for the support of the laity, monks and nuns are expected to live an austere life focused on the study of Buddhist doctrine, the practice of meditation, and the observance of good moral character. The relative degree of emphasis on meditation or study has often been debated in the Buddhist community. Many continued to keep a relationship with their original families.

A Bhikkhu or Bhikkhuni first ordains as a *Samanera* (novice) for a year or more. There are some conditions which must be met in order to be allowed into Buddhist monaticism, such as age between 7 and 70 and haven't broken sîla in some manners when undertaking them. Male novices often ordain at a very young age, but generally no younger than 8. Women usually choose to ordain as adults, since there is no expectation that they do so in childhood.

Samaneras live according to the Ten Precepts, but are not responsible for living by the full set of monastic rules, vinaya. Higher ordination, conferring the status of a full Bhikkhu or Bhikkhuni, is usually given only to those 20 or older. Women monastics follow a similar progression, but are required to live as Samaneras for a longer period of time, typically five years. In Thailand, monks are considered well supported by the community, and in return the monks offer guidance in life and in the Dharma. They can give the Bhikkhu or Bhikkhuni vows back and return to non-monastic living. According to the vinaya, the sangha should not accept a former Bhikkhuni to retake these vows, and for Bhikkhu up to taking three or seven times in a life. Breaking some important vinaya in manners according to the Vinaya Pitaka would not be accepted for monasticism again for a lifetime. In Burma, Taiwan and Hong Kong, there is sometimes short term monastic ordination available to lay buddhists to take some vows for a week up to month. In Thailand such arrangements are currently available for male only.

The disciplinary regulations for monks and nuns are intended to create a life that is simple and focused, rather than one of deprivation or severe asceticism. Celibacy is of primary importance in monastic discipline, seen as being the preeminent factor in separating the life of a monastic from that of a householder.[2] Depending on the tradition and the strictness of observation, monastics may eat only one meal a day, provided either by direct donations of food from lay supporters, or from a monastery kitchen that is stocked (and possibly staffed) by lay supporters.

Unlike Christian monastics, some schools of Buddhist monastics are not required to live a life of obedience to a superior. However, it is expected that monastics will offer respect to senior members of the Sangha (in Thai tradition, seniority is based on the number of rains retreats, vassas, that one has been ordained). The Buddha did not appoint a successor, nor did he specify rules mandating obedience in the monastic code. Individual groups of monastics are expected to make decisions collectively through regular gatherings of the community, at which decisions regarding violations of monastic rules and the dispositions of communal property are to be made. Individual relationships of teacher/ student, senior/junior, and preceptor/trainee may be observed among groups of monastics, but there are no formal positions, nor is there any authority to give orders or commands invested in senior monks. An abbess or abbot, typically a senior monastic still young enough to be active, is usually responsible for the day-to-day administration of the monastery, and may appoint others to assist with the work. In some traditions, the abbess/abbot is chosen by a vote of the monastics in a monastery. In other traditions (Thailand, for example), the abbot is chosen by the lay community.

LOCAL VARIATIONS

Monastic practices vary significantly according to location. In part, this can be attributed to differences in the scriptural and doctrinal traditions that were received in different parts of the Buddhist world. Additionally, local concessions to social, geographical, and climatic conditions have been adopted by most monastic orders in order to smooth the integration of monks into local communities, and to ensure that monks live in a safe and reasonable manner. In cold climates, for instance, monks are permitted to own and wear additional clothing not specified in the scriptures. In areas where begging rounds are impossible (due to traffic, geography, or disfavor by the lay community), monks more commonly employ a kitchen staff of monks or lay followers who are responsible for providing meals for the community.

Although there were a number of distinct vinaya traditions or ordination lineages, only three have survived to the present day: the Theravâda, Dharmaguptaka,Mûlasarvâstivâda.

Tibet

In Tibet, before the Communist invasion in the late 1940s and early 1950s, more than half of the country's male population was ordained. Today, this is no longer the case. While generally adhering to a Mahayana tradition that advocates the virtues of vegetarianism, Tibetan monks generally eat meat as a concession to climatic conditions that make a plant-based diet largely unfeasible. Tibetan monks follow the Mûlasarvâstivâda vinaya lineage.

Lamas who take bhikcu vows are not allowed to marry. The Nyingma school includes a mixture of bhikcus and non-celibate ngakpas, and it is not unusual for lamas to wear robes closely resembling monastic garb despite them not being bhikcus. Sakya school does not allow monks to get close to women after they have sons. Gelug school emphasized Vinaya ethics and monastic discipline; Choekyi Gyaltsen refused to wear monk clothing after he married. Kagyu monks are also required to return to non-monastic life to marry.

East Asia

In East Asia, monastics live in greater isolation from the lay population than is observed in most Theravada countries. Because of local conditions of geography and climate, as well as local attitudes towards begging, monks generally do not make begging rounds in China,Korea, Vietnam, and many parts of Japan. Instead, monasteries receive donations of bulk food (such as rice) and funds for the purchase of food that is then stored and prepared at the monastery. Many monks and nuns are vegetarians and, after Baizhang Huaihai, many monks farm food to eat; some work or sell. Most eat after noon. The management of the kitchen and monastery properties may be the purview of a specially designated layman or a monk who has been given a special role by the abbot of the monastery. Monks chant many mantras in regular living. Buddhist monks and nuns lived together in China in Lingshansi, Luming'an, Hong'ensi, Ciyunsi, Sandingsi, Chahuasi.

Monastics in Japan are particularly exceptional in the Buddhist tradition because the monks and nuns can marry after receiving their higher ordination. This idea is said to be introduced by Saichô, the founder of the Tendai school, who preferred ordaining monks under theBodhisattva vows rather than the traditional Vinaya. There had long been many instances of Jôdo Shinshû priests and priestesses marrying, influenced by the sect's founder Shinran, but it was not predominant until a government Nikujiku Saitai Law was passed during the Meiji Restoration that monks or priests of any Buddhist sect are free to seek wives. This practice influenced Korea and Taiwan. A nun in Taiwan gave birth. Some Korean monks live with wives in their monasteries.

Monks of some Chinese lay Buddhist sects may marry, such as in historical Yunnan, Lingnan and Taiwan.

Southeast Asia

In Sri Lanka, Thailand, Cambodia, Laos, and Myanmar, where the Theravada school is dominant, there is a long tradition of temporary ordination. During a school break, many young men usually ordain for a week or two to earn merit for loved ones and to gain knowledge of Buddhist teachings. In most countries, this temporary ordination occurs during the vassa retreat, which is regarded as a period of intensified spiritual effort by local Buddhists. Men in Thailand typically ordain only before being married; men in Laos and Myanmar could traditionally return to the monastery from time to time after being married, provided that they secured their wives' permission. Theravada monks are also most likely to engage in traditional practices of collecting alms, although the urbanization of parts of Southeast Asian (particularly Thailand) has presented a challenge to this practice.

In Thailand, where the Buddhist institution has traditionally been closely associated with the government and the institution of kingship, a more hierarchical structure has evolved to deal with the administration and regulation of monasteries. This system initially stemmed from a system of royal patronage, in which monks who were appointed the abbots of 'royal monasteries' (those endowed and supported by members of the royal family) were accorded greater respect than those who headed more conventional monasteries. This system remained fairly unstructured until the modernisation efforts of the 19th century, during which a more formal system of governance was created by the central government. Modern Thai monks are ranked according to their ability to pass examinations in Buddhist doctrine and the Palilanguage, and are appointed to successively higher positions in the ecclesiastic hierarchy on the basis of these exams, as well as their support among influential members of the royal family and government. Local affairs continue to be handled primarily by the local monastic and lay community, but nationwide efforts (such as curriculum decisions for monastic schools, and the authoritative form of scriptures and rituals) are typically made by the central hierarchy.

2013 MYANMAR ANTI-MUSLIM RIOTS

The 2013 Myanmar anti-Muslim riots were a series of conflicts in various cities throughout central and eastern Myanmar (Burma).

March riots in Meiktila

Tensions between Buddhist and Muslim ethnic groups flared into violent clashes in Meiktila, Mandalay Division on 20 March and continued until the 22nd, killing at least 40 and wounding 61 people. The violence started on 20 March after a Muslim gold shop owner, his wife, and two Muslim employees assaulted a Buddhist customer and her husband in an argument over a golden hairpin. A large mob formed and began to destroy the shop. The heavily outnumbered police reportedly told the mob to disperse after they had destroyed the shop. In the evening, a local Buddhist monk not involved in the incident was dragged from his bicycle, doused in petrol, and burnt alive by six Muslim youths at a nearby mosque. The killing of the monk caused the relatively contained situation to explode, greatly increasing intensity and violence.

The deadliest incident occurred when a Buddhist mob attacked and torched the Mingalar Zayone Islamic Boarding School. While outnumbered security forces stood by, rioters armed with machetes, metal pipes, chains, and stones killed 32 teenage students and four teachers.

On 25 March, communal rioting targeting Muslim houses and mosques spread to the towns of Othekone, Tatkone and Yamenthin. At least 9,000 residents were documented to have been displaced by the violence. In April, the BBC obtained a leaked police video showing outnumbered police officers standing by while rioters torched houses and businesses in Meiktila. The video also shows the burning and killing of at least two Muslim students at the hands of rioters, which included Buddhist monks. The video was captured to prosecute the perpetrators later in court. On the third day, the situation stabilised when the government declared state of emergency and deployed military troops.

On 21 May, seven Muslims, including the gold shop owner and those who perpetrated the murder of the monk, were convicted for inciting the unrest and jailed from 2 up to 28 years. In July, the Burmese courts sentenced 25 Buddhists to up to 15 years in prison for murder and other crimes during the riot.

April riots in Okkan

On 30 April 400 Buddhists armed with bricks and sticks overran mosques and torched more than 100 homes and shops in Okkan, killing two people and injuring at least ten more. Another 77 homes were destroyed in the nearby villages of Yadanakon, Panipin, Chaukthe and Thekon. The riot reportedly began when a Muslim girl on a bicycle bumped into a Buddhist monk, knocking over his alms bowl.

May riots in Lashio

On 29 May, violence broke out in Lashio, in Shan state bordering China, after reports that a 48-year-old Muslim man named Ne Win poured petrol on a young Buddhist woman with whom he was arguing and set her on fire. In response, a Buddhist mob armed with machetes and bamboo poles torched a mosque, a Muslim orphanage, and several shops after the police refused to surrender Ne Win. The Buddhists and Muslims continued to fight into the next day and at least one person died. Sword-wielding Buddhist gangs began patrolling the streets on motorbikes, forcing as many as 1,400 Muslims to take shelter in a Buddhist monastery until the police and army were able to restore order.

August riots in Kantbalu

On 24 August, violence once again flared up in Htan Gon village, 16 kilometres south of Kantbalu in the Sagaing Region, following rumors that a Muslim man tried to sexually assault a young Buddhist woman. Local monks led a 1,000-strong Buddhist mob to retaliate by burning down Muslim owned businesses and the village mosque. State television reported that 42 houses and 15 shops owned primarily by Muslims were razed during the three-hour riot. One firefighter and one civilian were injured in the incident. Police officers were powerless to contain the violence, but finally dispersed the mob by firing their pistols into the air.

October riots in Thandwe

Between 29 September and 2 October, Rakhine Buddhists have rioted and attacked Kamein Muslims in Thabyachaing and Linthi villages, about 20 kilometres north of the coastal town of Thandwe in Rakhine State. Seven Muslims and two Buddhists were killed and between 70 and 80 houses were set on fire. About 500 ethnic Kamein Muslims were forced to flee from their homes. Local residents were worried a further round of violence between Rakhine Buddhist and Muslim communities after two young Rakhine Buddhists girls aged five and six were found murdered on 17 and 18 November in separate incidents. One victim reportedly appeared to have been raped.

Spillover

- In April 2013, Muslim and Buddhist detainees from Burma clashed at a refugee camp in Indonesia. Eight Buddhists were killed and fifteen other people were wounded.Sources have asserted that the provocation for the riot was due to sexual harassment against female Rohingya Muslim inmates by the Rakhine Buddhist inmates. An Indonesian court jailed 14 Muslim Rohingya for nine months each in December. The sentence was lighter than the maximum penalty for violence resulting in death, which is 12 years. The men's lawyer said they would appeal for freedom because there was no real evidence shown during the trial.
- In May, two Muslims were arrested for planning to attack the Myanmar embassy in Jakarta, Indonesia with pipe-bombs. The mastermind of the plot said he was *still at war*with anyone oppressing Muslims.
- In June, at least four killings in Malaysia were linked to ethnic tensions in Myanmar. All the victims, including a man slashed to death by a machete-wielding mob in Kuala Lumpur, were Buddhists from Burma. Malaysian police had arrested approximately 60 Burmese immigrants in an attempt to control tensions.

- In July, Muslims were blamed for the Bodh Gaya bombings, targeting one of Buddhism's most revered sites.
- On 5 August, two pipe-bombs went off outside the Ekayana Buddhist Centre in West Jakarta as some 300 people gathered inside the temple for a sermon, injuring three people. There was a note from the perpetrators that read "We respond to the screams of the Rohingya".

BUDDHIST VIOLENCE IN MYANMAR HIGHLIGHTS RELIGIOUS MISCONCEPTIONS

A Pew Research Center polling study found that 35 percent of Americans believe that "Islam is more likely than others to encourage violence." American popular society oft-holds binary viewpoints on religion: Islam is associated with militancy, while other traditions, such as Buddhism, get painted as a universally-peaceful alternative to mainstream religious exploitation.

8,000 miles to the East in Myanmar (formerly Burma), however, current events back a different religious reality. The Rohingya, a Muslim minority, has suffered strong violence and persecution at the hands of the nation's Buddhist majority. Muslims have been lynched in periodic gang-attacks, which authorities have often overlooked due to most Rohingya's status as "non-citizens." Similarly, the UN Refugee agency categorizes approximately 514,000 Myanmar Rohingya's as "internally displaced," with many thousand members of the community undertaking perilous boat trips to refugee camps in neighboring nations such as Thailand.

"There's no doctrinal base in Buddhism that can legitimately support mass murder crusades," Charles Strain, a DePaul professor versed in Buddhist studies, said.

Rather, the issue highlights how, in Strain's words, "the ideology disease can infect (all) religious and secular ideologies." When describing the particular mechanics of the Buddhist-driven violence in Myanmar, he said, "It is people who are recognized as spiritual leaders who are (catalyzing) the mass riots, in which Rohingya have lost lives. The one percent can still stir up the other 99 percent of (common) religious followers. Monks are revered, and when they come out and exacerbate ethnic tensions, it can lead to mass rioting."

Such ideological tension between religions does not necessarily arise out of religious textual encouragement. Rather, as DePaul religious studies professor Yuki Miyamoto said, "There's always one rhetoric used in justifying (institutionalized) violence, which is 'protecting ourselves.' It's not so much about interpretation or the text itself; it's about people utilizing the sense of being threatened, of 'having to protect ourselves.'"

Buddhist right-wingers — many of whom are, as Strain mentioned, considered religious authority figures — have often utilized such rhetoric in attacks, for instance, while scapegoating local Rohingya's for local crimes such as rapes without the utilization of due-process.

As Miyamoto mentioned, it highlights the importance of nuanced Western viewpoints towards institutions — whether they be religious or secular.

"Think of nation-states and war; war is often the best mechanism to heighten people's solidarity or need to belong," Miaymoto said. "Japan used (rhetoric of preservation) even when they were the aggressor invading parts of Asia (in WWII), how their actions were 'protecting Asian people from Western colonization and hegemony.'"

Such types of binary viewpoints "create these polarities," Strain said. "Not only don't they do justice to the religions of the West (such as Christianity or Islam); they create a romanticized view of Buddhists." The opposite type of dualistic viewpoint could also occur in Southeast Asia with Buddhist directed blame, which would "ignore the examples of Buddhists worldwide that are disturbed with the Burmese violence ... In no way is there a monolithic response by the Buddhist community."

Nuanced understandings of religions, as they each believed, are necessary to understanding the actual sociological background causes behind human-rights issues, rather than dismissing them as results of "inherently violent ideologies." Only with nuanced understandings can human rights situations be properly addressed, either abroad or at home.

THE ROOTS OF RELIGIOUS CONFLICT IN MYANMAR

Understanding narratives is an important step to ending violence

Myanmar has been the site of serious conflicts between Buddhist and Muslim communities, particularly in Rakhine State where at least 146,000 persons have been displaced since the first riots in June 2012. This violence has prompted international organizations dedicated to early warning of mass violence to issue alarms, but the dynamics of this conflict are understood differently in Myanmar. In May, three Nobel laureates called violence and persecution of Muslims in Myanmar "nothing less than genocide." A few days later, U Zaw Aye Maung, the Rakhine Affairs Minister for Yangon Region, was quoted by the Reuters news agency as saying, "if genocide was taking place in Rakhine State, then it was against ethnic Rakhine Buddhists."

Such a statement is not simple intransigence in the face of external criticism. It illustrates a conception of victim and violator that is diametrically opposed to the one made visible in international discourse. In Myanmar's domestic context, such a conception is closer to the norm than otherwise. Other state authorities use similar rhetoric. Daw Aung San Suu Kyi, meanwhile, told the BBC in October 2013, "Fear is not just on the side of the Muslims, but on the side of the Buddhists as well. There's a perception that Muslim power, global Muslim power, is very great."

Over the last seven months, we have been conducting a 'Listening Project' seeking to understand how people talk about concerns for their local communities and country. In this research, conducted across six regions in Myanmar, we have regularly noted discourses that construct Muslims as an existential threat, in which Buddhism is vulnerable and needing protection lest Islam supplant it as the majority religion. Fear of a Muslim takeover is based on a conception of Islam as intrinsically violent, justified with arguments that are strikingly reminiscent of discourses common in the United States and other countries since September 11th

2001. People regularly raised examples of alleged violence by Muslims in Myanmar as well the actions of ISIS and Al Qaeda. Daw Aung San Suu Kyi was pilloried by non-Burmese observers for her 2013 interview, but in situating domestic fears in a global context she was descriptively accurate. Fear in Myanmar is not (only) of a small minority within Myanmar, but of a global threat felt to be both surrounding the country and growing within it.

Understanding these narratives is important because it helps to explain the ferocity of domestic backlash against international responses to recent violence: rejecting calls to recognize Rohingya citizenship is seen by many in Myanmar as integral to national security.

Rakhine State is often referred to as the country's "western gate," the front line in a battle to protect Myanmar from an invasion described as both external, via immigration from Bangladesh that is dated to the British colonial period, and internal, via expansion in domestic Muslim populations believed to be driven by large families, inter-faith marriage, and forced conversions. This narrative of threat also helps to justify discriminatory laws, disregard for the suffering of a religious other, and even violence as forms of virtuous self-defense. It should be no surprise, then, that perpetrators of anti-Muslim riots have been described shouting both "Muslims, be gone" and singing Myanmar's national anthem or shouting, "We are Buddhist martyrs."

Examining these narratives also highlights the ways in which they are emergent works in progress, as are the groups seeking to produce them. Many of the people we spoke with said things that matched the rhetoric of nationalist forces like 969 and Ma Ba Tha, but this was not the case for everyone. Similarly, while these groups present a view of long-standing and irreconcilable Buddhist-Muslim antagonism, many people still remember histories of religious co-existence. Relations between communities defined in religious terms are tense across Myanmar, not just in Rakhine State. But this has not always been so; a core component of conflict is erasing memories of everyday harmony and solidarities that crossed or blurred communal lines. It would be sad for Myanmar if these memories are forgotten, disavowed, or replaced.

Anyone interested in reducing conflict or promoting peace and reconciliation in Myanmar would do well to start by listening carefully to the ways people discuss violence in everyday life. Firstly, this reinforces the importance of backing local civil society efforts to counter narratives of threat and self-defense. This would not only include those who identify (or are identified) as peacemakers, but also those whose stated focus is elsewhere but who have the credibility, connections, and bravery to work for peace at the most difficult moments. These local actors exist, but they are not always the ones first identified by outsiders who would intervene. Local groups and individuals often have a greater understanding and sensitivity to the ways in which narratives of threat are mobilized, and how they may be countered – as well as who is (or is not) countering them.

Secondly, listening helps underscore the ways that discourse about violence in Myanmar can contribute to the mobilization of that violence. How are instances of riotous violence explained and who is identified as victim and aggressor? How is the historical lineage of contemporary conflict being constructed, and what beliefs about the irreconcilability of religious communities do this support? How is Islam being represented, and is it as a unitary and fearsome other? The ways in which influential actors in Myanmar society answer these questions helps to produce the narratives that can enable and legitimize violence. This is true of 969 and Ma Ba Tha, but it would be a mistake to make them the sole object of critique. When the arrests made after a riot disproportionately target one religious community, this operates as a powerful statement about who has been victimized and who must be defended against. So too are legislative and administrative moves that 'protect' one religion from another or privilege public speech and action by representatives of one religious group, along with implicit or explicit condoning of the rationale and rhetoric of 969 and Ma Ba Tha. Most dangerous of all are statements by authorities that imply or assert risks of 'Islamic terrorism' in Myanmar.

International discourses about conflict in Myanmar matter as well. Explanations for violence that focus only on the events immediately precipitating a given incident obscure questions about how violence is mobilized, who is involved, and with what direct or indirect support. Lazy historicization that equates contemporary violence with, for example, Indo-Burman riots in the 1930s reinforces attempts to present religious antagonism as inevitable and historically determined. Finally, writing and rhetoric about 'Islamic terrorism' has real impacts in Myanmar. Unsubstantiated headlines that crow of a terrorist threat in Myanmar, like those recently published by Newsweek and the Independent, are dangerous and irresponsible. And subtler trends in western discourses about Islam and terrorism are important, too. Myanmar is preparing for hotly contested national elections. We have identified the analogy between discourses in Myanmar and the US after 2001. In the US, similar sentiments and security rhetoric became an integral part of the 2004 elections, supporting political agendas while also demonizing Muslim communities in the US and worldwide; we should expect similar dynamics in Myanmar, while hoping for less violent outcomes.

Finally, listening is necessary as an ethical matter and as a way to de-escalate a growing sense in Myanmar that the fears and perceptions of Buddhists are being ignored. Listening need not equate with agreement, nor entail ignoring the voices of marginalized minorities. But it will lead to more informed responses. Without understanding the nature of narratives that posit Islam as an existential threat and the production and reinforcement of those narratives within Myanmar society, there is no hope for crafting responses that can promote peace and reconciliation, or decrease the likelihood of continued violence.

MYANMAR: TENSIONS HIGH AFTER BUDDHIST MOB ATTACKS VILLAGE MOSQUE

Authorities said an angry mob of around 200 Buddhists rampaged through a Muslim area of a village in Bago province following an argument between neighbours over the building of a Muslim school. It is the latest flare-up of anti-Muslim violence in Myanmar, which has seen sporadic bouts of religious bloodshed since 2012, with a surge of Buddhist nationalism presenting a key challenge for Aung San Suu Kyi's new government. Own Lwin, the local police chief, said the atmosphere remained tense with around 100 police officers deployed to keep the peace. He said there had been rumours that there might be more unrest, adding that no arrests have been made over the destruction of the mosque.

Win Shwe, the mosque's secretary, said Muslim residents feared for their safety and were planning to move to a nearby town until the tension cools. "Our situation is not safe and now we are planning to leave the village ... We still feel afraid," he said.

Strident anti-Muslim sentiment has fomented across Myanmar in recent years, with outbreaks of violencethreatening to unravel democratic gains since the former junta stepped down in 2011. The worst religious violence struck central Myanmar and western Rakhine State, which is home to the stateless Rohingya Muslim minority, tens of thousands of whom still languish in displacement camps after rioting. Hardline monks and Buddhist nationalists fiercely oppose moves to recognise the Rohingya as an official minority and insist on calling them "Bengalis" — shorthand for illegal migrants from the border with Bangladesh.

Ms Suu Kyi, a vocal champion for human rights, has been criticised for not taking a stronger stance on the Rohingya or the abuse they face. This month the UN warned violations against the group could amount to "crimes against humanity".

The Nobel Peace Prize laureate, now leading Myanmar's first civilian government in decades, asked for "space" while her administration sought to build trust between religious communities.

BUDDHIST MOB RANSACK MOSQUE AS VIOLENCE FLARES IN MYANMAR

Buddhist mob attacks a man for constructing a religious school inside his house, before going on to ransack a mosque and an under-construction school. A Buddhist mob destroyed a mosque in central Myanmar on Friday, forcing local Muslims to seek refuge overnight in a police station. A dispute between neighbours over the building of a madrasa, a religious Islamic school, spilled into religious violence, officials and residents said. Police said that the mob attacked and injured a Muslim man and destroyed the under-construction madrasa. Around 200 Buddhists then rampaged through the Muslim area of Thuye Tha Mein village in Bago province.

"It started when a Muslim man and a Buddhist women started to argue and then people came to fight him," Hla Tint, the village administrator, said. "Parts of the mosque were destroyed... they also destroyed the fence of the Muslim cemetery," he added.

A villager, Abdul Sharif, was accused of building a madrasa in his compound. In this village of 500 houses, 40 houses belong to Muslims. "He was taken to a hospital in Waw," Htay Khaing, officer-in-charge at the police station in Waw Township said. Security has been provided for his family members, he added.

"For his safety, we will not disclose where he is being kept," he said. "I do not understand why Abdul Sharif was attacked. He is a good man to neighbours," the victim's brother Abdul Shareek said while waiting at the police station to meet with his brother. He said that Abdul Sharif was building a new religious school at his house compound as an older madrasa in the mosque compound was unusable.

The villagers also destroyed the fence of a Muslim cemetery. The violence coincides with a rise in tensions over how to refer to the Rohingya, a 1.1-million group of Muslims living in fear miserable condition in Rakhine since an outbreak of violence in 2012. Around 70 Muslims, including children, were forced to seek shelter in a police station overnight on Thursday, he said. Police and the secretary of the mosque confirmed the damage, while a Muslim resident said that his community of around 150 people was now living in fear.

"We had to hide as some people were threatening to kill Muslims. The situation has never been like this before," Tin Shwe OO, 29, said, adding his family stayed at the small police station overnight. "I do not dare to stay at my house. For the safety of my family, I want to stay somewhere else for about a week or so." Outbreaks of deadly violence have become a threat for the country's nascent democratic gains since the army began loosening its stranglehold on the Myanmar in 2011. The worst violence struck central Myanmar and western Rakhine State. Tens of thousands of Rohingya still languish in displacement camps after rioting. Buddhist nationalists vigorously oppose moves to recognise the Rohingya as an official minority group, instead labelling them "Bengali" — shorthand for illegal migrants from the border with Bangladesh. Democracy champion Suu Kyi, who is currently visiting Thailand, has come under fire for her failure to speak up for the Rohingya. She recently caused uproar by using the incendiary term during a visit to Myanmar by America's top diplomat. Religious tensions pose a challenge to the new government and to Suu Kyi, a Nobel laureate once garlanded for her fight for rights for all.

Her party is dominated by ethnic Bamar Buddhists and did not field any Muslim MPs in the election last year that drove it to power. Hardline monks — known as the Ma Ba Tha — are accused of stoking violence and tensions with hate speech.

3

Violence of Buddhism in Sri Lanka

Theravada Buddhism is the religion of 70.1% of the number of inhabitants in Sri Lanka. The island has been a focal point of Buddhist grant and learning since the presentation of Buddhism in the third century BCE creating prominent researchers, for example, Buddhaghosa and safeguarding the unlimited Pâli Canon. All through the vast majority of its history, Sinhalese rulers have assumed a noteworthy part in the upkeep and recovery of the Buddhist organizations of the island. Amid the nineteenth century, a cutting edge Buddhist recovery occurred on the island which advanced Buddhist instruction and learning. There are around 6,000 Buddhist religious communities on Sri Lanka with roughly 15,000 ministers.

HISTORY

Presentation of Buddhism

As per conventional Sri Lankan annals, for example, the Dipavamsa, Buddhism was brought into Sri Lanka in the third century BCE after the Third Buddhist board by Mahinda Bhikkhu, child of Emperor Ashoka, amid the rule of Devanampiya Tissa of Anuradhapura. Amid this time, a sapling of the Bodhi Tree was brought to Sri Lanka and the main religious communities and Buddhist landmarks were built up. Among these, the Isurumuniya and the Vessagiri stay critical focuses of love. He is additionally credited with the development of the Pathamaka cetiya, the Jambukola vihâra and the Hatthâlhaka vihâra and the refectory. The Pali Canon, having beforehand been protected as an oral custom, was initially dedicated to writing in Sri Lanka around 30 BCE.

Mahavamsa §29 records that amid the tenet of the Greco-Bactrian King Menander I, a Yona head minister namedMahadharmaraksita drove 30,000 Buddhist friars from "the Greek city of Alasandra" (v, around 150 kilometers (93 mi) north of cutting edge Kabul, Afghanistan) to Sri Lanka for the commitment of the Ruwanwelisaya in Anuradhapura, showing that Greco-Buddhismcontributed to early Sri Lankan Buddhism.

Focal point of Pali writing

As an aftereffect of the work of Buddhaghosa and different compilers, for example, Dhammapala, Sri Lanka built up a solid convention of composed literary transmission of the Pali Canon. The accumulation of the Atthakatha (analyses) alongside the Nikâyas and different Pitakas were focused on composing without precedent for the Aluvihare Rock Temple amid the principal century BCE. Buddhist writing in Sinhalese additionally flourished and by 410, Sri Lankan friars voyaged generally all through India and Asia presenting their works.

Theravâda subdivisions

Over a great part of the early history of Buddhism in Sri Lanka, three subdivisions of Theravâda existed in Sri Lanka, comprising of the ministers of the three mahaviharas, Anuradhapura Maha Viharaya, Abhayagiri vihâra and Jetavanaramaya. The Anuradhapura Maha Viharaya was the main convention to be built up while Abhayagiri vihâra and Jetavanaramaya were set up by ministers who had split far from the Maha Viharaya custom. As indicated by A.K. Corrections officer, the Indian Mahîúâsaka built up itself in Sri Lanka nearby the Theravadas, into which they were later consumed. Northern locales of Sri Lanka likewise appear to have been surrendered to orders from India at specific times.

In the seventh century, Xuanzang composed of two noteworthy divisions of Theravada Buddhism in Sri Lanka, alluding to the Abhayagiri convention as the "Mahayana Sthaviras," and the Mahâvihâra custom as the "Hinayana Sthaviras." Abhayagiri seems to have been a middle for Mahayana andVajrayana lessons; Xuanzang composes, "The Mahâvihâravâsins reject the Mahâyâna and practice the Hînayâna, while the Abhayagirivihâravâsins study both Hînayâna and Mahâyâna lessons and spread the Tripimaka.

In the eighth century, both Mahayana and Vajrayana Buddhism were being honed in Sri Lanka, and two Indian friars in charge of spreading Vajrayana Buddhism in China, Vajrabodhi and Amoghavajra, went to the island amid this time.

In Pali commentaries, terms used for the Mahayanins of Abhayagiri were Vaitulya, Vaipulya and Vaidalya. According to HR Perera, the Theravada commentaries considered them heretical and their doctrines included:

They held the view that the Buddha, having been born in the Tusita heaven, lived there and never came down to earth and it was only a created form that appeared among men. This created form and Ânanda, who learned from it, preached the doctrine. They also held that nothing whatever given to the Order bears fruit, for the Sangha, which in the ultimate sense of the term meant only the path and fruitions, does not accept anything. According to them any human pair may enter upon sexual intercourse by mutual consent.

Accounts of Chinese pilgrims

In the 5th century, Faxian visited Sri Lanka and lived there for two years with the monks. Faxian obtained a Sanskrit copy of the Vinaya of theMahîúâsaka at the Abhayagiri vihâra c. 406. The Mahîúâsaka Vinaya was then translated into Chinese in 434 by Buddhajiva and Zhu Daosheng. This translation of the Mahîúâsaka Vinaya remains extant in the Chinese Buddhist canon as Taishô Tripimaka 1421.

The 7th century pilgrim Xuanzang first learned for several years at Nalanda and then intended to go to Sri Lanka to seek out further instruction. However, after meeting Sri Lankan monks in the Ċhola capital who were refugees, he decided not to visit: At the time of Hiuen Tsang's visit the capital was visited by 300 Bhikshus of Ceylon who had left the island in consequence of famineand revolution there. On the pilgrim telling them of his intended visit to Ceylon for instruction, they told him that there were no Brethren there superior to them. Then the pilgrim discussed some Yoga texts with them and found that their explanations could not excel those given to him by Úîlabhadra at Nâlandâ.

Decline and revival

From the 5th century to the eleventh century, the island of Sri Lanka saw continuous warfare between local kings, pretenders and foreign invaders such as the South Indian Chola and Pandyan dynasties. This warfare saw the sacking of viharas and made the situation for difficult for Buddhism. In 1070, Vijayabahu I of Polonnaruwa conquered the island and set about repairing the monasteries. The state of Sri Lankan Buddhism was so bad at this time that he could not find five bhikkhus in the whole island to ordain more monks and restore the monastic tradition; therefore, he sent an embassy to Burma, which sent back several eminent elders with Buddhist texts. The king oversaw the ordination of thousands of monks. The royal reforming of Sri Lankan Buddhism continued under Parakramabahu I (c. 1153), who restored many stupas and monasteries. During this period, Sri Lankan Buddhist literature thrived once again and the three greats writers Mahakassapa of Dimbulagala Raja Maha Vihara, Moggallana Thera and Sariputta Thera compiled Pali commentaries and sub-commentaries. Parakramabahu II of Dambadeniya (from c. 1236) was a learned king and wrote several Sinhalese Buddhist texts.

Abolition of other Theravada traditions

Before the 12th century, more rulers of Sri Lanka gave support and patronage to the Abhayagiris, and travelers such as Faxian saw the Abhayagiris as the main Buddhist tradition in Sri Lanka. The trend of Abhayagiri being the dominant sect changed in the 12th century, when the Maha Viharaya gained the political support of Parakramabahu I (1153–1186), who completely abolished the Abhayagiri and Jetavanaya traditions. The monks of these two traditions were then defrocked and given the choice of either returning to the laity permanently or attempting reordination under the Maha Viharaya tradition as sâmaGeras. Parakkamabâhu also appointed *asaEgharâja* "King of the Sangha," a monk who would preside over the Sangha and its ordinations in Sri Lanka with the assistance of two deputies.

Mahayana legacy

Veneration of Avalokiteœvara has continued to the present day in Sri Lanka, where he is called Nâtha. In more recent times, some western-educated Theravâdins have attempted to identify Nâtha with Maitreya. However, traditions and basic iconography, including an image of Amitâbha on his crown, identify Nâtha as Avalokiteœvara.

It is clear from sculptural evidence alone that the Mahâyâna was fairly widespread throughout [Sri Lanka], although the modern account of the history of Buddhism on the island presents an unbroken and pure lineage of Theravâda. (One can only assume that similar trends were transmitted to other parts of Southeast Asia with Sri Lankan ordination lineages.) Relics of an extensive cult of Avalokiteúvara can be seen in the present-day figure of Nâtha.

Early reports by Europeans from the 18th century describe the Buddhist monks of Sri Lanka as being engaged in the recitation of mantras and using Buddhist prayer beads for counting as practiced in Mahayana Buddhism.

Lineage continuity

Sri Lanka has the longest continuous history of Buddhism of any Buddhist nation, with the Sangha having existed in a largely unbroken lineage since its introduction in the 3rd century BCE. During periods of decline, the Sri Lankan monastic lineage was revived through contact with Burma and Thailand.

Colonialism and Christianity

From the 16th century onward, missionaries and Portuguese, Dutch and British colonizers of Sri Lanka have attempted to convert the local population to Christianity. The wars with the Portuguese and their allies weakened the Sangha. In 1592, Vimaladharmasuriya I of Kandy sought aid from Burma in order to ordain Buddhist monks on the island as there was hardly a single properly ordained monk left. From 1612 to 1658, the Dutch and the Portuguese fought over the island with the Sinhalese caught in the middle, the Dutch won and occupied the maritime sections of the island that had been occupied by the Portuguese until 1796 when they surrendered their territories to the British. The Dutch were less zealous than the Portuguese in their religious proselytizing, though they still discriminated against Buddhists which were not allowed to register with the local authorities therefore many Sinhalese pretended to be Protestant.During this period many religiously inclined Sinhalese rulers of the interior such as Vira Narendra Sinha of Kandy (1706-1739) and Sri Vijaya Rajasinha of Kandy (1739-1747) continued to patronize Buddhism, restoring temples and monasteries.

In the mid 18th century the higher ordination of Buddhist monks known as upasampada, which was defunct at the time, was revived with the help of Thai Buddhist monks on the initiatives taken by Weliwita Sri Saranankara Thero during the reign of king Kirthi Sri Rajasinghe.

In 1813 the American Ceylon Mission (Protestant) was established in Jaffna. In 1815 a British army captured Kandy and deposed the Sinhalese king ending a line of Buddhist kings lasting 2301 years, they retained Sri Lanka until 1948. Like the Dutch, the British refused to register unbaptized infants and to accept non-Christian marriages. They also always preferred Christians in government administration. The British also supported various Christian missionary groups who established schools on the island. Education in these schools (which disparaged Buddhism) were a requirement for government office. Missionaries also wrote tracts in Sinhalese attacking Buddhism and promoting Christianity

Buddhist revival

In the 19th century, a national Buddhist movement began as a response to Christian proselytizing, and was empowered by the results of the Panadura debate between Christian priests and Buddhist monks such as Migettuwatte Gunananda Thera andHikkaduwe Sri Sumangala Thera which was widely seen as a victory for the Buddhists. In 1880 Henry Steel Olcott arrived in Sri Lanka with Madame Blavatsky of the Theosophical Society; he had been inspired when he read about the Panadura debate and after learning about Buddhism converted to the religion. Olcott and the Sinhalese Buddhist leaders established the Buddhist Theosophical Society in 1880, with the goal of establishing Buddhist schools (there were only three at the time, by 1940, there were 429 Buddhist schools on the island). The society also had its own publications to promote Buddhism; the Sinhalese newspaper,*Sarasavisandarasa*, and its English counterpart, *The Buddhist*. As a result of their efforts, Vesak became a public holiday, Buddhist registrars of marriage were allowed, and interest in Buddhism increased. Another important figure in the revival is Anagarika Dharmapala, initially an interpreter for Olcott, who traveled around the island preaching and writing. After traveling to India, he established the Maha Bodhi Society in 1891 whose goal was to revive Buddhism in India, and restore the ancient Buddhist shrines atBodh Gaya, Sarnath and Kushinara. His efforts saw the restoration of these sites and a renewal of interest in Buddhism among some Indians. The associations of the Buddhist revival also contributed much to the publication of Buddhist texts, and promotion of Buddhist scholarship. Revivalist Buddhist scholars include Sir D. B. Jayatillake, F. R. Somnayake, Valisinha Harishchandra and W. A. de Silva. Several Buddhist shrines were also rebuilt. Buddhist leaders were also active in the movement for Sri Lankan independence. Since independence, Buddhism has continued to thrive on the island.

Since the Buddhist revival Sri Lanka has also been an important center of Western Buddhist scholarship. One of the first western bhikkhus, Nyanatiloka Mahathera studied in Sri Lanka, established the Island Hermitage there and ordained several western monks. Western monks who studied in the island hermitage such as Nanamoli Bhikkhu and Ven. Nyanaponika (who established theBuddhist Publication Society along with Bhikkhu Bodhi) were responsible for many important translations of the Pali Canon and other texts on Buddhism in English and German.

Bhikkhuni ordination

A few years after the arrival of Mahinda, Bhikkhuni Sanghamitta, who is also believed to be the daughter of Emperor Ashoka, came to Sri Lanka. She started the first nun's order in Sri Lanka, but this order of nuns died out in Sri Lanka in the 11th century.

Many women have been ordained in Sri Lanka since 1996. In 1996 through the efforts of Sakyadhita, an International Buddhist Women Association, Theravada bhikkhuni order was revived, when 11 Sri Lankan women received full ordination in Sarnath, India, in a procedure held by Ven. Dodangoda Revata Mahâthera and the late Ven. Mapalagama Vipulasâra Mahâthera of the Mahâbodhi Society in India with assistance from monks and nuns of Korean Chogyo order. Some bhikkhuni ordinations were carried out with the assistance of nuns from the East Asian tradition; others were carried out by the Theravada monk's Order alone. Since 2005, many ordination ceremonies for women have been organized by the head of the Dambulla chapter of the Siyam Nikaya in Sri Lanka.

BUDDHIST MONASTIC GROUPS

The different sects of the Sri Lankan Buddhist clergy are referred to as Nikayas, and three main Nikayas are:

- Siam Nikaya, founded in the 18th century by Ven. Upali Thera, a Siamese monk who was invited by the King Kirti Sri Rajasinha of Kandy, and on the initiative of Weliwita Sri Saranankara Thero.
- Amarapura Nikaya, founded in 1800 with higher ordination obtained from Myanmar (Burma)
- Ramanna Nikaya, founded in 1864 by Ambagahawatte Saranankara.

Within these three main divisions there are numerous other divisions, some of which are caste based. There are no doctrinal differences among any of them.

DEMOGRAPHICS

Buddhism in Sri Lanka is predominantly practised by the Sinhalese, however the 2012 Sri Lanka Census revealed a Buddhist population of 22,254, including eleven monks, amongst the Sri Lankan Tamil population, accounting to roughly 1% of all Sri Lankan Tamils in Sri Lanka. In 1988 almost 93% of the Sinhalese speaking population in Sri Lanka were Buddhist.

1915 CEYLONESE RIOTS

The 1915 Ceylonese riots (also known as the 1915 anti-Muslim riots or the 1915 Buddhist Mohammedan riots or the 1915 Sinhalese Muslim riots) was a widespread and prolonged ethnic riot in the island of Ceylon between SinhaleseBuddhists and the Ceylon Moors and the brutal suppression of it by the British colonial authorities.

The riots started in Kandy in the night of 28 May 1915 and spread to neighbouring villages on 30 May and to Colombo on 31 May and other towns there after. It was suppressed by 9 June with final incidents taking place on 11 May in Chilaw. Taking place at a time World War I was raging in Europe, the British feared the riots as a possible native upraising, martial law was first declared in the Western and Sabaragamuwa Provinces on 2 June, extended to other provinces in the following days, and terminated on 30 August, during which many summary executions and other atrocities where carried out by the colonial forces in attempts to subdue the riots.

Background

By the turn of the 20th century, Ceylon was a British colony. Since its last native kingdom, the Kingdom of Kandy was annexed to the British Empire, the island saw little conflict as in the century that past only two anti British uprisings (the Uva Rebellion and the Matale Rebellion) took place. Due to the relative peaceful nature of the colony, the last regular British Armyregiment was withdrawn from the island in 1881. Since then the Ceylon Police Force maintained law and order in the island. British military presence in the island was limited to a regular British Indian Army infantry regiment which would be circulated to Ceylon to supplement the garrison units that was made up of a company from the Royal Garrison Artillery, the Royal Engineers and other support units of the British Army. In addition the Ceylon Volunteers functioned as a volunteer reserve.

The native population of the island at this time was predominately Buddhist mostly from the ethnic group Sinhalese. There existed a Muslim minority known as the Moors. The Moor community consisted of two segments, the *Ceylon Moors* who originated from the Arab traders who settled in the Island about five or six centuries before and the *Indian Moors* who were at the time natives and residents of South India, who had come to Ceylon for trade. By 1915, the Ceylon Moors who had controlled trade in most parts of the island had been ousted by the Indian Moors. The 1911 Census indicates that Ceylon Moors numbered 232,927 and Indian Moors 33,527. Establishing them selfs rice importation, sale and distribution Indian Moors gained much wealth and established themselves across the country.

In Gampola, a dispute arose between the Indian Moors and the Buddhist Temple authorities of Wallahagoda Dewala. The Indian Moors objected to the Buddhist Perahera (religious pageant) procession traveling past their Mosque with music. The Buddhist authorities agreed to alter the time and day of the procession to avoid disruption to their worship, yet refused to conduct the procession without ceasing the music citing that it was a practice carried-out from time immemorial, safeguarded by the terms of theKandyan Convention. The Trustees of the Mosque refused to allow the Perahara procession to pass with music when though an other and older Mosques along the same route belonging to Ceylon Moors never objected. Due to this the procession was not held. In 1913, the Temple authorities filed action in the District Court of Kandy against the Crown for a declaration of this right. The judgment was given in favor of the Temple, however on appeal the Supreme Court, it dismissed the action, on the grounds that local legislation had modified religious privileges guaranteed to the Kandyan Sinhalese by the British under the Kandyan

Convention. An appeal to the Privy Council was filed against the decision of the Supreme Court by the bench of Justices Walter Shaw and Thomas De Sampayo.

Events

Rioting

The Supreme Court judgment encourage the Indian Moors to prevent Buddhist Perahera processions from passing their Mosque in Kandy. On the night of May 28, 1915 a Buddhist Perahera procession with music a police permit authorizing it was proceeding along Castle Hill Street, Kandy when it was opposed by Indian Moors who objected to the Perahera Procession passing their Mosque. At this point Police Inspector F. T. Coore, intervened and directed the procession to turn back. The procession turned back which was followed by hooting and derision of the Indian Moors which provoked the Sinhalese to return and a fight ensued about midnight. The crowd entered the Mosque and did some damage. Several Sinhalese and Moors were injured as well as the Police Inspector Coore and many arrested.

On May 29 the first cases of violence was reported with Sinhalese attacking the Moorish bazaars. The first bloodshed of the riots was reported when an Indian Moors shot dead a Sinhalese boy in Colombo Street, Kandy and the murderer was not arrested. This aggravated the situation and rioting escalated. Shops in the bazaars were damaged, Sinhalese bazaars were attacked by Moors, Moorish buildings in Katugastota and Mahaiyawa were damaged. In Kandy the police took steps to control the rioting and police reinforcements where brought in from Colombo. Soon Sir Robert Chalmers, the British Governor of Ceylon; Herbert Dowbiggin, the Inspector General of Police and Brigadier General H. H. L. Malcolm, Officer Commanding the Troops in Ceylon; proceed to Kandy with a military contingent from the 28th Punjabis to take control of the situation.

As the situation escalated due to the initial inaction of the police, and rioting spread to Colombo by the June 31, the Governor dispatched Brigadier Malcolm back to Colombo to take control of the situation. The 28th Punjabis of the British Indian Army under the command of Lieutenant Colonel A G de V Chichester, was the only regular regiment stationed in Ceylon at the time and was called out in force along with European and Ceylonese sections of the Colombo Town Guard, and the Ceylon Volunteers to suppress the rioting.

During the next nine days or so the clashes and assaults spread through the Central, North Western, Western, Southern and Sabaragamuwa Provinces; and at one point, on the 2nd June, were reported to be occurring simultaneously at 116 centres. Large crowds were involved in the attacks on the Moors; mobs of over a thousand were reported atMatale, Wattegama, Kadugannawa, Gampola, Rambukkana, Panadura, Godapitiya and Akuressa. Areas where large populations of Moors saw fighting with Moors attacking Sinhalese and elsewhere Sinhalese mobs attacked Moors with Tamils joining in. The police and military came down hard on the riots with many Sinhalese shot and arrested. As they cleared towns of riots, the riots spread to villages where the Punjabis who were also Muslims came down hard on the villages.

Martial law

Fearing that the riots would turn out of control, Sir Robert Chalmers still in Kandy declared martial law on June 2, 1915 in several provinces and down with a heavy hand on the Sinhalese community. There was a belief in higher echelons of the administration that the riots were per-planned and seditious, some believed that there was a German link and the riots was the start of an upraising against British rule. Auxiliaries units on the lines of the Colombo Town Guard was formed in the local towns with European volunteers recruited from planters and mercantile executives. Special constables were appointed from among the European planters in remote areas. Officer Commanding the Troops, Brigadier Malcolm ordered the police and the military to shoot any one who they deemed a rioter without a trial. It was reported that Brigadier Malcolm had ordered his troops to "not to waste ammunition, but to shoot through the heart any Sinhalese that may be found on the streets," and IGP Dowbiggin had given instructions to their armed constables to "shoot down, without a challenge , certain people whose identity was to be gathered from description, if they were found in the streets after hours". Hundreds of Sinhalese peasants were shot down throughout the country. Persons who couldn't answer a challenge due to language differences of the Europeans and Punjabis were shot. In villages males slept in the verandas of their huts, villages who slept as such were shot on the account that martial law dictated that all sleep indoors.

Prosecution

Police and Punjabi soldiers set about searching villages for looted items, with the later in tern looting the villages and harassing women. Summary police courts were conducted on case of looting at police stations by passing legal procedure. Thousands were arrested in some cased whole villages, its men, women and boys, on charges of looting and being in possession of stolen property, and no bail allowed. These were immediately tried and in certain instances sentenced to lashing and/or imprisonment.

J. G. Eraser, Government Agent, Western Province, was appointed Commissioner by the Government to inquire into the riots. At the same time Special Commissioners (Military Commissioners) with extraordinary punitive powers were appointed by Brigadier Malcolm. These Special Commissioners were mostly Government Agents or Military Officers who had powers to threaten penalties to gain information about the riots. They gained valuation of damage and looted items by the Moors themselves and demanded compensation from the local Sinhalese, failure of payment to the *Riot Fund* resulted in arrest and subjected to court martials. Those who paid were pardoned. R. W. Byrde,Mayor of Colombo and Special Commissioner proposed a levy on Sinhalese in the wards of Colombo to pay in proportion to their wealth as compensation to the Moormen.

In the early stages of the rioting prominent Sinhalese were arrested on accusations on inciting the riots while as others volunteered to disperse the crowds peacefully. F. B. Walgampahe, Basnayaka Nilame (the Lay Chief) of the Ancient Temple of

Gadaladeniya, Gampola was taken in to custody by Punjabi soldiers and was found dead on arrival in Kandy.

The colonial authorities had the house of many prominent Sinhalese searched and many were arrested on charges of treason within days of the riots. These included F R Senanayake, D.S. Senanayake (later the first prime minister of Ceylon), D B Jayatilaka, W A de Silva, F R Dias Bandaranaike, E T de Silva, Dr Casius Ferreira, C Batuvantudawe, D P A Wijewardene, John de Silva, W H W Perera, Martinus Perera, John M Senivaratne, Arthur V. Dias, H Amarasurya, D E Weerasuriya, Reverent G D Lanerolle, E A P Wijeyeratne, Harry Mel, A H E Molamure, A E Goonesinha, Battaramulla Unanse - a monk, Edmund and Dr C A Hewavitharatne, the brothers of Anagarika Dharmapala, who was also interned in Calcutta, where he had been during the unrest. After the arrests, riot compensation was exacted under threat of force.

The colonial authorities suspected the temperance movement led by educated middle class Ceylonese to be supporting the Germans in Great war that was ragging at the time.

Field general court martials were established and handed out summary judgments under martial law on arrested Sinhalese civilians and some military personal. Several where executed swiftly before appeals could be made, this included Captain Henry Pedris who was found guilty of treason and executed by firing squad. Others such as Edmund Hewavitarne were imprisoned and died in prison. Many respected Sinhalese were removed from appointments of state such as Hulugalle Adigar who was stripped of his title of Adigar on the account he was not present in his home area during the riots.

Casualties and damage

According to some official estimates, which must be taken as approximate, there were 25 murdered, 189 wounded, 4 incidents of rape associated with the riots. 4075 houses and boutiques looted, 250 houses and boutiques burned down, 17 mosques burnt and 86 mosques otherwise damaged. Other official figures place total of 116 people were killed, 63 by military and Police forces.

Aftermath

The heavy handed actions of colonial authorities to suppress the riots and the punishments handed down by it where heavy criticized by those such as popular Tamil politicianSir Ponnambalam Ramanathan gain much national popularity. A secret memorandum initiated and drafted by Sir James Peiris to the Secretary of State for the Colonies, pleading for the repeal of martial law and describing atrocities claimed to have been committed by the authorities was carried in the soles of the shoes braving mine and submarine-infested seas (as well as the Police) by E. W. Perera, a lawyer from Kotte.

The colonial administration established a Police Inquiry Commission to inquire into the riots in late 1915 made up five members with Chief Justis Sir Alexander Wood Renton as Chairman and it contained one Sinhalese member Sir Solomon Obeyesekere. The findings were published in 1916.

In September 1915, Brigadier Malcolm was transferred to the western front as a Brigade Commander in the British Expeditionary Force where he served unit December 1915. The 28th Punjabis regiment was transferred to the Middle Eastern theatre by January 1916 where it was to take part in the mesopotamian campaign suffering a total of 1423 casualties by the end of the war.

Governor Chalmers was removed from the post in December 1915 and made Under-Secretary to the Lord Lieutenant of Ireland Lord Wimborne. The British Home Government did not appoint a Royal Commission of Inquiry as requested for by the Ceylonese.

Sir John Anderson who succeeded Chalmers as Governor appointed a Commission on October 26, 1916 to inquire into and report upon the circumstances connected with the shooting of L Romanis Perera, Telenis Appu, Podi Sinno, James Bass, Juvanis Fernando, W G Serahamy, Pugoda Peter, Uduwa Arachchi and Juwanis Appu. The Commissioners were Chief Justis Sir Alexander Wood Renton and G. S. Schnieder. The Commission found that, "In each of the cases that have been under investigation the act of shooting cannot be justified on the ground of existence of Martial Law; in short, it had no legal justification.' But, they said, they were bona fide for the maintenance of good order and government and for the public safety of the Colony, and, that action was protected by the Ceylon Indemnity order in Council, 1915."

Legacy

After 1915 a number of Sinhalese leaders gradually emerged from the educated middle class, who were to leave an indelible mark on the political life of the country. It marked the beginning of the independence movement with the educated middle class demanding more legislative power that lead to the Donoughmore Commission and the Soulbury Commission which lead to Ceylon gaining independence in 1948.

The events of 1915 would ultimately be what would be called the unfolding of explicit manifestation of ethnic tensions in the country which was to increase in number and intensity once the country attained independence. Sinhalese Buddhist nationalism took hold, in the beginning led by reformers in the name of religion. The event also led to a major distrust between the Tamil and the Moor community who shared a common native language and strong cultural traditions. Also Muslims would side up with the Sinhalese against the indigenous Tamils to protect their political turf and business interests in the later ethnic conflict that would take place between the two communities after the country's independence.

MAWANELLA RIOTS

The Mawanella riots was a series of planned attacks on the Sri Lankan Muslim minority by the majority Sinhalese in the town ofMawanella, that resulted in the deaths of two people and left more than 15 injured in the clashes and also leading to destruction of millions of rupees worth property in the region.

Incident

On April 30, 2001, a group of thugs entered a hotel owned by a Muslim, took some cigarettes without paying, and then menaced the cashier to hand over money. When he refused to oblige, the cashier was seized, dragged outside, tied to an iron fence and had his mouth slashed with a knife. Three policemen saw the incident but stood by and did nothing to help the victim. The injured youth could only be hospitalised after the attackers left.

When efforts taken by the hotel owners to persuade the Police to arrest those responsible went in vain, hundreds of Muslims took to the streets in protest demanding the criminals be brought to justice.

According to some eyewitnesses in Mawanella, the initial attack was instigated by a gang that included the bodyguards of Mahipala Herath, a government minister from the Kegalle District. But the minister denied these charges as baseless.

Only when the protests intensified, the police promised to take action.

However as the crowd was dispersing, a Sinhala mob, several hundred strong, descended on the area and went on a rampage, setting fire to Muslim-owned shops, houses, businesses and mosques. One group entered the town's main mosque dragged out the cleric and burned furniture, a funeral casket and a copy of the Koran. Police were accused of helping the mob enter a hardware store by shooting off its padlock.

In retaliation a group of Muslims stoned the police station and attacked several Sinhalese-owned shops. The police in an attempt to disperse the protestors, fired into the crowd, killing two people, including 55-year-old Haniffa Mohamed, and injuring 15 others.

Aftermath

Muslim Protests erupted in the wake of the incident, in various places including Colombo, Puttalam and Batticaloa. Shops of Sinhalese people were attacked and the roads were blocked by burning tyres. Clashes took place outside the Maradana police station in Colombo, where police tear-gassed demonstrators and baton charged the crowd. Fifteen people were injured, two seriously. Police took some drastic measures to quell the protests. Scores of people were arrested, including Mujibur Rahuman, leader of the Muslim United Liberation Front (MULF), who was later released on bail.

Reactions

Sri Lankan Government

The government reacted to the unrest by imposing a 12-hour curfew in Colombo and throughout the adjoining Western Province. The government has announced the formation of a "peace committee" in the Mawanella area to include representatives of the Sinhala and Muslim communities as well as local police chiefs. It has also promised to pay compensation to those whose property was damaged.

SLMC

Members of the Sri Lanka Muslim Congress blamed the Government for instigating and being indifferent to the riots.

A month later after the incident, the Sri Lanka Muslim Congress, a party formed in the 1980s to give voice to the Muslims of the east, broke from the PA coalition it earlier belonged to.

2014 ANTI-MUSLIM RIOTS IN SRI LANKA

The 2014 anti-Muslim riots in Sri Lanka were religious and ethnic riots in June 2014 in south-western Sri Lanka. Muslims and their property were attacked by Sinhalese Buddhists in the towns of Aluthgama, Beruwala and Dharga Town in Kalutara District. At least four people were killed and 80 injured. Hundreds were made homeless following attacks on homes, shops, factories, mosques and a nursery. 10,000 people (8,000 Muslims and 2,000 Sinhalese) were displaced by the riots. The riots followed rallies by Bodu Bala Sena (BBS), a hard line Buddhist group. The BBS was widely blamed for inciting the riots but it has denied responsibility. The mainstream media in Sri Lanka censored news about the riots following orders from the Sri Lankan government.

Background

Since 2012 there have been a number of attacks against Sri Lanka's Muslim minority by the majority Buddhists. Bodu Bala Sena (BBS) has engaged in various anti-Muslim campaigns.

On Poson Poya (12 June 2014) Buddhist monk Ayagama Samitha and his driver were allegedly assaulted by Muslims in Dharga Town. A mob from Samitha's temple, together with the priest, stormed Aluthgama Police Station demanding that immediate action be taken. Three Muslims were arrested and remanded until 25 June 2014 by the courts. That evening a tense situation arose in Aluthgama as a group of Sinhalese Buddhists started protesting against the alleged assault. The protest turned violent and the mob started throwing stones at the police and attacking Muslim shops. Government ministers Kumara Welgama andRohitha Abeygunawardena visited the scene to sort out the situation but Welgama's vehicle was stoned by the mob. The police were forced to use tear gas against the protesters. Three people were arrested over the violence.

On 15 June 2014 the BBS staged rallies in Aluthgama, Beruwala and Dharga Town in Kalutara District. Addressing a cheering crowd in Aluthgama, BBS leader Galagoda Aththe Gnanasaara threatened "In this country we still have a Sinhala police; we still have aSinhala army. After today if a single Marakkalaya [Muslim, in context used derogatorily] or some other paraya [alien, outcast, also a derogatory term] touches a single Sinhalese.....it will be their end."

Riots

After its rally the BBS drove into Dharga Town chanting anti-Muslim slogans. Local residents started throwing stones at the BBS convoy which resulted in violent clashes erupting between the two groups. Eyewitnesses reported Muslim homes and a mosque being stoned. Muslims were pulled off buses and assaulted whilst the Buddhist mob threw Molotov cocktails, burning and looting Muslim shops and homes. Muslim residents were forced to flee from their homes and seek shelter in mosques and community centres. There was rioting in Beruwala as well.

Special Task Force personnel were deployed to control the situation. The police imposed an indefinite curfew in Aluthgama at 6:45pm on 15 June 2014 and at 8:00pm in Beruwala. Despite the curfew BBS supporters wielding weapons were seen in the area.

Muslim residents stated that the curfew was only for the Muslims, not for the rioters. According to local residents the police did nothing to help them. Some residents accused the police of helping the BBS.

Three men who were trying to protect Welipitiya mosque in Dharga Town were shot dead in the early hours of 16 June 2014 by a group travelling in a vehicle. The victims were identified as labourer Mohammed Shiraz (30), shop keeper Mohammed Sahuran (40) and tile layer Mohammed Imran (41).

More than 80 people were injured. The injured were taken to several local hospitals. 36 people, including seven who had been shot, were taken to Kalutara Base Hospital while seven others, including a police officer, were taken to Beruwala District Hospital. 10,000 people (8,000 Muslims and 2,000 Sinhalese) displaced by the riots sought shelter in schools, mosques and other community facilities.

The curfew was later extended. By 16 June 2014 no arrests had been made in relation to the violence. After the police failed to restore order, around 50 military personnel were deployed in Aluthgama, Beruwala, Dharga Town, Maggona and Welipenna to maintain order. Local schools were closed on 16 June 2014.

On the night of 16 June 2014 the riots spread to the Welipenna where a mob of 50-60 men armed with Guns, Molotov cocktails and Knives destroyed 26 shops and nine houses. Karuppan Sivalingam (58), an unarmed Tamil guard, was hacked to death and a Sinhalese farm worker seriously injured when a mob raided a Muslim owned chicken farm in Henagama near Welipenna. The curfew was temporarily lifted at 8.00am on 17 June 2014 before being re-imposed at 12.00pm. By 17 June 2014 10,000 police and Special Task Force personnel had been deployed in the area. According to the police 41 people had been arrested by 17 June 2014. The number of arrested later rose to 49. By 21 June 2014 58 people had been arrested, 36 of whom were remanded whilst the rest were released on police bail.

Journalists covering the riots were also attacked by the mob. *Sunday Leader* journalist Binoy Suriarachchi was held hostage for several hours and his driver Upul was attacked. *Sunday Times* journalist Sarath Siriwardana was attacked by a mob in Aluthgama on the night of 15 June 2014. An *Al Jazeera* crew travelling between Mathugama and Aluthgama on 17 June 2014 were attacked by a mob who damaged their vehicle's windscreen.

On 17 June 2014 the police obtained court order preventing the BBS from holding a rally in Mawanella. The curfew in Aluthgama and Beruwala was lifted at 8.00am on 18 June 2014.

Aftermath

President Mahinda Rajapaksa, accompanied by government minister Mervyn Silva, visited Beruwala on 18 June 2014 to meet victims of the riots and promised an impartial inquiry. According to the president, the government would re-build homes and business destroyed by the riots. The president announced via social media on 21 June 2014 that he would appoint a high-level panel to investigate the riots. At a meeting in Badulla on 21 June 2014 Rajapaksa blamed "international forces" for a "concerted efforts to destabilise the country" and ordered a crackdown on hate groups. Former President Chandrika Kumaratunga and various other parliamentary ministers also condemned the attack.

Moderate Buddhist monk Watareka Vijitha, who had been critical of the BBS, was abducted and assaulted in the Bandaragama area on 19 June 2014. Vijitha had been forcibly circumcised. The police later stated they would take action against Vijitha for giving false statements, saying that his injuries were self-inflicted. Vijitha was later charged by the police for making false allegations. Vijitha had been threatened by BBS leader Galagoda Aththe Gnanasaara in April 2014. He had gone into hiding following attempted assaults.

Muslim businesses in Colombo, Eastern Province and Northern Province staged a hartal on 19 June 2014 as protest against the riots. Contrary to fears there was no violence after Jumma prayers on 20 June 2014.

The Muslim owned *No-Limit* clothing store in Panadura was destroyed by fire in the early hours of 21 June 2014, causing Rs.400 million in damage. Witnesses reported seeing petrol bombs being thrown into the store. Police and Special Task Force personnel were deployed in the area. Schools in the riot affected re-opened on 23 June 2014. Sporadic attacks against Muslim targets continued in the days after the riots.

Reaction

President Rajapaksa, who was in Bolivia for the Group of 77 summit, issued statements via social media urging restraint and promising an investigation. The governmentthen urged the media not to publish news about the riots which could cause "disharmony" amongst religious groups in the country. As a result, there was a virtual blackoutabout the violence in the mainstream media in Sri Lanka.

Rajapaksa's United People's Freedom Alliance (UPFA) government was divided over the riots. Rauff Hakeem, Minister of Justice and leader of the Sri Lanka Muslim Congress, has called for "an independent and transparent inquiry" into the riots which would bring to justice not just those responsible for the violence but also those allowed or encouraged religious zealotry. Risad Badhiutheen, Minister of Industry and Commerce and leader of the All Ceylon Muslim Congress, accused the BBS of instigating racial tensions and called upon the government to ban the BBS and take legal action against its leader Gnanasara. Vasudeva Nanayakkara, Minister of National Languages and Social Integration and leader of the Democratic Left Front has called for BBS leader Gnanasaara and other BBS members to be arrested for instigating racial tensions which led to the riots. However, Champika Ranawaka, Minister of Technology, Research and Atomic Energy and leading member of the Jathika Hela Urumaya, blamed the violence on Muslim extremists and accused the United States of nurturing a Taliban in Sri Lanka. Rajapaksa has criticised ministers who were critical of the government's and police's response. At the 26 regular session of the United Nations Human Rights Council on 20 June 2014 the Sri Lankan government blamed Muslims for the riots.

The BBS has denied responsibility for the riots, saying it did not organise the rally in Aluthgama on 15 June 2014. The main opposition United National Party (UNP) condemned the riots and blamed the governing United People's Freedom Alliance for instigating the violence. UNP MPMangala Samaraweera, a vocal critic of the Rajapaksa government, went as far as to name three senior military intelligence officers - General (retd) Kapila Hendawitharana (defence ministry advisor), Colonel Suresh Salley and Deputy Inspector General Chandra Wakishta (deputy chief of the State Intelligence Service) - whom he accused of instigating the violence. The violence was also condemned by religious leaders and civil society groups.

UN Secretary General Ban Ki-moon expressed concern at the communal violence and urged the government to ensure the safety of all Sri Lankans. UN High Commissioner for Human Rights Navi Pillay issued a statement on 16 June 2014 expressing alarm at the riots and urging the government to halt the violence and hate speech and bring the perpetrators to book. The European Union delegation in Colombo, with the support of the Norwegian, Swiss and Turkish embassies, issued a statement on 20 June 2014 condemning the violence and urging the government to uphold the rule of law. Organisation of Islamic Co-operation Secretary General Iyad bin Amin Madani expressed serious concern at the violence against Muslims and observed a rising trend of violence by extremists.

The US embassy in Colombo also a statement on 16 June 2014 condemning the violence and urging the government to restore order and bring the perpetrators to justice. The following day United States Department of State spokesperson Jen Psaki stated that the US condemned the violence and blamed it on recent "inflammatory rhetoric". Canada's Ambassador for Religious Freedom Andrew P. W. Bennett issued a statement on 16 June 2014 condemning the communal violence against Muslims and calling for a swift and transparent investigation into the violence.

Amnesty International urged the government to take action to end the violence immediately, rein in groups targeting religious minorities, protect Muslims and bring to account those responsible for the violence. Human Rights Watch has urged the government to urgently investigate the violence, and identify and investigative those responsible for the attacks on Muslims. The riots took place in a popular tourist area which prompted some foreign governments to issue travel advisories to their citizens.

SRI LANKA'S VIOLENT BUDDHISTS

When I met Watareka Vijitha Thero in early 2014 in a suburb of Colombo, the Sri Lankan capital, he had been in hiding for nearly five months.

The gentle-voiced monk had spoken out against anti-Muslim fearmongering by a hard-line group called the Buddhist Power Force, known by its Sinhalese initials B.B.S. Mr. Vijitha's car was attacked in retaliation, and he narrowly escaped. "What does it mean for Buddhism if those that speak for communal harmony have to hide in fear?" he asked me. "What does it mean for my country that the government lets these lawless thugs have a free run?"

Six months later, Mr. Vijitha was found on a road near Colombo stripped naked and bloody, his hands and legs bound. The B.B.S. denied involvement.

When the monk filed a complaint, the police threw him in jail for 12 days on charges of self-inflicted violence — a warning to others who dared to criticize hard-line Buddhists. Three years ago, the B.B.S and other hard-line groups were fringe elements. Today, they are a powerful force, and their aggressive assertion of Sinhalese Buddhist dominance, in a country that is 70 percent Buddhist, is increasingly mirrored in government-approved revisionist histories of Sri Lanka.

Now, with the country's president, Mahinda Rajapaksa, facing a challenger in elections on Thursday, hard-line Buddhist groups have mobilized to support him. A wave of populist chauvinism has engulfed the country and sidelined the Tamil and Muslim minorities that make up over a quarter of the population. If it continues unchecked, Sri Lanka will face more instability, ethnic polarization and suppression of dissent.

Extremist Buddhist monks are confounding; they directly contradict a canonically nonviolent religion often perceived as apolitical. Like radical monks in Thailand and Myanmar, Sri Lankan hard-liners reserve special ire for Muslims. The B.B.S. and its counterparts have incited mobs to demolish mosques. A June speech by the B.B.S. chief Galagodaththe Gnanasara triggered anti-Muslim rioting in Sri Lanka's southern villages; thugs burned homes, four people were killed and at least 80 were injured. But instead of arresting Mr. Gnanasara, the president simply urged "all parties concerned to act in restraint."

In Sri Lanka, monks have long been involved in efforts to bolster Buddhist primacy. In the 19th century, amid fears that European colonizers and Christian missionaries were diluting Sri Lankan identity, monks led a Buddhist revival, followed by a cultural movement for the dominance of the Sinhalese language over English. These efforts produced a Buddhist nationalism that persisted after independence in 1948 (Buddhism itself is accorded primacy in the Sri Lankan Constitution).

In the last decade, activism by Buddhist monks has grown more overtly political. In 2004, they founded the National Heritage Party, known by the initials J.H.U., and contested elections for the first time; nine monks won parliamentary seats. Though it never espoused violence, the J.H.U. supported the Sri Lanka Freedom Party of Mr. Rajapaksa. As the government intensified its battle against the separatist Tamil Tigers, the monks' backing gave religious legitimacy to the state's claim of protecting the island for the Sinhalese Buddhist majority.

The defeat of the Tamil rebels in 2009 ended the country's nearly 30-year-long civil war. The B.B.S. emerged during this postwar high, deploying a selective reading of Sri Lanka's origins — excluding the contributions of indigenous and non-Sinhalese communities — to fan fears of an existential threat to Buddhism and justify its acts of violence.

At a rally in 2012, the B.B.S. leader Mr. Gnanasara likened the Sri Lankan military's victory to the ancient conquest of a Tamil chief by a beloved Sinhalese king. The spectators knew the story and cheered at the comparison. "Tamils have been taught a lesson twice," he said; so would other minorities if they tried to "challenge Sri Lankan culture."

In the past two years, hard-line groups have consolidated their political power. The B.B.S. has even used the state-owned cellular network to raise funds. Sri Lanka's defense secretary, Gotabaya Rajapaksa, the president's brother, has attended some of their events. The government, meanwhile, denies any links to them.

By instruction or apathy, the police and army look away when hard-line monks incite riots, and fail to thoroughly investigate complaints. While the B.B.S. is not the sole voice of Sri Lankan Buddhists, its recourse to violence has increasingly forced secular liberals and pacifist Buddhists into silence.

More perniciously, a nostalgia for Buddhist supremacy is now widespread. Today, a revisionist version of history is celebrated in films, books, TV programs and state-run newspapers. In the Tamil-dominated north, and in the east, where most of the country's Muslims live, national monuments have been erected to honor Buddhist kings.

Government offices frequently announce "rediscoveries" of long-lost Buddhist temples and Buddha statues are placed in areas sacred to Muslims or Tamils. In the Kanniya hot springs in the east, a sign in Sinhalese and English explains that the site — considered among Tamils to be linked to a Hindu myth— had been part of an ancient Buddhist monastery.

In Kuragala in the central hills, the culture ministry built a Buddhist stupa at a Sufi Muslim cave, declaring it an ancient monastery site. These claims aren't based on new archeological findings; the Sri Lankan government is simply rewriting history with a more politically expedient narrative.

In November, Mr. Rajapaksa's health minister, Maithripala Sirisena,unexpectedly defected and announced his candidacy for president. The B.B.S. denounced him as a Western stooge and gave its support to Mr. Rajapaksa, but the J.H.U. has said it will oppose Mr. Rajapaksa's undemocratic ways by backing his opponent.

Mr. Sirisena is likely aware that he must play up his Buddhist allegiances if he hopes to defeat Mr. Rajapaksa — a strategy that will only strengthen chauvinist groups. He has sworn to preserve

Buddhism's constitutional prominence, and rejected Tamil demands for greater autonomy. With little choice, Tamil and Muslim parties now back Mr. Sirisena.

No matter who wins in January, the message is unmistakable: To be truly considered Sri Lankan these days, one must accept the primacy and glory of the country's Sinhalese Buddhist past. Unless it is challenged, this mindset will pose a far greater danger to Sri Lanka than the blows of hard-line thugs.

4

The Darker Side of Buddhism

The rule of peacefulness is vital to Buddhist lessons, yet in Sri Lanka some Buddhist ministers are being blamed for mixing up antagonistic vibe towards different beliefs and ethnic minorities. Their hard line is bringing on expanding concern. The little sanctuary in suburbia of Colombo is calm. A picture of the Buddha is encompassed with purple and white lotus blooms. Littler Buddhas line the dividers.

Yet, upstairs, a husky minister in a brilliant orange robe holds forward - for this is one of the fundamental workplaces of a hard-line Buddhist association, the Bodu Bala Sena or Buddhist Power Force (BBS).

The tranquil statutes for which Buddhism is broadly known scarcely figure in his words. Rather, the minister, Galagoda Aththe Gnanasara Thero, discusses his Buddhism as far as race. Most Buddhists here are ethnically Sinhalese, and Sinhalese make up 75% of the island's populace. "This nation has a place with the Sinhalese, and the Sinhalese developed its civilisation, society and settlements. The white individuals made every one of the issues," says Gnanasara Thero furiously.

He says the nation was annihilated by the British colonialists, and its present issues are additionally the work of what he calls "untouchables". He implies Tamils and Muslims.

Truth be told, while a minority of the Tamils did for sure originate from India as tea ranch laborers, the greater part of them, and the vast majority of the Muslims, are as Sri Lankan as the

Sinhalese, with hundreds of years old roots here. "We are attempting to... do a reversal to the nation of the Sinhalese," says Gnanasara Thero. "Until we adjust this, we are going to battle."

This torch strain of Buddhism is not new to Sri Lanka. A key Buddhist Pentecostal figure of the mid twentieth Century, Anagarika Dharmapala, was not exactly complimentary about non-Sinhalese individuals. He held that the "Aryan Sinhalese" had made the island into Paradise which was then annihilated by Christianity and polytheism. He focused on Muslims saying they had "by Shylockian strategies" flourished to the detriment of the "children of the dirt".

Furthermore, later, in 1959 Prime Minister SWRD Bandaranaike was killed by a Buddhist friar - the conditions were cloudy yet one disagreeable issue was the administration's inability to do what's necessary to guarantee the privileges of the Sinhala individuals.

The long war against the Tamil Tigers - a savage revolutionary gathering implying to represent the Tamil minority - brought the hard-line Buddhists into their own particular yet again. Depicting the war as a mission to ensure the Sinhalese and Buddhism, in 2004 nine friars were chosen to parliament on a patriot stage. What's more, it was from the friars' principle party that Gnanasara Thero later split away, in time shaping the BBS. It is currently the most conspicuous of a few associations sharing a comparative philosophy.

Since 2012, the BBS has grasped direct activity, taking after the case of other similarly invested bunches. It attacked Muslim-possessed butcher houses guaranteeing, erroneously, that they were infringing upon the law. Individuals showed outside a law school asserting, again erroneously, that exam results were being contorted for Muslims.

Since a Tamil foe has been vanquished, Muslims appear to be these patriots' fundamental focus, alongside zealous Christians whom they blame for misleadingly and cleverly changing over individuals far from Buddhism.

Be that as it may, can the BBS be called vicious? "At whatever point there is something incorrectly done by a Buddhist minister everything [is faulted on] us on account of our prominence," says BBS representative Dilantha Withanage.

"BBS is not a fear association, BBS is not advancing brutality against anybody... yet, we are against sure things." He refers to dangers by Islamic State to pronounce the entire of Asia a Muslim domain. On numerous occasions he and his partner section "Muslim" together with "fanatic".

They are by all account not the only Sinhalese who express uneasiness at an unmistakable ascent in Muslim social conservatism in Sri Lanka. A larger number of ladies are concealing than before and in parts of the nation Saudi-affected Wahabi Muslims are shaking with more liberal ones. However there is no confirmation of fierce fanaticism among Sri Lankan Muslims. Or maybe, they have been forced to bear assaults from different parts of society.

In the small town of Aluthgama last June, three people died in clashes that started when the BBS and other Buddhist monks led an anti-Muslim rally in a Muslim area. At the time, I met Muslim families whose homes and shops had been burnt and utterly destroyed, and who were cowering in schools as temporary refugees. Moderate Buddhists have also been targeted by hard-line ones. Last year Rev Wathareka Vijitha Thero was abducted, rendered unconscious, tied up and forcibly circumcised - he says this was meant as a gesture of ridicule because he had worked for closer cooperation between Buddhists and Muslims.

He believes Buddhist monks - he doesn't know who or whether they were aligned with any particular group - were responsible. In a separate case, a few weeks earlier, Vijitha Thero had held a news conference to highlight the grievances of the Muslim community - the gathering was broken up by the BBS. Gnanasara had hurled insults and threatened him: "If you are involved in this type of stupid treachery again, you will be taken and put in the Mahaweli River," he said. The reference to the Mahaweli is significant - there was a left wing insurrection against the Sri Lankan government in 1989 - it's estimated 60,000 people disappeared and many dead bodies were dumped in the river.

Another country where fierce Buddhism has recently made headlines is Myanmar, formerly known as Burma. A Buddhist faction there, the 969 movement, is known for strident anti-Muslim campaigns that have triggered widespread violence. Its leader, Shin Wirathu, was recently invited to Sri Lanka by the BBS. Both organisations say that even if Buddhism predominates in their own countries, overall it is under threat. "We want to protect it, therefore we signed a memorandum of understanding on forming alliances in the Asian region," says Withanage. In January, Sri Lanka unexpectedly elected a new president, Maithripala Sirisena. He told me that "everybody knows" who gave rise to the BBS - implying that it was the administration of his predecessor, Mahinda Rajapaksa. The previous government was, at least, strongly supportive of the organisation.

And the group thrived because the rule of law had broken down, according to the new minister for Buddhist affairs, Karu Jayasuriya. He has told me that the BBS will be reined in. On Tuesday, Gnanasara Thero was arrested for taking part in an unauthorised demonstration but later freed on bail. Thus far, the new government - which, like the old one, includes a strongly Buddhist nationalist party - seems timid about taking on the men in orange.

BUDDHIST MONKS ATTACKING MUSLIMS?

Of all the moral precepts instilled in Buddhist monks the promise not to kill comes first, and the principle of non-violence is arguably more central to Buddhism than any other major religion. So why have monks been using hate speech against Muslims and joining mobs that have left dozens dead? This is happening in two countries separated by well over 1,000 miles of Indian Ocean - Burma and Sri Lanka. It is puzzling because neither country is facing an Islamist militant threat. Muslims in both places are a generally peaceable and small minority.

In Sri Lanka, the issue of halal slaughter has been a flashpoint. Led by monks, members of the Bodu Bala Sena - the Buddhist Brigade - hold rallies, call for direct action and the boycotting of Muslim businesses, and rail against the size of Muslim families. While no Muslims have been killed in Sri Lanka, the Burmese situation is far more serious. Here the antagonism is spearheaded by the 969 group, led by a monk, Ashin Wirathu, who was jailed in 2003 for inciting religious hatred. Released in 2012, he has referred to himself bizarrely as "the Burmese Bin Laden".

Buddhism and non-violence

Buddhist teachings were handed down orally and not written until centuries after the Buddha's lifetime. The principle of non-violence is intrinsic to the doctrine, as stressed in the Dhammapada, a collection of sayings attributed to the Buddha.

Its first verse teaches that a person is made up of the sum of his thoughts: "If a man speaks or acts with an evil thought, pain follows him, as the wheel follows the foot of the ox that draws the carriage."

The most basic principles of Buddhist morality are expressed in five precepts, which monks are obliged - and laymen encouraged - to follow. The first is to abstain from killing living creatures. One objective of Buddhist meditation is to produce a state of "loving kindness" for all beings. Verse five of the Dhammapada tells us that: "Hatred does not cease by hatred at any time: hatred ceases by love, this is an eternal rule."

BBC Religion - Buddhism

March saw an outbreak of mob violence directed against Muslims in the town of Meiktila, in central Burma, which left at least 40 dead. Tellingly, the violence began in a gold shop. The movements in both countries exploit a sense of economic grievance - a religious minority is used as the scapegoat for the frustrated aspirations of the majority.

On Tuesday, Buddhist mobs attacked mosques and burned more than 70 homes in Oakkan, north of Rangoon, after a Muslim girl on a bicycle collided with a monk. One person died and nine were injured.

But aren't Buddhist monks meant to be the good guys of religion? Aggressive thoughts are inimical to all Buddhist teachings. Buddhism even comes equipped with a practical way to eliminate them. Through meditation the distinction between your feelings and those of others should begin to dissolve, while your compassion for all living things grows.

Of course, there is a strong strain of pacifism in Christian teachings too: "Love your enemies and pray for those who persecute you," were the words of Jesus in the Sermon on the Mount.

But however any religion starts out, sooner or later it enters into a Faustian pact with state power. Buddhist monks looked to kings, the ultimate wielders of violence, for the support, patronage and order that only they could provide. Kings looked to monks to provide the popular legitimacy that only such a high moral vision can confer. The result can seem ironic. If you have a strong sense of the overriding moral superiority of your worldview, then the need to protect and advance it can seem the most important duty of all.

Christian crusaders, Islamist militants, or the leaders of "freedom-loving nations", all justify what they see as necessary violence in the name of a higher good. Buddhist rulers and monks have been no exception.

One of the most famous kings in Sri Lankan history is Dutugamanu, whose unification of the island in the 2nd Century BC is related in an important chronicle, the Mahavamsa. It says that he placed a Buddhist relic in his spear and took 500 monks with him along to war against a non-Buddhist king.

He destroyed his opponents. After the bloodshed, some enlightened ones consoled him that the slain "were like animals; you will make the Buddha's faith shine".

Burmese rulers, known as "kings of righteousness", justified wars in the name of what they called true Buddhist doctrine.

In Japan, many samurai were devotees of Zen Buddhism and various arguments sustained them - killing a man about to commit a dreadful crime was an act of compassion, for example. Such reasoning surfaced again when Japan mobilised for World War II.

Buddhism took a leading role in the nationalist movements that emerged as Burma and Sri Lanka sought to throw off the yoke of the British Empire. Occasionally this spilled out into violence. In 1930s Rangoon, amid resorts to direct action, monks knifed four

Europeans. More importantly, many came to feel Buddhism was integral to their national identity - and the position of minorities in these newly independent nations was an uncomfortable one.

In 1983, Sri Lanka's ethnic tensions broke out into civil war. Following anti-Tamil pogroms, separatist Tamil groups in the north and east of the island sought to break away from the Sinhalese majority government. During the war, the worst violence against Sri Lankan Muslims came at the hands of the Tamil rebels. But after the fighting came to a bloody end with the defeat of the rebels in 2009, it seems that majority communal passions have found a new target in the Muslim minority.

In Burma, monks wielded their moral authority to challenge the military junta and argue for democracy in the Saffron Revolution of 2007. Peaceful protest was the main weapon of choice this time, and monks paid with their lives. Now some monks are using their moral authority to serve a quite different end. They may be a minority, but the 500,000-strong monkhood, which includes many deposited in monasteries as children to escape poverty or as orphans, certainly has its fair share of angry young men.

The exact nature of the relationship between the Buddhist extremists and the ruling parties in both countries is unclear. Sri Lanka's powerful Defence Secretary Gotabhaya Rajapaksa was guest of honour at the opening of a Buddhist Brigade training school, and referred to the monks as those who "protect our country, religion and race".

But the anti-Muslim message seems to have struck a chord with parts of the population. Even though they form a majority in both countries, many Buddhists share a sense that their nations must be unified and that their religion is under threat.

The global climate is crucial. People believe radical Islam to be at the centre of the many of the most violent conflicts around the world. They feel they are at the receiving end of conversion drives by the much more evangelical monotheistic faiths. And they feel that if other religions are going to get tough, they had better follow suit.

5

Buddhist Extremism and the Hypocrisy of 'Religious and Violence'

This apparently harmless scene was in actuality a meeting between agents of two profoundly radical Theravada ascetic gatherings: Ashin Wirathu Thero of the 696 Movement in Burma (Myanmar) and Dilantha Withanag of the Bodhu Bala Sena (BBS) bunch in Sri Lanka. These gatherings assume a main part in the rising tide of religious fanaticism in their separate nations and have been dynamic in advancing the rough belief system that has prompted many passings in Sri Lanka and what some have called "genocide" in the western Rakhine condition of Myanmar.

It doesn't take much information of Buddhism to acknowledge exactly how beyond reconciliation the reasoning of Buddhist fanatics gatherings are with what the Buddha Gotama educated and the way Buddhism is honed all through a large portion of the world. The principal statute of Thervada Buddhism is not to slaughter any living being, and all through the Pali Cannon this idea is extended to say one ought not wish hurt upon another or loathe any being in any state. Religious narrow mindedness is not present in anything the Buddha educated.

Clearly, religious wonders are once in a while represented by plan of action to the foundational reports of that religion. Buddhist radicalism has emerged out of a political connection of expanded ethnic patriotism and the conspicuous part persuasive ministers regularly play in some Theravada social orders. Clarifying the ethnic purifying of the Muslim Rohingya in Rakhine is more about racial governmental issues than it is about religion. None of Myanmar's ethnic minorities have gotten away oppression from the nation's Burman greater part government throughout the years - be they Christian, Animist, Muslim or Buddhist.

All things considered, it merits inquiring as to why these demonstrations of brutality have not corrupted the way the West sees Buddhism? All things considered, the Western media has more than once shown itself inclined toward becoming tied up with sentimentality when it comes religion - for example, Time magazine ran a sensational spread picture including Wirathu's face with the feature, "The Face of Buddhist Terror" back in June 2013. But we keep on viewing Buddhism as a quiet religion, despite the pictures of ministers in robes hacking individuals to death with cleavers.

What's more, in fact, numerous white nonbelievers who are intractably restricted to religion talk enthusiastically of Buddhism and are progressively eager to go to Vipassana reflection withdraws. So why are we arranged to separate a few religions from demonstrations of brutality, and not others?

Like their Islamic partners, Buddhist radical gatherings utilize their religion as avocation for savagery. Wirathu contends that Buddhism is serene by nature, however that it is important to depend on savagery with a specific end goal to oppose the danger of Islam - to abstain from having the tranquil religion "wiped out," indicating Buddhism's verifiable noticeable quality in focal Asia before the ascent of Islam.

His rationale is entirely thin, particularly given the absence of Muslims or brutality from Islamic gatherings in Myanmar, yet he has by and by taken advantage of a group of people of religiously faithful and socially traditionalist Burmese ultranationalists. These gatherings are battling a social fight to shape the fabric of Burmese society as it experiences a time of progress, with the lifting of Western authorizations consequently for the still sketchy guarantees of vote based "change." There is a reasonable feeling of advantage about a significant part of the dialect utilized by Buddhist radicals bunches, which is acquired specifically from the way the West talks about Islam.

In spite of Buddhism's place in the decolonisation battle in different nations, religion did not play the same wide bringing together part crosswise over Asia in the way that it did in the Middle East. But then the "conflict of civilisations" story that is progressively prominent in Western talk about Islam is not utilized with regards to Buddhism. In addition, notwithstanding the way that conventional Tibetan social Buddhism could be seen as far expelled from European society as most Middle Eastern Islamic social customs, Tibetan Buddhism is to a great extent grasped by the West.

It is likewise important how geopolitical interests bolster into this situation, and how the latent picture of Buddhism would change on the off chance that we were frequently and reliably required in military clash in sincere Buddhist nations.

When I was in Jakarta not long ago, I listened to Ihsan Alief, a specialist and establishing individual from Liberal Islam Network, give a discussion on a contextual analysis examination they had done on different instances of religious savagery all through Indonesia. Separating every case - whether they be assaults on Christian places of worship or the murdering of adherents of the minority Ahamdiyah order of Islam - he demonstrated the basic strains at play, which had little to do with religion. There were area possession clashes, pressure amongst transients and nearby government authorities looking to politicize strains in the number one spot up to decisions.

The size of the viciousness for every situation was generally dictated by the way nearby law authorization offices and government responded and whether they remained by, incite or diffuse strains.

A recent example of the simplistic Western media "religious violence" narrative is the ongoing conflict in Yemen that escalated in recent months with Saudi Arabia's military intervention. The media exhibits neither the patience nor the care to actually understand the crisis; instead, they merely consign the violence to yet another "Sunni-Shi'a" conflict and move on.

When I interviewed a number of people who came out to protest against what they called the "Islamisation of Australia" at the recent Reclaim Australia rallies, I found that the problem of "religious violence" was often cited. I remember talking to a man who didn't know if Kenya was in east or west of Africa, but was sure that the massacre of 140 students at Garissa University in Kenya was evidence Muslims shouldn't be allowed in Australia.

We paint with broad strokes a picture of "religious violence," while ignoring the complexities of each given situation. This narrative fits the popular idea of a "clash of civilisations" and confirms the popular assumption that Islam is inherently violent, instead of recognising the Middle East and north Africa as places of immense turmoil. In so doing, we take the cheap option of blaming religion instead of making the effort to understand.

THE SERENE-LOOKING BUDDHIST MONK ACCUSED OF INCITING BURMA'S SECTARIAN VIOLENCE

The recent flood of Rohingya refugees streaming out of Burma at the hands of ruthless smugglers, who imprison them in death camps or leave them stranded on ramshackle ships, has onlookers questioning what could drive people to such desperate measures.

Part of the answer, human rights activists say, is Ashin Wirathu, a Buddhist monk who is accused of inciting waves of violence against a groupfrequently called "one of the most persecuted minorities in the world."

"Wirathu plays a central role with his hate speech and the Islamophobia that it creates, given that the Rohingya are surrounded by a hostile community that can be whipped into violence very quickly," Penny Green, director of the International State Crime Initiative at Queen Mary University of London and author of a forthcoming report on Burma, told the Los Angeles Times. "Why are these people leaving on boats? Why would people risk certain death on the high seas? Because the existence they have, and the lack of a future, is worse."

By all appearances, Wirathu seems an unlikely leader of sectarian violence. He speaks in soft, measured tones, clasping his hands thoughtfully. Like all Burmese Buddhist monks, his head is shaved and he is draped in a simple saffron robe. He teaches at a quiet and dimly lit monastery in Mandalay where monks kneel in study or prayer and flowers and images of religious figures decorate the walls. It's every bit the Western stereotype of Buddhist tranquility.

But the exterior of the monastery is gruesome, coated with propaganda posters depicting violence he claims has been perpetrated by the Rohingya, Burma's Muslim ethnic minority: collapsed temples and blood-streaked bodies.

"These pictures are here to protect our religion and our national interest," the monk calmly explained to a BBC reporter in a 2013 documentary. "If we do not protect our own people we will become weak, and we will face more mass killings of this kind when they grow to outnumber us."

"Muslims are only well behaved when they are weak," he adds, contemplating another poster. "When they are strong they are like a wolf or a jackal, in large packs they hunt down other animals."

Wirathu is the leader of Burma's 969 movement, a radical nationalist group that's been accused of inciting violence against the Rohingya. Rights activists have called him a neo-Nazi and Time ran a 2013 profile of him under the headline "The Face of Buddhist Terror." In that article, Time said he had "taken the title of 'the Burmese bin Laden.'" Wirathu contested the quote, but it was too late. The moniker stuck.

The Rohingya, who live mostly in Burma's western Rakhine State, have been persecuted long before Wirathu arrived on the scene. Despite the fact that many Rohingya have been in the country for generations, the Burmese government considers them illegal immigrants from Bangladesh — sectarians like Wirathu often refer to them derogatorily as "Bengalis." The Rohingya have been denied Burmese citizenship since 1982.

But their situation deteriorated drastically in 2012, when clashes broke out between the Rohingya and Rankhine Buddhists. With much of the state in shambles, the government quickly moved to put Rohingya in internally displaced person camps — which critics say are more like concentration camps. The following year, violence against Burmese Muslims spilled beyond Rankhine into the rest of the country — thousands more people were displaced, hundreds of homes and businesses destroyed, and scores killed, including 20 students who were massacred at an Islamic school. Those who could escape, did. The United Nations estimates that 120,000 Rohingya have fled the country during the past three years.

In 2003, Wirathu was imprisoned by Burma's military junta — who he says defrocked him and tortured him in jail. But at the same time that the conflicts between Burma's Buddhists and the Rohingya began to escalate, Wirathu wasreleased as part of a 2012 general amnesty. He began traveling the country, giving sermons and distributing DVDs that Rangoon-based writer Alex Bookbinder said in the Atlantic "would not be out of place at the Nuremberg rallies."

"You can be full of kindness and love, but you cannot sleep next to a mad dog," he said of Muslims at a 2013 sermon reported by the New York Times. Later, to reporters, he added, "I am proud to be called a radical Buddhist."

A catchy pop tune titled "Song to Whip Up Religious Blood" is often played at 969 rallies. The movement is named for three digits that monks say symbolize the virtues of the Buddha, Buddhist practices and the Buddhist community, but its theme song is far from devotional. The lyrics reference people who "live in our land, drink our water, and are ungrateful to us," according to the Times. And the chorus, "We will build a fence with our bones if necessary," is repeated over and over again.

Wirathu claims that his movement is not responsible for the violence against the Rohingya. But he does repeatedly insist that Muslims — whom he often calls "kalars," a derogatory term roughly equivalent to the N-word — need to be kept in their place. He calls for boycotts of Muslim-owned businesses,warns Buddhists to protect their women from Muslim rapists and was a vocal backer of a law restricting marriages between Buddhists and Muslims. And outbreaks of violence often coincide with Wirathu's speeches or posts on the 969 Facebook page, the U.S.-based rights group Justice Trust said. "The fact that all these episodes showed the same recurrent pattern — including speaking tours by Wirathu ... just before the outbreak of violence — indicates a deliberate strategy to foment such violence," the group wrote in a March report.

In light of all this, Osama bin Laden isn't the only person Wirathu gets compared to. Muang Zarni, a Burmese democracy activist based in London, said that Wirathu's movement against Muslims resembles Hitler's rhetoric against the Jews in Nazi Germany. "Their intent is genocidal in the sense that the Muslims of Burma — all of them, including the ethnically Burmese — are considered leeches in our society the way the Jews were considered leeches and bloodsuckers during the Third Reich when Nazism was taking root," he told Vice in 2013.

But inside Burma, Wirathu has few vocal critics. Many speculate that the Burmese government supports the radical monk in hopes that his rhetoric will distract Burmese citizens from the country's other pressing issues and give a nationalist boost to the ruling party ahead of this year's election. Even celebrated democracy activist Aung San Suu Kyi has offered only muted criticism of the violence, earning her condemnation from both sides.

"I think she has seriously miscalculated her response to anti-Muslim violence in Burma," Mark Farmaner, director of Burma Campaign UK, told GQ. "She has ended up with the worst of both worlds. On the one hand, she hasn't spoken up for an oppressed and endangered minority, on the other hand, she's still being attacked by the 969 movement and losing support because there remains a perception that she's friendly to Muslims."

The Dalai Lama has condemned Burma's anti-Muslim violence, asserting in a 2013 speech at the University of Maryland that conflict serves political purposes, not spiritual ones. "Really, killing people in the name of religion is unthinkable," he said, according to Reuters.

For his part, Wirathu rejects the allegations that he is a bad Buddhist, a terrorist or a government pawn. In 2013, when a reporter for GQ asked him about his connection to the military, he ended the interview. When Time published its 2013 profile comparing him to bin Laden, he wrote the reporter abizarre message lamenting, "You are not a gentle lady as I thought but of the same flock with extremist Kalars." He has accused the media of being controlled by Muslims and purposefully framing him as a hatemonger. "Look at my face," he told the Los Angeles Times recently. "I don't have any hatred at all."

MYANMAR BUDDHIST MONKS THREATEN DEMOCRACY WITH SUPPORT FOR ANTI-MUSLIM LAWS

More than 10,000 Buddhist monks and nuns rallied recently to celebrate Myanmar's restrictive new race and religion laws, packing themselves into an indoor soccer stadium to cheer and chant nationalist slogans.

The event, held last month in Myanmar's commercial capital, was a dramatic display of a rising force in Myanmar's political landscape — a group of ultra-nationalist Buddhists called the Ma Ba Tha, whom analysts say could pose a threat to the country's shaky hopes for democracy.

Voters in Myanmar, or Burma, head to the polls Sunday in a landmark election that is the first since the military junta eased their control and began democratic overhauls in 2010. Reliable polling is scarce, but Aung San Suu Kyi, the country's Nobel laureate, has been drawing large crowds as she campaigns across the country for her National League for Democracy party.

Meanwhile, leaders of the Ma Ba Tha, which translates to the Association for the Protection of Race and Religion, have thrown their support to President Thein Sein, the former general, and his military-backed ruling party. The movement's growing influence and its support for laws restricting religious freedom have troubled Myanmar's advocates in the United States, who saw the country as a potential model for democratic overhauls and an Obama administration success story.

Tom Malinowski, assistant U.S. secretary of state for democracy, human rights and labour, said there were two narratives in the election.

"There is the narrative of democracy vs. dictatorship and then a competing narrative which aims to convince voters this is an election about protecting the vast majority of Burmese who are Buddhists against what has been characterized as an existential threat from a tiny minority that is Muslim," Malinowski said. "That gives rise to worries many people have about potential violence down the road. You can't invent such a narrative for an election and then forget about it the day after."

Ashin Wirathu, the firebrand Buddhist monk who is a leader in the Ma Ba Tha, said that the group is supporting Thein Sein because his government passed the legislation governing interfaith marriage, family size and religious conversion that many say targets the Muslim minority.

"As President Thein Sein implemented the race and religion protection laws without caring about international pressure, we see him as a special one," Wirathu said in an interview. If Suu Kyi and her party come to power, he said, Myanmar would have "female dictatorship." Suu Kyi is technically barred from the presidency by a constitutional provision, but she has said she will lead the country anyway if her party wins a majority.

"The way she behaves, the way she treats the people inside the party and the audience, and the small parties, she has more percentage on the authoritarian side," the monk said. "So, if she is in power, I can imagine that a female dictatorship country will emerge in the world."

Ashin Wirathu, 47, is one of the Ma Ba Tha's most outspoken advocates. He has called Muslims mad dogs and the United Nations envoy for human rights a "bitch" and a "whore." He has been dubbed the "Burmese bin Laden," a label he once rejected but says no longer troubles him.

"About the election," he says. "Ma Ba Tha just hopes for security and peace." Myanmar, a predominantly Buddhist country of 51 million, was under military rule for more than a quarter-century until Thein Sein's quasi-civilian government released Suu Kyi from house arrest, freed other political prisoners and relaxed censorship. The actions paved the way for the United States and other countries to ease sanctions and resulted in millions in foreign investment. Analysts say that lifting controls allowed some free speech for the first time in decades, but also permitted radical monks such as Ashin Wirathu to flourish on Facebook and elsewhere. Ashin Wirathu began advocating avoiding Muslim businesses as part of the "969 Movement," a precursor to Ma Ba Tha.

Radical monks have been accused by human rights organizations of hate speech that fomented violence in Rakhine State in 2012, which left more than 200 dead and displaced more than a quarter-million. Many were the stateless Rohingya Muslims. About 140,000 Rohingya continue to live as virtual prisoners, ostensibly for their own safety, in fetid camps. They were stripped of voting rights earlier this year.

On a recent campaign swing through Rakhine State, Suu Kyi did not speak directly about the plight of the Rohingya but was peppered with questions from local Buddhists asking if Muslims would have greater power if her party ran the country. Her party has not fielded any Muslim candidates, in part to avoid criticism from the Ma Ba Tha.

"If we choose Muslim candidates, Ma Ba Tha points their fingers at us so we have to avoid it," NLD leader Win Htein told UCA news, the Asian Catholic news agency.

Myanmar Muslims who are citizens said they too had been subject to growing incidents of racism, saying that Buddhists refuse to patronize their stores and they have had trouble getting identity cards.

Ashin Wirathu argues that the Buddhists are the targets. "It is more than a threat, they are harming us physically," he said, noting that in 2012 eight villages were destroyed in Rakhine and Buddhists were killed and attacked.

Observers say that the Ma Ba Tha has amassed grass-roots support, a broad donor base and increasingly tech-savvy volunteers since it was formed in 2013. Burmese scholar Maung Zarni said they are a puppet of the military, noting the impressive array of military men who showed up for the Oct. 4 rally. Election observers for the Carter Center — the nonprofit public policy center founded by former president Jimmy Carter — also raised concerns about the rally and the "potentially disruptive use of nationalist and religious rhetoric during the campaign" in a recent report. The group has received four official complaints of misuse of religion in the campaign, including members of the Ma Ba Tha passing out materials that target candidates. Monks are technically prohibited from participating in political activities.

On a recent day, the headquarters for the Ma Ba Tha movement located in a monastery in Yangon's Insein Township was quiet, its nearby temple holding only a few worshipers of a large reclining Buddha. A pink-robed nun enthusiastically ushered guests into a small bookshop to show off a variety of nationalist tomes.

"We need these laws to safeguard our own race and religion. Buddhism has almost been swallowed completely around the country," the nun, Khay Mar Thi, said.

A gong sounded, and dozens of monks emerged on their way to afternoon study. Some said they didn't know much about this group in their midst; others said they didn't want to talk. But a few were only too happy to share what they had learned.

"Muslims are dangerous," said novice monk Shin Thu Mana. "They're not like other religions."

BUDDHISM AND HINDUISM

Hinduism and Buddhism are two closely related Dharmic religions that are in some ways parallel to each other and in other ways divergent in theology and practice.

Hinduism, like Buddhism under Sakyamuni Buddha, is a post-Vedic religion and some would say a post-Buddhist religion as mention of the Buddha is found in most of the Puranas. The word "Hindu" finds no mention in any pre-Gupta period.

Hiuen Tsang who visited India country between AD 630 and 645 says that while the word "Shin-tu" (Chinese for "Hindu") could be heard outside our borders, it was unknown within the country..

The word *Sanatana Dharma*, is used by many Hindus to identify their religion, but it was used by all Dharmic religions and found in the Buddhist text, Dhammapada, with the Dhamma or law in Vedic thought being identified as being eternal law and the King of Kings in such texts as the Brihadaranyaka Upanishads. Buddhism has no singular founder by tradition as Buddhism is a continuation of a long line of Buddhas, this is similar to the claim of Jains and Hindus who claim their teachings are from a long line of sages.

The Vedic, Buddhist and Jains also share a common regional culture situated near and around north eastern India — modern day eastern Uttar Pradesh, Bihar and Nepal. It was in this region that the first Upanishad, the Brihadaranyaka Upanishad, considered to be the oldest Upanishad, under King Janaka of Mithila was compiled.

Both Siddhartha who became the Buddha and Mahavira who was latest sage of Jainism also hailed from this region.

According to the Buddhist tradition, Siddhartha Gautama was born as a Kshatriya prince to the Shakya clan in modern day Nepal, at the beginning of the Magadha period (546–324 BCE), in the plains of Lumbini, modern day Nepal region of the Indian subcontinent. Siddhartha Gautama is known as the *Shakyamuni* (literally *"the sage of the Shakya clan"*). Under a fig tree (held sacred by most religions and in India Vedic people know this tree as the tree of Vishnu) known to Buddhists as the Bodhi tree, he vowed to meditate until he discovered the truth. At the age of 35, he attained Enlightenment.

Siddhartha Gautama was then known as *"Buddha"*, which translates to *"the enlightened one."* For the remaining 45 years of his life, he travelled the Gangetic Plain of central India, teaching his doctrine and discipline to a diverse range of people.

Nastik Buddhists believe the Buddha, like Vidyaranya, accepted and incorporated many tenets of Hinduism in his doctrine, but also taught that to achieve salvation one did not have to accept the authority of the scriptures or even the existence of God. Many Indians converted to Buddhism. Buddhism had a great influence on Hinduism, from the way it used parables and stories as a means of religious instruction, to its influence on Indian art, sculpture and education.

SIMILARITIES BETWEEN HINDUISM AND BUDDHISM

Siddhartha Gautama

Siddhartha was born in Lumbini, under the full moon of the sixth lunar month, in the spring.

His father was Suddhodana (Pali Suddhodana), of the Vedic Kcatriya varna which according to texts such as the Brihadaranyaka Upanishads, Buddhist and Jain sources, the highest varna, was the chief (raja, or king) of the Sakya nation, one of several ancient tribes on the margins of the growing state of Koshala (Pali Kosala). His mother was Mayadevi, King Sudhodhana's wife.

Ahimsa

Ahimsa is a religious concept which advocates non-violence and a respect for all life. *Ahimsa* is Sanskrit for avoidance of *himsa*, or injury. It is most often interpreted as meaning peace and reverence toward all sentient beings. Ahinsa is an important doctrine of Hinduism, Jainism, and Buddhism. Its first mention in Indian philosophy is found in the Vedic scriptures called the Upanishads, the oldest of which date to about 800 BCE and others dating much later.

Idol Worship

A murti (also spelled *murthi* or *murthy*) typically refers to an image in which the Divine Spirit is 'murta', or expressed. A murti becomes worshippable after the Divine is invoked in it for the purpose of offering worship. Thus the murti is treated as the Deity of the Divine. Buddhists during view statues of deities as points of meditational focus as well as a reminder of the ultimate goal, Buddhahood.

Buddhists venerate many deities which were common to the Indian subcontinent in Vedic tradition, even deities that Hindus themselves no longer worship, including that of Indra. Indra is venerated by the Chinese, Korean and Japanese as Taishakuten while Ganesh is worshipped as Lord Shoten.

In "Ganesh, studies of an Asian God", edited by Robert L. BROWN, State University of New York Press, 1992, page 241-242, he wrote that in the Tibetan Kanjur, it is said that the Buddha had taught the Ganapati Hridaya Mantra (or Aryaganapatimantra) to disciple Ananda. However, having taken the vows of refuge, a Buddhist does not rely on such deities for enlightenemnt or liberation but simply to aid them in worldly life for such material things as wealth, food and shelter which provides conducive conditions for practising. As for Ganesh, the a Tibetan tradition holds that Chenrezig out of compassion dissolved an emanation of himself into Ganesh, thereby blessing him to support Buddhist practitioners. It is taken that this particular Ganesh is the one venerated by Buddhists and is seen to have gained enlightenment by now. Thus, another Ganesh has taken the former's position and the new Ganesh is not venerated by Buddhists.

Karma

Karma is a word of ancient origin meaning *action* or *activity* and its subsequent results (also called karma-phala, "the fruits of action"). It is commonly understood as a term to denote the entire cycle of cause and effect as described in the philosophies of a number of Dharmic Religions such as Hinduism and Buddhism. Karma originated in the Vedic system of religion, which became Hinduism. Karma is a sum of all that an individual has done, is currently doing and will do. Individuals go through certain processes and accompanying experiences throughout their lives which they have chosen, and those would be based on the results of their own creations. Karma is not about retribution, vengeance, punishment or reward. Karma simply deals with what is. The effects of all deeds actively create past, present and future experiences, thus making one responsible for one's own life, and the pain and joy it brings to others. In religions that incorporate reincarnation, karma extends through one's present life and all past and future lives as well.

Dharma

Dharma means Natural Law or Reality, and with respect to its significance for spirituality and religion might be considered the Way of the Higher Truths. Dharma was first described in Hinduism. Hinduism is called *Sanatana Dharma* which translates to "the eternal dharma." Dharma forms the basis for philosophies, beliefs and practices originating in India. The four main ones are Hinduism, Buddhism, Jainism, and Sikhism, all of whom retain the centrality of Dharma in their teachings. In these traditions, beings that live in harmony with Dharma proceed more quickly toward Dharma Yukam, Moksha, Nirvana (personal liberation). Dharma also refers to the teachings and doctrines of the various founders of Dharmic traditions, such as Vidyaranya, Kumarila Bhatta, Gautama Buddha and Mahavira. As the religious and moral doctrine of the rights and duties of each individual. Dharma can refer generally to religious duty, and also mean social order, right conduct, or simply virtue.

Aum

In Buddhism and Hinduism, the term *bija* is used for mystical "seed syllables" contained with mantras. These seeds do not have precise meanings, but are thought to carry connections to spiritual principles. The best-known *bija* syllable is Om, which first is seen in the Hindu scriptures known as the Upanishads.

Mantra

A mantra is a religious syllable or poem, typically from the Sanskrit language. Their use varies according to the school and philosophy associated with the mantra. They are primarily used as spiritual conduits, words or vibrations that instill one-pointed concentration in the devotee. Other purposes have included religious ceremonies to accumulate wealth, avoid danger, or eliminate enemies. Mantras originated in India with Vedic Hinduism and were later adopted by Buddhists, Sikhs and Jains, now popular in various modern forms of spiritual practice which are loosely based on practices of these Eastern religions.

Yogic Traditions

Yoga, meaning 'yoke' in Sanskrit, is a family of ancient spiritual practices originating in India. It is one of the six schools of Hindu Philosophy, in which it is often paired with Samkhya, and they are referred together as the Samkhya-Yoga school. The diversity within Yoga philosophy itself is traditionally classified into four main braches: Karma Yoga (yoga of action), Jnana Yoga (yoga of knowledge), Bhakti Yoga (yoga of devotion), and Raja Yoga (yoga of meditation), but other classifications do exist. It remains a vibrant living tradition in which the common goal of all branches is liberation from suffering by attainment of enlightenment.

There is a considerable overlap between Yoga and Buddhism. Of particular interest is a comparison of the Buddhist eight-fold path and the eight limbs of Patanjali's Yoga. Their moral precepts (the *sila* of Buddhism, the *yama* and *niyama* of yoga) share the Hindu principle of non-violence (*ahimsa*); their final steps point towards a common goal-6. Buddhist *Samma Vayama* (Effort) vs Yogic *Dharana* (Concentration), 7. Buddhist *Samma Sati* (Mindfulness) vs Yogic *Dhyana* (Meditation) and 8. Buddhist *Samma Samadhi* vs Yogic *Samadhi*. An in relation to views of the Self, yoga's *asmita-samapatti* is designed to eradicate the wrong views on the Self much in the same way Buddha did it in *Anatta-lakkhana-sutta*. The correlation between Yoga and Buddhism seems to be particularly strong in Tibetan Buddhism, due to various historical events including the influence of Tantra on Tibetan traditions. For example, a system of 108 bodily postures practiced with breath and heart rhythm timing in movement exercises is known as Trul khor or union of moon and sun (channel) prajna energies, and the body postures of Tibetan ancient yogis are depicted on the walls of the Dalai Lama's summer temple of Lukhang.

Prominent Tibetan Buddhist Yoga schools Six yogas of Naropa, Tumo and Tsa lung Trul khor.

Dhyana

Dhyana's beginings are traced to Hinduism, where it is considered to be an instrument to gain self knowledge, thereby seperating maya from reality and helping attain the ultimate goal of Moksha. Depictions of hindu yogis performing dhyana are found in ancient texts and in statues and frescoes of ancient India temples. Siddhartha Gautama studied dhyana during his early years away from his kingdom.

Reincarnation

In India the concept of reincarnation is first recorded in the Upanishads (c. 800 BCE), which are philosophical and religious texts composed in Sanskrit. According to Hinduism, the soul (atman) is immortal, while the body is subject to birth and death. The Bhagavad Gita states that: Worn-out garments are shed by the body; Worn-out bodies are shed by the dweller within the body. New bodies are donned by the dweller, like garments. The idea that the soul (of any living being-including animals, humans and plants) reincarnates is intricately linked to karma, another concept first introduced in the Upanishads.

Karma (literally: action) is the sum of one's actions, and the force that determines one's next reincarnation. The cycle of death and rebirth, governed by karma, is referred to as samsara.

Buddhism believes in the anatta. Buddhists also believe that a new-born child may be the reincarnation of some important departed lama. In Tibetan Buddhism, the substance that make up the impermanent "self" (skandha) of an important lama (like the Dalai Lama) is said to be reborn into an infant born nine months after his decease. This process is said to occurs after years of crystallization of the skandhas through mental cultivation. And when the body dies, some of the crystallized skandhas (which normally dissolves at death), is said to attach itself to the consciousness. So that when the next rebirth occurs, the new person will have some of the old characters. This belief, however, does not contradict with Buddha's teaching on the impermanent nature of the self.

Nirvana

The Sanskrit term "Nirvana" was nothing a the time of Buddha, as Hindu scriptures concentrated on this principle. Parinirvana, in Hinduism is known as Mahasamadhi. Although in modern-day terms, Buddhism is different from Hinduism, in which the Nirvana is Brahma-Nirvana. Buddhists today argue whether the Buddha has eternally remained a Buddha, come down as humans only to show humans that this eternal bliss is achievable by anyone. This form of Buddha in Buddhism is known as Dharmakaya Buddha.

It was Buddha who is remembered for saying, "*You are a Buddha, I am the Buddha.*"

JAINISM AND BUDDHISM

Jainism and Buddhism are the two branches of the Shramana tradition that still exist today. Until recently Jainism was largely confined to India, while Buddhism has largely flourished in countries outside of India. However the two traditions share remarkable similarities.

Buddhism separates itself from the Jain tradition by teaching an alternative to "extreme asceticism". Even though it is said that, during Buddha's life he undertook many fasts, penances and austerities, the descriptions of which are elsewhere found only in the Jain tradition (for example, the penance by five fires, plucking of hair, and the consumption of food using only one's cupped hands), ultimately Buddha abandoned these methods on his discovery of the Middle Way (Magga). To this day, many Buddhist teachings, principles, and terms used in Buddhism are identical to those of Jainism, but they may hold very different meanings for each.

However, it is interesting to note that even under the Jain tradition, there exist a non-extreme pathway. While the Jain Sadhu and Sadhvi are referred to as the Sramans and Sramanis, the Shravak and Shravika are household men and women (Grihastha), respectively, who have not abandoned the worldly affairs, i.e. not having obtained "Diksha", but are still following the religious guidelines, in the given constraints. There are separate norms that have been prescribed for the Shravak and Shravika under the Jain tradition.

Whether or not it was an influence of Jain culture and philosophy in ancient Bihar that gave rise to Buddhism is unclear, but there are some striking similarities between the two traditions, and Buddhism may have adopted many of its ideas and traditions from pre-existing ones held by the Jains. The two groups are so similar that early western archaeologists working in India often attributed Buddhist art and historical sites as being of Jain origin. Buddhist texts often mention Jain philosophy, and it seems likely that the latter was a well established tradition before the rise of Buddhism.

The Buddhists have always maintained that by the time Buddha and Mahavira were alive, Jainism was already an entrenched faith and culture in the region. Buddhist scriptures record philosophical dialogues between the wandering seeker Siddartha Gautama (Buddha) and Udaka Ramaputta, who was likely a Jain, and the first of several teachers that young Siddartha Gautama studied with before his enlightenment. Buddhist scriptures attest that some of the first Buddhists were in fact Jains (*Nirgranthas* as they were then called, meaning "the unbonded ones") who "converted", but were encouraged by Buddha to maintain their Jain identity and practises such as giving alms to Jain monks and nuns.

Buddhists recorded that Mahavira preached the "four-fold restraint" of the Nirgrantha tradition — a clear reference to the teachings of Mahavira's predecessor Lord Parshva (877-777 BC), traditionally the 23rd Tirthankara of Jainism — who propounded the four vows of Ahinsa (Ahimsa), Satya (truth), Aparigraha (non-possessiveness), and Asteya (non-stealing), which may have been the template for the Five Precepts of Buddhism. Additionally, the Buddhist *Anguttara Nikaya* scripture quotes the independent philosopher Purana Kashyapa (the sixth century BC founder of a now extinct order) as listing the Nirgranthas as one of the six major classifications of humanity. Mahavira and Buddha were contemporaries, however there is no mention of the two teachers ever meeting. The Pali texts mention the Buddha referring to the liberation of Mahavira (referred to as Nigganthа Nataputta) at Pava.

The possibilities of Jainism and Buddhism being similar and not necessarily an offshoot is the spiritual path to gain Moksha is similar and hence the teachings and the beliefs are so similar.

The common concepts in Jainism and Buddhism:

- Shramana
- Nirvana: (the definition is different in the two traditions)
- Arhat: the term is used somewhat similarly.
- Dharma

- Jina
- Acharya (chief of the orders)
- Sutra (scriptures)
- Indra/Shakra (chief of the gods).

The terms that are used with different meanings:

- Pudgala
- Siddha.

Common Symbols:

- Pratima, foot prints
- Stupa
- The dharma-chakra
- The swastika
- The trirathna
- The ashta-mangalas
- Minor devas.

Vegetarianism is required for both monks and laity in Jainism. In Buddhism, the monks in China, Japan, Korea and Vietnam are vegetarian; however vegetarianism is not required.

It has also been suggested that the influence of Jain culture and philosophy in ancient Bihar may have given rise to Buddhism. Buddhist scriptures describe various penances (*tapas*) undertaken by Gautama Siddhartha which appear identical to Jain penances (e.g., cupping the hands to consume alms, plucking of hair, the penance by five fires, etc.). These penances were later renounced by Gautama as activities not leading to Nirvana (Final Liberation). Buddhist writings reflect that Jainism was an already established faith — rather than a newly founded or reformist one — by the time Buddha lived. Early Buddhists posited the existence of 24 previous Buddhas (Buddhas who walked the earth prior to Siddhartha Gautama, as established in the Buddhist text *Mahavanso* 1:100:1 among others) many of whose names are identical to those of the 24 Jain *Tirthankaras* and other traditional Jain figures. Suggesting close correlations between the teachings of the Jains and Buddha, the *Majjhima Nikaya* relates dialogues between Buddha and several members of the *Nigantha* (Jain) community, sometimes resulting in the latter's acceptance of Buddha as a teacher. In many instances, both philosophies continue to share similar Prakrit terminology for important themes and teachings but may differ significantly in interpretation and meaning. This method of teaching adopted by the Buddha points to the pragmatic aspect of Buddha's style of teaching wherein the Buddha uses words and terms that are familiar to the audience instead of introducing new and complex technical jargon. In this way, Buddhism sought to appeal to a broad audience.

Jainism is an ancient religion and school of thought that predates Buddhism. One of its two most revered teachers, Mahavira (599-527 BCE according to Jains, though some scholars prefer 549-477 BCE), was possibly a senior contemporary of the Buddha whose philosophy, sometimes described as dynamism or vitalism, was a blend of the earlier Jain teacher Parúvanatha's (877-777 BCE) order and the reforms instituted by Mahavira himself. (The *Majjhima Nikaya* relates an incident wherein a disciple brings Buddha the news that the Nigantha Nattaputta, i.e. Mahavira, had died, thereby suggesting the latter's seniority.) Debates between Buddhists and Jains are recorded in Jain texts, and dialogues between Jains and the Buddha are included in Buddhist texts. This article helped me a lot in completing my project. Shubhasis Debata (Stewart School, Orissa)

Indian Buddhist tradition categorized all non-Buddhist schools of thought as "Pasanda" (Pasanda means to throw a noose or pasha — since these schools foster wrong view which tend to bind and ensnare rather than free the mind). The difference between the schools of thought are outlined in the Saamannaphala Sutta of the Digha Nikaya.

NONTHEISM

Nontheism covers a range of concepts regarding spirituality and religion which do not include the idea of a deity — a theistic God or theistic gods. It can be applied to atheism (both strong and weak) and agnosticism, as well as certain Eastern religions including Confucianism, Taoism, and Buddhism. It also has links and similarities to Christian existentialism.

Nontheism in Christianity

Certain liberal Christian theologians, including Episcopal bishop John Shelby Spong and Anglican bishop John A.T. Robinson define a "nontheistic God" as "the ground of all being" rather than as a personal divine being. Spong refers to a theistic God as "a personal being with expanded supernatural, human, and parental qualities, which has shaped every religious idea of the Western world."

Both Robinson and Spong owe much of their theology to the work of Christian existentialist philosopher Paul Tillich, including the phrase "the ground of all being". Another quotation from Tillich is, "God does not exist. He is being itself beyond essence and existence.

Therefore to argue that God exists is to deny him." This Tillich quotation summarizes his conception of God. He does not think of God as a being which exists in time and space, because that constrains God, and makes God finite. But all beings are finite, and if God is the Creator of all beings, God cannot logically be finite since a finite being cannot be the sustainer of an infinite variety of finite things. Thus God is considered beyond being, above finitude and limitation, the power or essence of being itself.

Secular humanist Sidney Hook wrote in an essay called *"The Atheism of Paul Tillich"*:

With amazing courage Tillich boldly says that the God of the multitudes does not exist, and further, that to believe in His existence is to believe in an idol and ultimately to embrace superstition. God cannot be an entity among entities, even the highest. He is being-in-itself. In this sense Tillich's God is like the God of Spinoza and the God of Hegel. Both Spinoza and Hegel were denounced for their atheism by the theologians of the past because their God was not a Being or an Entity. Tillich, however, is one of the foremost theologians of our time.

John Dominic Crossan and Robert Funk cofounded the Jesus Seminar, a group of academic scholars who seek, following Rudolf Bultmann, to "demythologize" Jesus. Some also consider this work to be a nontheistic examination of the life and work of Jesus.

Nontheism in Buddhism

The first historically significant nontheist was probably Gautama Buddha, who, when asked whether God existed, or any similar question of metaphysics, usually responded with complete silence. These questions became known as the Fourteen Indeterminates.

On one occasion, when presented with a problem of metaphysics by the monk Malunkyaputta, Buddha responded with a story of a man shot with a poisoned arrow. The man's family summons the doctor to have the poison removed, and the man given an antidote: "But the man refuses to let the doctor do anything before certain questions can be answered. The wounded man demands to know who shot the arrow, what his caste and job is, and why he shot him. He wants to know what kind of bow the man used and how he acquired the ingredients used in preparing the poison. Malunkyaputta, such a man will die before getting the answers to his questions. It is no different for one who follows the Way. I teach only those things necessary to realize the Way. Things which are not helpful or necessary, I do not teach."

Although Buddhism has a vast number of scriptures and practices, the fundamental core of Buddhism, the Four Noble Truths and the Noble Eightfold Path, are distinguished in the world of religion as being absent any mention of God(s) or any notion or worship of any deity. They are purely ethical and meditative guidelines based on the truths of psychological suffering due to impermanence.

Zen Master Bassui (1327-1387) had strong words for those applying notions of divinity to any separate beings, such as bodhisattvas: "... so you should realize that all the names of the bodhisattvas are just different names for the nature of mind. As an expedient in the World-Honoured-One's sermons, he defined things using certain names, and with these names he pointed to the truth. Ordinary people, unaware of this truth, become attached to the names and, in the hopes of attaining Buddhahood, seek the Buddha and Dharma outside their minds. It's like cooking sand in the hopes of producing rice."

Despite an involved Buddhist cosmology, the creation of Things, along with their attachments and aversions (the illusion of maya), is attributed to ignorance or avidya; and attaining to Buddhahood is the end of such ignorance. This technical emphasis on creation, within the mind, contrasts with the notion of any God initating a cosmological creation story, as in theistic traditions.

Nontheism remains a common element of many schools of Buddhism. However, many theologians have argued that Buddhists have merely transferred their theistic devotion to ancestors, bodhisattvas, kami, and other alleged "deity surrogates". Other observers have dismissed these practices as mere folk traditions, analogous to the pagan undertones present in European Christian worship, and not a feature of higher religion. Most modern Buddhist teachers, such as Soyen Shaku and Robert Baker Aitken, avoid addressing the existence or nonexistence of deities, regarding the issue as an indulgence and a distraction.

BUDDHISM AND OTHER RELIGIONS

The Buddha-Dhamma, or Buddhism, can be related to other religions in many ways. Here, only a few main points of comparison will be sketched.

Buddhism is a graduated system of moral and mental training with Nibbana, the highest happiness, as its goal. It is founded upon the principle of causality, the law of cause and effect in the moral domain, that is, in the field of human behavior. Above all, it is a path to liberation from suffering, a goal to be won by cultivating the Noble Eightfold Path in its three stages of morality, concentration, and wisdom *(sila, samadhi, pañña).*

Religion lays down the general lines of conduct by which a person will live his daily life; it lays down rules in such matters as respect for the lives of others, intoxicating liquors, marriage, divorce, and means of livelihood. For the believer it thus colors his or her whole attitude towards matters like birth, sex, family limitation, death, and the afterlife. Transgression of the religious code entails feelings of guilt, so the religion that one follows has a profound influence, shaping one's entire outlook on life as well as one's attitudes, whether in wholesome ways or in unwholesome ways.

Against this background, we can now see how the Buddha-Dhamma is related to other religions.

As stated earlier, the Buddhist way to Nibbana is the Noble Eightfold Path. The question then arises as to whether arahantship — perfect holiness — or Nibbana is possible outside this path. The Buddha's answer to Subhadda's question, just before he passed away, clarifies our problem: "In whatever teaching, O Subhadda, there exists the Noble Eightfold Path, there is the first saint *(sotapanna),* there is the second saint *(sakadagami),* there is the third saint *(anagami),* there is the fourth saint *(arahant).* An arahant is a perfect saint. Elsewhere there are mere semblances of saints." As the Noble Eightfold Path is found only in Buddhism, in the Buddha's own words "the other teachings are empty of true saints."

They therefore err who say that all spiritual paths lead to the same summit and that the view from the top is identical for all. The reason is simple: the Buddha saw the true nature of things clearly and completely with his own independent supramundane insight — his perfect enlightenment — and so his teaching is an exact reflection of reality, while other religious teachers had only an imperfect view of reality, with eyes dimmed by various forms and degrees of ignorance *(avijja).*

This, however, does not imply that Buddhism is intolerant of other religions. Neither the Buddha nor his followers ever imposed his system of thought or his way of life on anyone who would not accept it of his or her own volition. Acceptance was a purely voluntary matter. Even if accepted, how much of it one should practice is one's own responsibility. But regardless of one's personal inclinations, the universal moral laws operate objectively — action being followed by due reaction, deeds by their fruits. The Buddha merely reveals the laws of life, and the more faithfully we follow them, the better it is for us, for then we act according to the Dhamma.

This peaceful policy of non-compulsion and tolerance, characteristic of the Master's teaching, is born partly of compassion and partly of understanding human nature and the nature of truth. If the vision of some is dimmed as to the merits of the teaching it is one's duty to help them to see. But one must stop there: one should not coerce others or persecute those who refuse to accept one's own beliefs. Wisdom, the ability to see things as they truly are, cannot be imposed on others from the outside. It must grow from within the individual, out of the developing sensitivity and refinement of human nature. This takes time. At any given period only few will be capable of genuinely appreciating, understanding, and realizing the Buddha's teaching, as human beings vary widely in their intellectual, moral, and spiritual capabilities. Unethical conversions are therefore unheard of in Buddhism.

Buddhist tolerance, however, should not mean apathy and indifference. That would be a misinterpretation of the term. When erroneous statements about Buddhism were made by people in the Buddha's time, the Master kindly corrected them. He even expelled his cousin Devadatta from the Sangha when occasion demanded it to preserve the purity of the Doctrine and the unity of the Sangha. Yet the Buddha was the perfect example of tolerance and compassion. Likewise monk and laity should be always watchful and should emulate the Buddha. Otherwise their case would go by default, for which they alone are to be blamed. Today various proposals are being made to create an all-embracing system of religion, the idea being simply to absorb all other religions into one's own. However, a universal religious consciousness can never be created because: (1) the various religions have fundamentally different conceptions of reality; (2) the concept and content of the good life vary between different religions — the good means one thing to a Buddhist, and another to a Christian, and yet another to a Muslim; and (3) no adherent of a religion wants his religion to be absorbed by another body. Is it not deeply rooted in human nature to believe that no other religion in the world compares with one's own?

Taking Buddhism specifically — and in detail — it is unique, a thing apart from all other religions in the world. It teaches the formula of conditioned arising *(paticca-samuppada)* and its reversal by human effort; craving as the creator of life instead of a creator God; a becoming *(bhava)* without a self *(atta);* personal evolution according to the quality of one's own deeds *(kamma);* an impersonal moral order *(kamma-niyama)* with moral values and moral responsibility; free will, within limits, and therewith the possibility of a good life; survival after death by the continuity of the individual life-flux without transmigration of an individual, immutable, immortal soul; and a transcendental reality (Nibbana), realizable here and now solely by one's own effort. As such, there are major and unbridgeable differences between Buddhism and the other world religions and spiritual philosophies. The attempt to find a common denominator in the uncommon, or to adapt the Dhamma so that it does not differ from the other religions, must necessarily fail. It will only end in the debasement of the Buddha-Dhamma or in its total extinction by painless absorption.

The idea of a universal religion is both unrealistic and impracticable, a mere mirage and an idle delusion. In contrast, over 2500 years ago, the Buddha offered another way of relating religions to each other based on mutual respect yet maintaining the separate identity of each religion. To practice this method one need not become a Buddhist. It is also very practical, effective, and does no violence or offense to anyone. It is simply to cultivate regularly four basic social and ethical attitudes: (1) *metta* — a friendly feeling of loving-kindness to all beings in every situation regardless of race, creed, or caste; (2) *karuna*— compassion for all who suffer, and to take practical steps whenever possible to eliminate or alleviate those sufferings; (3) *mudita* — altruistic joy, to be happy in others' happiness, in their prosperity and success, thereby counteracting feelings of jealousy and unhealthy rivalry between individuals and groups; and (4) *upekkha* — equanimity, the maintenance of an even mind when faced with the ups and downs inherent in life. By practicing these virtues daily, a Christian becomes a better Christian, a Hindu a better Hindu, a Muslim a better Muslim. All of these qualities convey a universal message that make the practitioners universal human beings. Surely, this is universalism in religion par excellence.

This is the most satisfactory way of living harmoniously with one's fellow men and women of all faiths, fostering inter-religious goodwill and avoiding religious conflicts. By pursuing this policy for over 2500 years, there have been no religious wars in Buddhism. It is also the best method of relating the Buddha's Teaching to other religions.

Buddhism, to repeat, is unique — a thing apart from all other religions in the world. While at all times maintaining its separate identity, it should peacefully coexist with other religions, following a policy of live-and-let-live. Such a policy has paid rich dividends in the past and will continue to do so in the future. Monks and laypersons in Sri Lanka should remember this, for the good of the Sasana and the well-being of the country.

In addition, every Buddhist should:

1. live his daily life in accordance with the Master's Teaching by observing the Five Precepts, thereby showing to all that the Buddha-Dhamma yet lives and daily rules his life;
2. support only genuine bhikkhus who observe the rules of discipline (Vinaya) to ensure the purity of the Sangha;
3. give with discrimination to Buddhist causes and to humanitarian projects, as cautioned by the Buddha — to the most deserving the things most needed, as funds are limited;
4. help make known abroad his message of wisdom and compassion.

A TASTE OF THE HOLY LIFE

An Account of an International Ordination in Myanmar

"Ehi bhikkhu!" "Come, monk!" With these simple but portentous words, the Buddha founded the Sangha, the Order of bhikkhus, which has preserved and practiced his doctrine from that day to this.

With that *"Ehi bhikkhu!"* the Buddha conferred ordination upon the first monk, the Venerable Kondañña, at Isipatana near Benares. At the conclusion of the Buddha's first discourse Kondañña had asked to be ordained, and the Buddha, simply by calling him a bhikkhu, transformed him into one. The Buddha went on to say:

"The Dhamma has been well expounded. Practice the holy life rightly to make an end of suffering." That was the ultimate, the highest aim of becoming a monk then as it is now: liberation from all *dukkha,* the suffering of repeated becoming in the cycle of rebirth, *samsara.*

During the Buddha's life, and since, the procedure to become a Buddhist monk evolved into a series of steps often involving large numbers of bhikkhus and lay people. Modern ordination ceremonies clearly express the interdependent relationship of monks and lay people supporting each other in their efforts to put an end to suffering. The bhikkhus, by their conduct, must inspire faith in the lay people. The householders in turn show deep respect for the Order by honoring the individual bhikkhus who in turn determine to make themselves worthy of the respect and support they receive from the laity.

The Buddha could only ordain a few bhikkhus with the phrase *"Ehi bhikkhu."* Such instantaneous ordination required that the man had cultivated certain *paramis* (perfections, good qualities) in the past. Chief amongst the good kammas needed for the Buddha to accept someone as a monk in this way, tradition says, was having been a bhikkhu in previous lives and/or having helped others to ordain. This is one of the reasons why laymen in Myanmar ordain temporarily, and why they obtain such lavish help from lay people, notably their families, when they undertake temporary ordination.

Because they are closely based on the Vinaya Pitaka, the ordination ceremonies in the different Theravada countries are almost identical. Whether the bhikkhus expect to remain in robes for the remainder of their lives or are "temporary" monks (a common practice in Myanmar and Thailand) makes no difference to the procedure. But national variations, especially in the lay aspects of the events, do lend color and specific points of interest to the solemn ceremony.

In January 1994 a mass ordination of foreign men was held in Yangon, Myanmar (the former Rangoon, Burma) under the combined auspices of the Myanmar Department of Religious Affairs and the International Meditation Centre, Yangon. This event, unusual in its location, scale, and international scope, will be described below along with a summary of the week these men were in robes.

All the detailed arrangements of place, transport, requisites, and the like had been made by the hosts beforehand for seven boys aged 9-14 to become samaneras or novices and forty-nine foreign men and one Myanmar to take the full *upasampada* ordination. They would remain in robes for about a week, in accordance with the Myanmar custom of temporary ordination. In that land it is considered essential for every Buddhist male to become a samanera as a boy and a bhikkhu as a man at least for some short period of his life, for the reason explained above and to earn a very high kind of merit, *puñña.* All those in this group who were to be ordained were meditation students of Mother Sayamagyi and Sayagyi U Chit Tin, direct disciples of the late Sayagyi U Ba Khin, renowned lay teacher of Vipassana meditation in Myanmar. They were associated with the International Meditation Centers in that tradition around the world, and the small original IMC, atop a low hill in suburban Yangon's diplomatic area, was the focus for most of the activities.

The shaving of heads, preliminary to every ordination, was set up just outside the wall surrounding the Light of the Dhamma Pagoda at the Centre. About six life-long bhikkhus from the preceptor's monastery came to help shave the heads of the ordinands. Shaded from the hot afternoon sun by a permanent awning, the men doused their heads with water from plastic buckets, then the brown-haired Europeans, blond Americans, black- and grey-haired Asians and Australians sat on low stools. Two people, including the man's wife if she was available, held a piece of white cloth beneath the candidate's chin to catch the locks of hair as they fell from the blade. The bhikkhus swiftly used the straight razors the foreigners had imported, while guiding the movements of their assistants through gesture when they did not share a common language.

The men were meditating, on the parts of the body or the breath or the significance of ordaining. Well aware that this was the start of an important ceremony, everyone quietly reflected on its value. It took perhaps an hour before all were shorn. As a man's head was finished, he took a shower and changed into fresh clothes in preparation for the *pabbajja* ("going forth," the preliminary ordination) ceremony which was to take place that evening in the Center's Dhamma Hall. The organizers knew that the men would be hungry so they were given an early evening meal since they would not be able to eat again that day after they had taken the novice's Ten Precepts, the sixth of which requires abstaining from food after midday.

It had already been a long day of celebration and religious activity. Early in the morning the children in the group, four girls and seven boys, had been dressed as princesses and princes in gilt and silk costumes that included fanciful high crowns, sequined *lungis* with long trains for the girls, makeup and decorations imitating precious jewelry. The princes were going to become samaneras, novices, in the evening and the dressing up was part of the build up, so they would enjoy themselves and keep happy memories of the day. The royal attire also symbolized the renunciation of the princely life by the Bodhisatta Siddhattha — the future Buddha — when he went forth from the palace to find the way to liberation.

Before 8 am, the children were lifted up into the backs of small open pickup trucks and seated on upholstered chairs by the individuals from the Centre who had been assigned to be their foster parents for the day. The real parents, perhaps a bit nervous about how their children would behave, carried the bundle of their sons' robes along with some small white orchids. It was a landmark event in the lives of these Western Buddhist families. The boys' trucks were adorned with tall golden umbrellas proclaiming the ordination procession to passers by. The rest of the group followed in cars and coaches. They moved at a stately pace through Yangon to the Shwe Dagon Pagoda, where several hairs of the Buddha are enshrined. At the head of the motorcade a uniformed Myanmar band standing in a truck played the typical raucous music of the land and sang about the Great Renunciation. A dancer performed in the jerky bent knee and elbow style of Southeast Asia. This too was part of the traditional way to celebrate the boys' going forth. The 130-strong group found the route up to Shwe Dagon, Myanmar's most revered Buddhist site, clear of other devotees. Single file, barefoot, contented and chatting a little, each carrying a purple orchid spray offering, they proceeded up the series of long escalators to the level of the walkway. This is situated perhaps halfway between ground level and the peak of the spire with the golden umbrella. The wide band is paved in marble and much of it is covered with pagodas, cetiyas, and sculptures, notably of the stylized lions who seem to be guardians of the sacred shrine. There were many bhikkhus and lay families at the pagoda although it was not crowded. They showed mild curiosity about the large group of outsiders. The international contingent was dressed for the occasion in proper Myanmar attire, the men in plaid *lungis* and short white jackets, the women in heavy woven cotton *lungis* all of one pattern in various dark colors. The group was led by their teachers and the princes and princesses as it respectfully and mindfully circumambulated the golden dome. The atmosphere was informal and comfortable, the meditators appreciating the beauty and peace of the scene.

After a short meditation session in a side chamber, they left Shwe Dagon and drove to an audience with the fifteen leading sayadaws, renowned senior bhikkhus, who were in office by turns from among the country's State Sangha Maha Nayakas, the Central Executive Body of the Sangha. The group had been allotted a narrow window in the busy schedules of the sayadaws, the Central Executive Body of the Sangha, to pay respects. The theras sat on chairs in the front of the room with an ornate shrine behind them, and were formally introduced in English to the meditators. The foreigners, the teachers and Myanmar hosts accompanying them all paid respects to the sayadaws by bowing with their foreheads to the floor. They then repeated "Namo Tassa Bhagavato" and other devotional verses after the chief sayadaw.

The focus of events shifted to the meditation centre for the rest of the day. In the early afternoon there was an ear-boring ceremony for the four girls aged 5-13. Since the Order of bhikkhunis (nuns) has died out and, according to Theravada orthodoxy, cannot be revived for lack of bhikkhunis to ordain others, girls in Myanmar undergo this simple ritual, generally when a brother is becoming a samanera. At IMC's Dhamma Hall, there was some chanting as the girls sat proudly before the assembly in their slightly rumpled princess outfits. A Myanmar woman doctor put earrings in each girl's ears and they were free to change out of the fancy but inconvenient clothes. For the girls this was the conclusion of their ceremony.

The head shaving of boys and men followed as already described. After their supper, the men came into the Dhamma Hall, their skulls shining, where they were seated on the rugs in rows in age order, facing a line of senior sayadaws. They received a bundle of brown robes neatly rolled together and tied with the red cloth belt worn by Myanmar bhikkhus. Everyone else sat at the back of the hall meditating and observing the proceedings. The ceremony, which had been explained in advance, went on in a combination of Pali, Myanmar and English. Small groups of the samaneras-to-be offered their robes to their preceptor, who accepted them; then they requested the robes back from him so they could go forth, and he returned the robes. Now they all changed out of their lay clothes into the robes. (The shirts and *lungis* were put in labeled bags to be washed and ironed by wives or female volunteers and returned at the time of disrobing.) Most of these men (and one of the boys) had ordained previously, and many had done so several times. But they were all anxious to have another opportunity to practice the strict purity of a member of the Sangha in Myanmar, the land they cherished as the home of the pure Buddha Dhamma which they had been practicing, some for over twenty years. They each formally requested to be ordained as novices and then took the Ten Precepts from U Pandicca, their preceptor, and underwent a few other short formalities. They were given their bhikkhu names from a list considered appropriate for the day of the week of their birth. There was a short discourse of advice for the samaneras and the sayadaws chanted several *paritta suttas* (discourses of protection), for the well being of all. With that, the novitiation was complete.

Later in the evening there was the usual group meditation in the Dhamma Hall, with the new samaneras seated at the front, in order of seniority, which in almost all cases was age. The boys formed the last row and behind them were laymen, two or three from abroad, the rest from Myanmar. Next came the foreign women who had also come for the two weeks at the Centre, about forty-five of them. Filling the back to capacity were Myanmar ladies. This formal meditation hour was repeated three times a day for the two weeks the foreigners were in Yangon.

The men's full ordination *(upasampada),* their entry into the life of bhikkhus, took place on Sunday the 9th of January. The *upasampada* had to be in a monastery, so with the sponsorship and help of the Myanmar Department of Religious Affairs, the ordinations took place at Kaba Aye. This complex had originally been constructed to accommodate thousands of members of the Buddhist Sangha who gathered in Myanmar from all over the world in the mid-1950s to recite and purify the Pali canon at the Sixth Great Buddhist Council.

Because of the large number of people to undergo full ordination at the Kaba Aye ordination hall *(sima),* they were divided into morning and afternoon batches. The motorcade left IMC right after breakfast. The men and boys had been offered their first meal as samaneras in their dining room at the Centre. After the food had been placed on the low round tables and the samaneras had all sat on mats on the floor, upasakas, while bowing, gently lifted each laden table up several inches, symbolically offering the food to the novices in Myanmar fashion.

When they reached the Kaba Aye *sima,* shoes were left in the buses and the samaneras, followed by the laypeople, formed a procession from the gateway. The *sima* is a large circular structure surmounted by a small golden pagoda. The line was led by five Burmese men dressed in fantastic gilt deva costumes holding ten foot tall white cloth sunshades dangling with small metallic Bodhi leaves. The sayadaws, samaneras and lay meditators walked slowly up a red carpet runner on the broad flight of stairs, into the *sima.*

The interior is 150 feet in diameter with a truly colossal golden Buddha statue on a nearly fifteen foot high throne at the front. It is flanked slightly below by statues of the two Chief Disciples, the Elders Sariputta and Maha-moggallana, paying respects among various devotional objects: a tasteful grand scale shrine. The ceiling must be thirty feet high, supported on six massive columns decorated with bands of mirror inlay. A frieze goes around the perimeter, level with the Buddha's throne, composed of some hundred bhikkhu statues, perhaps half life-size, seated in meditation. Screened doors open outside at equal intervals; thick carpets cover the floor for the comfort of all; low, movable, decorative section dividers separate the Sangha from householders and men from women. The foreign women sat behind Mother Sayamagyi at the left and watched the proceedings while the samaneras were seated in the central section of the *sima* several meters away from and facing their preceptor and other sayadaws participating in the ordination ceremony. Laymen occupied another back section.

When everyone had settled in the proper place, the ceremony began. In groups of three, starting with the eldest samaneras, the foreigners approached the elder monks to seek full ordination. From the remote viewpoint of the lay people, it was difficult to understand everything that was going on, but following details was not essential as they were there to witness the event and share in the making of good kamma. The samaneras could understand as they had been trained beforehand. They were being asked the questions put to prospective bhikkhus ever since the Sangha became fully organized in the Buddha's lifetime: about their health, their sex, whether they were free and not in debt, if they were really human beings, etc. They replied appropriately. When they had all completed the answers, the groups again went up to the theras to request full ordination. When they had been accepted into the Order, each trio moved to join the Myanmar lifetime bhikkhus seated just to the side of the sayadaws conducting the proceedings. At times permanent bhikkhus had to bodily manipulate the foreigners into their proper places because they could not communicate through the language barrier.

The afternoon proceedings were similar except that a large number of outsiders also came to the *sima* to participate in the meritorious actions of supporting an ordination and of giving alms to the new monks afterwards. The atmosphere was quite special, generated by the commitment the men were making to the pure Buddha Dhamma and by the intention of everyone in the crowd to create *kusala,* good deeds, by participating in the proceedings.

The Deputy Minister for Religious Affairs spent several hours observing the ordinations and the Minister himself came to lead off the offering of *dana* to the newly ordained monks outside the *sima* in the late afternoon. The general public too was welcome to participate in these activities. Many who had just read about it in the newspaper came, having bought some small item to donate, or put some cash into an envelope to give (the standard way around the fact that monks are not supposed to touch gold or silver, i.e. money). All the International Meditation Centers (Yangon, U.K., U.S.A., Austria, and Western and Eastern Australia) had their own tables loaded with a particular item to be given to the monks. These had been purchased in Myanmar out of funds donated by members of the centers. Also various associations of the city participated in this *dana,* Yangon University lecturers, for example, came together. In all, many hundred laypeople lined the path from the ordination hall to the street, standing and waiting in the hot sunshine, or patches of shade.

Inside the building, the bhikkhus were grouped by nationality behind labeled placards carried by young men. Each monk had a Myanmar layman bearing a tall white sunshade behind him and two of them on each side. These pairs of upasakas carried large white sacks. As *dana* items piled up on the monks' bowls, they carefully placed them in the bags, making sure they did not touch the ground. All these male workers wore badges for identification.

The senior sayadaws emerged first and slowly filed through the crowd, looking neither right nor left but just before them, not acknowledging the laypeople making their donations into the big black lacquer almsbowls. The feeling in the area switched from anticipation to reverence for the Sangha, respect for this institution which protects and follows the Buddha's teachings to the full. As the newly ordained bhikkhus passed through the line of donors, they responded to this awe for the robes they were now honored to wear, keenly aware of their obligation to conduct themselves as proper monks. Only in this way would they be worthy of the respect they were being shown, not let down their teachers and hosts, and not disillusion the laity, who were so sincere in their honor.

The laypeople slipped off their shoes, picked up a packet from the table behind them, and with both hands, carefully placed it in the bowl of the monk as he passed in front of them. (The women took extra care not to touch or brush against any bhikkhu or his robes in the crowd.) The giving was done systematically, rotating through each small cluster so that every lay person had equal chance to earn merit. The almsround right after monks have been ordained is considered sure to bring donors extra merit. The new bhikkhus looked radiantly pure, with their shaven heads, lowered eyes, and restrained demeanor.

The final event of this day was held from five to six in the evening in Moguk Hall nearby in the same Kaba Aye complex. Here about a thousand lay devotees, mostly local, sat on the floor while the sayadaws and the junior monks sat on chairs at the front of the room facing them. The golden shrine was behind the bhikkhus. They recited Namo Tassa Bhagavato, the Refuges and the Precepts after the head sayadaw of the Kaba Aye monastery, and then a libation ceremony of pouring out water was held to symbolize sharing the merits made that day. This was invisible to most of the lay people but was held in the front of the hall using several sets of silver vessels.

A tired, happy serenity was felt at IMC afterwards, born of the knowledge that so much *kusala* had been generated by so many people that day.

For the remainder of the week of the ordination course, the new bhikkhus stayed at the meditation centre. They lived in their own dormitories at one end of the grounds, under the watchful eye of their assistant preceptor, the Venerable U Chanda Siri, who had also helped in all the earlier ordinations organized by the IMCs. They made good use of their time in robes free of worldly affairs by meditating many hours a day— observing the breath to develop sharp *samadhi* and then applying the concentrated mind to the sensations rising and vanishing in their bodies to penetrate the *anicca* (impermanent)— and so *dukkha* (unsatisfactory) and *anatta* (impersonal) — nature of mind and body as deeply as they could. All was done as taught in the tradition of Sayagyi U Ba Khin, in strict accordance with the teachings of the Buddha.

Every evening there was a confession also in the hall. As there were so many bhikkhus, U Chanda Siri heard the confessions of half of the men and one of the older of the foreigners heard the confessions of the remainder. The bhikkhus got up from their seats on the floor, straightened their robes and worked their way to the front of the hall in pairs to recite the short Pali catechism admitting to miscellaneous errors and accepting admonition to try to do better in the future. In this orderly way it took about twenty minutes to finish all of the monks each evening. Sometimes the confession was followed by a short discourse by U Chanda Siri or one of the meditation teachers. One talk was about the *"dullabhas,"* or states difficult to obtain, the most rare of which is being a bhikkhu. Another was an explanation of the origins of the questions the samaneras had to answer before being ordained as full bhikkhus. Those had been instituted by the Buddha in response to specific situations which arose, just as all the rules for the Sangha had been.

Following the bhikkhus' confession, the young samaneras came forward to recite the Refuges, Ten Precepts, etc., after U Chanda Siri. He was very particular that they pronounce each syllable in exactly the correct way, and they would repeat difficult words over and over until the result was as perfect as the preceptor wanted. The samaneras had their own bedroom and activities which included daily visits to the Shwe Dagon Pagoda.

The bhikkhus were fed in a separate upstairs dining hall on choice Myanmar and Chinese vegetarian food. Often some special dish — such as ice cream — had been donated by someone. People were always looking for more ways to earn merit by helping the bhikkhus, and other meditators, at the Centre. The Myanmar Buddhists exhibit great generosity, cultivating the *dana parami.*

The offerings the bhikkhus had received at the *sima* were sorted out by lay people one evening. The cash was totaled up and donated to certain pagodas and monasteries in Yangon, and the monks could take whatever they wanted of the remainder. Most of the things actually went out to vicars (monasteries) where lifetime bhikkhus would have more use for them than foreigners returning to lay life in their own countries in a few days.

The week as bhikkhus was interspersed with several events. One morning a *pindapata* (almsround) was held at IMC itself. Monks from U Pandicca's monastery had come to wrap the temporary monks' robes in the complex way, modestly covering the neck and both shoulders, appropriate for "going among the houses." The line of donors wound around the pagoda and Dhamma Hall. This time most of the items were food, since it was before noon. The atmosphere was more like a community event since the Centre was "home" to all the participants. The lay people again were dressed in fine Myanmar clothes to honor the bhikkhus. One afternoon, Myanmar TV conducted interviews with six of the bhikkhus, and two of the foreign laywomen, in the Dhamma Hall. (Actually, TV crews, local and Japanese, had been covering most of the events of the ordination week and everyone was familiar with bright lights — from external sources — while they were meditating in the Dhamma Hall.) The questionnaire which had been given to the interviewees was quite serious and the bhikkhus especially had a good opportunity to express their views on the situation of Buddha Dhamma in the West and in Myanmar and about what they had personally gained from practicing this meditation. If the interviews were shown in full, some profound Buddha Dhamma would have come over that most unlikely of media.

The boys took off their robes on Saturday the 15th; the bhikkhus did so precisely a week after the ordination. On that Sunday afternoon the confession was held early, at four, and immediately afterwards they agreed aloud that they were prepared to return to lay life.

They then requested to be regarded as samaneras. They removed the robes and changed back into their lay clothes and then asked to be recognized as laymen again — in both Pali and English. Finally U Chanda Siri gave them a discourse as laymen, urging them to cooperate in spreading the Buddha Dhamma in their own countries and always to follow the advice of Mother Sayamagyi and their other teachers.

The temporary bhikkhus returned to lay life with satisfaction at having done what is so hard to do: to be a good Buddhist monk. They were glad to have had even that short chance to know life without the entanglements, the "dust" as the Buddha called it, of household affairs. Some of them were a bit sorry at its ending. Most will probably try to take ordination again in this lifetime to earn still more merit. Their families were joyous to see how they had matured from the experience. Everyone had the assurance that comes from the performance of meritorious deeds dedicated towards purification of mind and the attainment of Nibbana, the cessation of all suffering.

BUDDHA AS VIEWED BY OTHER RELIGIONS

Hinduism

Buddhism is a dharmic religion. The systems of Buddhism and Hinduism, some say, must not be considered to be either contradictory to one another or completely self contained. Coomaraswamy wrote:

> *"The more superficially one studies Buddhism, the more it seems to differ from Brahmanism in which it originated; the more profound our study, the more difficult it becomes to distinguish Buddhism from Brahmanism, or to say in what respects, if any, Buddhism is really unorthodox."*

Buddhist scholar Rahula Vipola wrote that the Buddha was trying to shed the true meaning of the Vedas. Buddha is said to be a knower of the Veda (vedajna) or of the Vedanta (vedantajna) *(Sa.myutta, i. 168) and (Sutta Nipata, 463).*

Hinduism and Buddhism share many common features including Sanskrit, yoga, karma and dharma.

Taoism, Confucianism and Shintoism

The arrival of Buddhism caused Taoism to renew and restructure itself and address existential questions raised by Buddhism. Buddhism was seen as a kind of foreign Taoism and its scriptures were translated into Chinese with Taoist vocabulary. Chan (Seon, Thien, or Zen) Buddhism in particular holds many beliefs in common with philosophical Taoism. Some early Chinese Taoist-Buddhists thought Buddha to be a reincarnation of Lao Tzu born in the land of barbarians.

Buddhism shares many commonalities with Neo-Confucianism, which is Confucianism with more religious elements. In fact, the ritual of ancestor worship normally practiced by Confucianists, has been adapted to Chinese Buddhist beliefs.

In the Japanese religion of Shinto, the long coexistence of Buddhism and Shintoism resulted in the merging of Shintoism and Buddhism. Gods in Shintoism were given a position similar to the Hindu gods in Buddhism. Moreover, because one of Mahayana Buddha's (Dainichi Nyorai) symbols was the sun, many equated Amaterasu, the Sun Goddess, as the previous reincarnation (bodhisattva) of Dainichi Nyorai.

However, the Tokugawa Shogunate era saw a revival movement within Shinto. Some Shinto scholars started to argue that Buddhas were previous incarnations of Shinto gods, thus turning the position of Shintoism and Buddhism upside down. Shinto and Buddhism were officially separated after the Meiji Restoration.

Islam

> *"If you desire to see the most noble of mankind, look at the king in beggar's clothing; it is he whose sanctity is great among men." —Abdul Atahiya, Arab Poet.*

The Buddhist monastic class flowed into what came to be called Islamic monasticism — Sufism — which has given many poets and scientists to both Islam and the world. The Qalandariyah Sufi Order, a Muslim mystical movement, attracted many Buddhist monks. This order arose in 9th century as a result of the Malamatiyya, and became established in Khorasan (Eastern Persia) as early in the 11th century.

Ascetic practices within the Sufi philosophy are associated with Buddhism. The notion of purification (cleaning one's soul from all evil things and trying to reach Nirvana and to become immortal in Nirvana) plays an important role in Buddhism. The same idea shows itself in the belief of *vuslat* (communion with God) in Sufi philosophy.

> *"The mission of the Buddha was quite unique in its character, and therefore it stands quite apart from the many other religions of the world. His mission was to bring the birds of idealism flying in the air nearer to the earth, because the food for their bodies belonged to the earth." —Hazrat Inayat Khan.*

The Indian scholar Maulana Abul Kalam Azad proposed in a commentary on the *Qur'an* that Siddhartha Gautama is the prophet of Islam *Dhû'l-Kifl* referred to in Sura 21 and Sura 38 of the Qur'an together with the Biblical characters Ishmael, Idris (Enoch), and Elisha. Azad suggested that the *Kifl* in *Dhû'l-Kifl* (Ar: "possessor of a double portion") is an Arabic pronunciation of Kapilavastu, where the Buddha spent his early life. Azad did not, however, provide direct historical evidence to support his speculation. According to other ancient Muslim scholars *Dhû'l-Kifl* was either a righteous man and not a prophet, or he was the prophet called Ezekiel in the Bible.

6

Buddhist, Beliefs and Violence

Buddhism shows that people must beat enduring with a specific end goal to achieve nirvana and end the cycle of death and resurrection. As viciousness is a noteworthy wellspring of human enduring, Buddhists battle to overcome and maintain a strategic distance from it at whatever point conceivable. This is a rule shared by all Buddhists paying little respect to group, and it shapes the premise for Buddhist morals.

Compassion

Most Buddhists trust that empathy is a prime ethicalness of Buddhism. A few entries in Buddhist sacred writing advise Buddhists to fight the temptation to battle on occasion of war and rather attempt to feel empathy for others. Buddhists ought to hold the sentiment empathy regardless of the fact that they are harmed by others. This is on the grounds that Buddhists trust that viciousness dependably aims more savagery and just empathy and adoration can end the cycle. This is valid in all circumstances, and even in self-preservation, a Buddhist should never execute another person.

Reciprocity

In Buddhism, the Three Practices - Sila, Samadhi and Prajna - are three methods for carrying on with one's life that will help the individual conquer enduring and accomplish nirvana. Sila bargains only with Buddhist profound quality and behavior. As indicated by Sila, people must take after the standard of correspondence and treat others the same way they need others to treat them. This is like the Golden Rule in Christianity, and gives an ethical establishment that rejects viciousness towards others. Buddhists likewise extend this guideline to every single living being, which as indicated by Buddhist statutes are equivalent.

Avoiding Suffering

The evasion of misery, both in oneself as well as other people, is the central objective of Buddhism, and taking after a way of peacefulness is a critical part in accomplishing this objective. Taking after a way of peacefulness towards all life, particularly slaughtering, will help the individual stay away from sentiments of regret or blame. Thus, war makes victors and failures, and the washout will live in a condition of misery after annihilation, so it is best to keep away from war inside and out. The craving to keep away from brutality is likewise found in the educating of hand to hand fighting. Military specialists are instructed to utilize their abilities just in self-protection and to utilize the littlest measure of power important to repulse the aggressor.

Contradictions

Albeit Buddhist convictions don't bolster brutality, a few Buddhists have generally tested this conviction. Some Japanese Zen experts bolstered Japanese war animosity by guaranteeing brutality was adequate when coordinated towards individuals who disturb open request. There are likewise recorded case of Buddhist followers taking part in savagery or war, for example, the war in Sri Lanka between the Sinhalese and the Tamils. Be that as it may, most by far of Buddhists test these special cases and don't trust they are perfect with Buddhist reasoning.

EXTREMISM RISES AMONG MYANMAR BUDDHISTS

After a ritual prayer atoning for past sins, Ashin Wirathu, a Buddhist monk with a rock-star following in Myanmar, sat before an overflowing crowd of thousands of devotees and launched into a rant against what he called "the enemy" — the country's Muslim minority.

"You can be full of kindness and love, but you cannot sleep next to a mad dog," Ashin Wirathu said, referring to Muslims.

"I call them troublemakers, because they are troublemakers," Ashin Wirathu told a reporter after his two-hour sermon. "I am proud to be called a radical Buddhist."

The world has grown accustomed to a gentle image of Buddhism defined by the self-effacing words of the Dalai Lama, the global popularity of Buddhist-inspired meditation and postcard-perfect scenes from Southeast Asia and beyond of crimson-robed, barefoot monks receiving alms from villagers at dawn.

But over the past year, images of rampaging Burmese Buddhists carrying swords and the vituperative sermons of monks like Ashin Wirathu have underlined the rise of extreme Buddhism in Myanmar — and revealed a darker side of the country's greater freedoms after decades of military rule. Buddhist lynch mobs have killed more than 200 Muslims and forced more than 150,000 people, mostly Muslims, from their homes.

Ashin Wirathu denies any role in the riots. But his critics say that at the very least his anti-Muslim preaching is helping to inspire the violence.

What began last year on the fringes of Burmese society has grown into a nationwide movement whose agenda now includes boycotts of Muslim-made goods. Its message is spreading through regular sermons across the country that draw thousands of people and through widely distributed DVDs of those talks. Buddhist monasteries associated with the movement are also opening community centers and a Sunday school program for 60,000 Buddhist children nationwide.

The hate-filled speeches and violence have endangered Myanmar's path to democracy, raising questions about the government's ability to keep the country's towns and cities safe and its willingness to crack down or prosecute Buddhists in a Buddhist-majority country. The killings have also reverberated in

Muslim countries across the region, tarnishing what was almost universally seen abroad as a remarkable and rare peaceful transition from military rule to democracy. In May, the Indonesian authorities foiled what they said was a plot to bomb the Myanmar Embassy in Jakarta in retaliation for the assaults on Muslims.

Ashin Wirathu, the spiritual leader of the radical movement, skates a thin line between free speech and incitement, taking advantage of loosened restrictions on expression during a fragile time of transition. He was himself jailed for eight years by the now-defunct military junta for inciting hatred. Last year, as part of a release of hundreds of political prisoners, he was freed.

In his recent sermon, he described the reported massacre of schoolchildrenand other Muslim inhabitants in the central city of Meiktila in March,documented by a human rights group, as a show of strength.

"If we are weak," he said, "our land will become Muslim." Buddhism would seem to have a secure place in Myanmar. Nine in 10 people are Buddhist, as are nearly all the top leaders in the business world, the government, the military and the police. Estimates of the Muslim minority range from 4 percent to 8 percent of Myanmar's roughly 55 million people while the rest are mostly Christian or Hindu.

But Ashin Wirathu, who describes himself as a nationalist, says Buddhism is under siege by Muslims who are having more children than Buddhists and buying up Buddhist-owned land. In part, he is tapping into historical grievances that date from British colonial days when Indians, many of them Muslims, were brought into the country as civil servants and soldiers.

The muscular and nationalist messages he has spread have alarmed Buddhists in other countries.

The Dalai Lama, after the riots in March, said killing in the name of religion was "unthinkable" and urged Myanmar's Buddhists to contemplate the face of the Buddha for guidance.

Phra Paisal Visalo, a Buddhist scholar and prominent monk in neighboring Thailand, says the notion of "us and them" promoted by Myanmar's radical monks is anathema to Buddhism.

But he lamented that his criticism and that of other leading Buddhists outside the country have had "very little impact."

"Myanmar monks are quite isolated and have a thin relationship with Buddhists in other parts of the world," Phra Paisal said. One exception is Sri Lanka, another country historically bedeviled by ethnic strife. Burmese monks have been inspired by the assertive political role played by monks from Sri Lanka's Sinhalese majority.

As Myanmar has grown more polarized, there have been nascent signs of a backlash against the anti-Muslim preaching. Among the most disappointed with the outbreaks of violence and hateful rhetoric are some of the leaders of the 2007 Saffron Revolution, a peaceful uprising led by Buddhist monks against military rule.

"We were not expecting this violence when we chanted for peace and reconciliation in 2007," said the abbot of Pauk Jadi monastery, Ashin Nyana Nika, 55, who attended a meeting earlier this month sponsored by Muslim groups to discuss the issue. (Ashin is the honorific for Burmese monks.) Ashin Sanda Wara, the head of a monastic school in Yangon, says the monks in the country are divided nearly equally between moderates and extremists.

He considers himself in the moderate camp. But as a measure of the deeply ingrained suspicions toward Muslims in the society, he said he was "afraid of Muslims because their population is increasing so rapidly."

Ashin Wirathu has tapped into that anxiety, which some describe as the "demographic pressures" coming from neighboring Bangladesh. There is wide disdain in Myanmar for a group of about one million stateless Muslims, who call themselves Rohingya, some of whom migrated from Bangladesh. Clashes between the Rohingya and Buddhists last year in western Myanmar roiled the Buddhist community and appear to have played a role in later outbreaks of violence throughout the country. Ashin Wirathu said they served as his inspiration to spread his teachings.

The theme song to Ashin Wirathu's movement speaks of people who "live in our land, drink our water, and are ungrateful to us."

"We will build a fence with our bones if necessary," runs the song's refrain. Muslims are not explicitly mentioned in the song but Ashin Wirathu said the lyrics refer to them.

Pamphlets handed out at his sermon demonizing Muslims said that "Myanmar is currently facing a most dangerous and fearful poison that is severe enough to eradicate all civilization."

Many in Myanmar speculate, without offering proof, that Ashin Wirathu is allied with hard-line Buddhist elements in the country who want to harness the nationalism of his movement to rally support ahead of elections in 2015. Ashin Wirathu denies any such links.

But the government has done little to rein him in. During Ashin Wirathu's visit here in Taunggyi, traffic policemen cleared intersections for his motorcade. Once inside the monastery, as part of a highly choreographed visit, his followers led a procession through crowds of followers who prostrated themselves as he passed.

Ashin Wirathu's movement calls itself 969, three digits that monks say symbolize the virtues of the Buddha, Buddhist practices and the Buddhist community.

Stickers with the movement's logo are now ubiquitous nationwide on cars, motorcycles and shops. The movement has also begun a signature campaign calling for a ban on interfaith marriages, and pamphlets are distributed at sermons listing Muslim brands and shops to be avoided.

In Mawlamyine, a multicultural city southeast of Yangon, a monastery linked to the 969 movement has established the courses of Buddhist instruction for children, which it calls "Sunday dhamma schools." Leaders of the monasteries there seek to portray their campaign as a sort of Buddhist revivalist movement.

"The main thing is that our religion and our nationality don't disappear," said Ashin Zadila, a senior monk at the Myazedi Nanoo monastery outside the city.

Yet despite efforts at describing the movement as nonthreatening, many Muslims are worried.

Two hours before Ashin Wirathu rolled into Taunggyi in a motorcade that included 60 honking motorcycles, Tun Tun Naing, a Muslim vendor in the city's central market, spoke of the visit in a whisper.

"I'm really frightened," he said, stopping in midsentence when customers entered his shop. "We tell the children not to go outside unless absolutely necessary."

7

Myanmar's Buddhist and Terrorism

Myanmar's President Thein Sein repealed a voting rights offer to the nation's Rohingya people group in the midst of extraordinary weight from far-right Buddhist gatherings. A week ago many Buddhists rioted to censure the continuation of a 2010 law that extended the privilege to vote to the nation's more than 1 million ethnic Rohingya. Myanmar does not view the minority bunch as natives.

The viciousness coordinated toward the Muslim Rohingya people group has been portrayed in the media as Buddhism's fear based oppression issue. In any case, the religious depiction of the Rohingya emergency depreciates the political and social subtleties important to comprehension the contention.

The 'Burmese container Laden'

The Rohingya are a standout amongst the most oppressed gatherings on the planet. Stripped of citizenship in the 1980s, the Rohingya have been a subject of incessant bigot promulgation and rankling brutality. For quite a long time various human rights associations have archived the oppression of the Rohingya in Myanmar's northern Rakhine state. The people group keeps on living under steady dangers, with couple of lawful rights.

The battle against the Rohingya and Muslims in Myanmar is led by dubious minister Ashin Wirathu. When alluded to as the "Burmese container Laden," he is the pioneer of a ultranationalist bunch called 969, which contradicts the development of Islam in Myanmar. He was imprisoned in 2003 for impelling disdain and mixing partisan conflicts and discharged in 2010.

Wirathu has cautioned against a looming Muslim takeover of Myanmar. In 2012 the assault of a Buddhist lady in northern Rakhine prompted fierce assaults that left many regular folks dead and more than 125,000 Rohingya and different Muslims uprooted. Human Rights Watch depicted the helpful emergency as "ethnic purifying."

Myanmar's administration and neighborhood powers have for some time been complicit in the viciousness against the Rohingya and other minority bunches. "Burmese authorities, group pioneers and Buddhist ministers sorted out and empowered ethnic Arakanese upheld by state security powers to lead facilitated assaults on Muslim neighborhoods and towns in October 2012 to threaten and coercively move the populace," HRW said in a point by point report in 2013. "Incorporated into the loss of life were 28 kids who were hacked to death, including 13 under age 5. "

Wirathu advocated the viciousness saying the Rohingya were wanting to set up an Islamic state in Rakhine. He has since asked non-Muslims to blacklist Muslim shops and abstain from working with Muslims. "Your buys spent in their shops will profit the foe," Wirathu said in a 2013 YouTube video. "So work with just shops with 969 signs."

The Rohingya-Buddhist conflict in Rakhine dates to the 17thcentury. The animosity between Muslims and Buddhists in western Myanmar has roots in a history of successive invasions by the British and Muslims. "Rakhine identity ... has been partially built around a feeling of being besieged (and conquered) by Muslim kingdoms to the west and Burman (Buddhist but ethnically different) kingdoms to the east," according to Oxford University researcher Matthew J. Walton.

Walton is not alone in highlighting the political nature of this conflict. "It's more about politics," former United Nations Ambassador Nyunt Maung Shein said of the conflict in 2013. "It is not due to a crisis of religion ... It is a political play, not due to the discrimination and religion."

In 1982 authorities in Myanmar stripped the Rohingya of Burmese nationality under the country's Citizenship Law, often referring to them as "resident foreigners" and "Bengalis." The move was part of the ruling elite's xenophobic refusal to recognize other ethnicities, including ethnic Chinese minorities. Ironically, Gen. Ne Win's government,which promulgated the law, was famous for its socialist program and lack of clear interest in promoting the edicts of Buddhism. Meanwhile, the lack of international spotlight has allowed radical monks such as Wirathu to legitimize their vitriolic rhetoric, ethnic cleansing and massacres against Rohingya.

The negligence and blatant collusion of the Burmese state and its policies is far more problematic than demonization campaigns by ultra-Buddhist nationalist groups. The existence of contentious legislation such as the Citizenship Law means the Rohingya will continue to remain stateless, with few to no legal rights.

Meek responses

Over the last few years, entire villages inhibited by Rohingya Muslims have been razed or forcibly displaced. Amid the coverage of conflicts in Syria, Nigeria and Ukraine, the Rohingya crisis has received scant mainstream media attention. Myanmar's opposition leader and democracy icon Aung San Suu Kyi has been mum on the issue, perhaps deterred by the growing tensions between the majority Buddhist population and the minority Muslim community.

Similarly, President Barack Obama, who has visited the country twice in the last seven years, has been meek in his response, refusing to openly condemn Myanmar's failure to end the violence.

"Discrimination against a Rohingya or any other religious minority ... does not express the kind of country that Burma over the long term wants to be," Obama said during a trip to Myanmar last year. His use of the word Rohingya was considered a bold gesture and resulted in street protests there.

Minority radical monks have used Buddhism to promote violence against the Rohingya. However, not all Buddhists are promoting religious intolerance. For example, the Dalai Lama has unequivocally condemned extremist monkssuch as Wirathu and

Myanmar's leaders for failing to end the attacks against Muslims. Besides, a closer look at the Rohingya crisis reveals a checkered and complicated history that goes beyond a religious spat.

Burmese activists and leaders such as Suu Kyi must stand up for the human rights of the Rohingya community. In the face of such travesties, the international community must also break its silence and pressure Thein Sein to protect religious and ethnic minorities in Myanmar.

TERROR IN BURMA: BUDDHISTS VS. MUSLIMS

For a devoutly Buddhist country, Burma has lots of people who hedge their bets. Animism is still a force in the country, especially in the villages, and animist beliefs have been incorporated into Burma's brand of Theravada Buddhism for centuries (thirty-seven Great Nats, or spirits, are recognized as guardians of Buddhist temples). Fortune telling and astrology are widely practiced, and many Burmese employ astrological charts in naming their children. Numerology has also long figured into decisionmaking in the country, sometimes in ways that to outsiders seem downright bizarre.

On the advice of astrologers, for instance, the country became formally independent from Great Britain at exactly 4:20 a.m. on January 4, 1948 (the Brits had pushed for January 1st). The military leaders who ruled the country from 1962 until 2011—Ne Win and Than Shwe in particular—often seemed obsessed with lucky numbers. Ne Win's lucky number was nine, the principal reason that he introduced currency in loopy 45-kyat and 90-kyat units in 1987. The number eleven was Than Shwe's favorite; hence the origin of the sixty-five-year prison sentences handed out in 2008 to fourteen prominent pro-democracy activists. Six plus five makes eleven—get it?

And there is also the so-called "8888 Uprising" that got its name because it was timed to begin on August 8, 1988, a date seen as propitious in Burma (and other parts of Asia). Not to be upstaged, General Saw Maung, Ne Win's cat's-paw, crushed the uprising on September 18th. (September is the ninth month, and one plus eight equals nine.) In a disingenuous concession to the activists, the government (then known as the State Law and Order Restoration Council, or SLORC) later scheduled a general election—the first since 1962—for Sunday, May 27, 1990. Why? In the Gregorian calendar, which is used formally in Burma, it was the fourth Sunday of the fifth month. There's that nine again.

So numbers matter in Burma, and, unfortunately, two numbers that matter a lot in Burma today are 969 and 786. Much has been written this year about the 969 movement, led by Buddhist nationalists, that, according to many observers, is fomenting—or, at the very least, supporting—a broad range of anti-Muslim activities, including violent ones, across much of Burma.

Although the Burmese monk Ashin Wirathu (known just as Wirathu) has become "the face of Buddhist terror," as *Time* magazine recently put it, the writings in the 1990s of another Burmese monk, Kyaw Lwin, were instrumental in creating the ideological basis for today's 969 movement. If Wirathu is "the Burmese bin Laden"—as the monk has referred to himself—Kyaw Lwin is the 969 movement's equivalent to Sayyid Qutb, the intellectual godfather of jihadism.

Doing the numbers is crucial for understanding Burmese politics. In fact, 786 became significant before 969. The number 786 is derived from the numerical value in the Arabic Abjad numeral system of the opening passage of the Koran. In the Abjad system, all twenty-eight letters in the Arabic alphabet are assigned numeric values. The Koran opens with the words "In the name of Allah, the beneficent, the merciful." The numerical value of these words in the Abjad system comes to 786. In parts of the Muslim world, especially in South Asia and Burma, the number 786 has come to be posted on shops, stores, buildings, etc., as a kind of signaling mechanism to denote, "This place is Muslim."

But in the increasingly tense ethno-cultural atmosphere in numerological-fixated Burma of recent decades, the number 786 has been interpreted by some Buddhists as possessing a coded meaning over and above this simple ethnic identification. Because seven plus eight plus six equals twenty-one, Muslims, in posting the number publicly, are said by some Buddhists to be pronouncing that they will dominate the world in the twenty-first century.

Buddhist ideologues in Burma came up with 969 as a political counterpunch. These numbers are said to capture in symbolic form the key virtues of Buddhism. The Lord Buddha has nine special attributes. There are said to be six special attributes to Buddhist teachings, and Buddhist monks, too, possess special attributes—nine in fact. Thus 969, a number that also happens to be much larger than the Muslim 786.

Reading political developments in Burma is never easy, but getting a handle on the 969 movement is especially tricky. Its origins can be traced back to the early 1990s. In response to the 8888 Uprising and the pro-democracy agitation in the years thereafter, the generals in charge of the country, hoping at once to split apart and co-opt some part of the community of Buddhist monks involved in anti-government activism, began promoting what was touted as a Buddhist renewal movement. The movement's ideology combined Buddhist religious fanaticism with intense Burmese nationalism and more than a tinge of ethnic chauvinism. Not surprisingly, it became strongest—perhaps I should say most virulent—among the Bamar, the principal ethnic group in Burma, accounting for about two-thirds of the country's population, and especially prominent in the lowlands of the Irrawaddy Basin. The vast majority of the Bamar are Theravada Buddhists.

The main message of 969 was (and is) Burma for Buddhists, particularly for Buddhists who are Bamar rather than members of other ethnic groups. Shortly after the movement began, a monk named Kyaw Lwin became a central figure, and his writings were distilled and distributed by a unit of the official Religious Ministry, first as "How to Live as a Good Buddhist" (1992) and later as "The Best Buddhist" (2000). After Kyaw Lwin's death in 2001, at the age of seventy, Wirathu—who had known Kyaw Lwin for a number of years—along with a number of other monks, picked up the mantle and began elaborating upon the dead monk's thoughts, albeit with a more explicitly and aggressively anti-Muslim message.

The movement gained momentum in Burma in 2001, helping to precipitate an upsurge of anti-Muslim activity (the destruction of the Bamiyan Buddhas in Afghanistan by the Islamist Taliban in March played an incendiary role). Such activity included anti-

Muslim riots, most notably in Sittwe, capital of Rakhine State, in February 2001, and in Taungoo, in the Bago Region of south-central Burma, about two hundred and twenty kilometers north-northeast of what was then the Burmese capital, Yangon, in May 2001. In the latter, more than two hundred Muslims were killed and eleven mosques destroyed. All of this happened even before September 11th exacerbated anti-Muslim sentiment in Burma and elsewhere.

Violence against Muslims continued intermittently after Sittwe and Taungoo—I myself witnessed several such incidents while visiting the ancient temple complex at Mrauk U, in Rakhine State, in January 2002—and Wirathu, who had been fanning the flames, was arrested in 2003 for inciting anti-Muslim riots in his hometown near Mandalay, riots in which Buddhists killed ten Muslims. Wirathu was sentenced to twenty-five years in prison, but was released as part of a broader amnesty in 2011, shortly before the latest surge of anti-Muslim activity in the country, which spiked in the period from fall 2012 through summer 2013. During this spike, Kyaw Lwin's ideas, mediated by Wirathu, became increasingly salient, and the 969 appeared menacingly all over the country.

Since November 2012, more than two hundred and fifty people have been killed and many more injured—the vast majority of them Muslims—as a result of a series of acts of what some have labeled Buddhist terror, mostly in the west and in central Burma. In addition, somewhere between about one hundred and forty thousand and two hundred and fifty thousand Muslims—estimates vary dramatically—have been displaced, mostly from their homes in Rakhine State (formerly Arakan State), the western part of which abuts Bangladesh. The 969 movement is deeply involved, but it is a politically and culturally complex situation.

It seems pretty clear that what is going on in most of Burma right now is more akin to terrorism than to sectarian conflict, as some have preferred to style it. Even in Rakhine State, where there is a large Muslim minority and the violence is somewhat less one-sided, the power of the Buddhist majority—supported, when necessary, by the Buddhist Bamar-controlled government—is ironhanded. To be sure, Muslims have often been accused of instigating specific incidents across Burma—there have been an uncanny number of rumors of Muslim men attempting to rape Buddhist women, for example—but the weight of the evidence suggests that such rumors are more often than not fictions useful primarily for provocation or to rationalize Buddhist promoting, or at least supporting, violence.

To those with only a casual interest in Asian affairs, the notion of Buddhist terrorism seems something of an oxymoron. For example, in Time magazine's much-discussed story on the country ("The Face of Buddhist Terror," July 1, 2013), there is a pullout quote on the first page that reads: "It's a faith famous for its pacifism and tolerance. But in several of Asia's Buddhist-majority nations, monks are inciting bigotry and violence—mostly against Muslims." Later in the piece, another line reads: "To much of the world, it [Buddhism] is synonymous with nonviolence and loving kindness, concepts propagated by Siddhartha Gautama, the Buddha, 2,500 years ago." This sentence is qualified immediately by another: "But like adherents of any other religion, Buddhists and their holy men are not immune to politics and, on occasion, the lure of sectarian chauvinism."

A brief glimpse back at Burma's history shows how true, and truly complex, this idea is. During the British colonial period, Burmese, by which we generally mean Buddhist Bamar, periodically denounced and rose up against the relatively small communities of indigenous Muslims and especially against Muslim immigrants from South Asia whose arrival was encouraged by the British rulers. Some of the actions ostensibly directed against Muslim migrants were actually animated by anger toward the British for "Indicizing" the country, purportedly to the economic detriment of the Bamar (among other native-born ethnic groups).

The South Asians who migrated to Burma in the nineteenth century and early twentieth century came mainly from Madras, Bengal, and Ceylon. Over half of them were Muslim and they took up residence mainly in cities and labor-scarce areas in Lower Burma. Over time, they came to play important roles in the country as seasonal labor in agriculture, in transportation and construction, as workers in rice mills, as stevedores (dockworkers), as merchants and moneylenders, as well as in the British civil service and the British military. There was a lot of turnover, with most South Asian migrants arriving by sea for short-term, often seasonal stints, then returning back to their homeland. Many immigrants also arrived in western Burma from Chittagong and other parts of Bengal via overland routes. While some of these migrants later quit Burma as well, a substantial number remained in Arakan, now Rakhine State, which has remained a flash point in ethnic-religious conflict even today.

There were instances of the (overwhelmingly Buddhist) Bamar lashing out against South Asian immigrant communities, sometimes violently, as in 1926, 1930, and 1938, but it was not clear whether these outbreaks had to do mainly with economic resentments or were manifestations of political opposition to the British colonizers and their South Asian confederates. Or what role "race" and "color" played. The Bamar are of East Asian origin—their language is considered Sino-Tibetan—and they are generally lighter-skinned than South Asians in Burma, who are sometimes referred to pejoratively in the Burmese language as *kala*, a term that can be loosely translated as "dark-skinned foreigner."

The South Asian and Muslim presence—and the "problem" it represented in Burma—receded considerably as a result of the Great Depression, World War II, and the end of colonial rule. With the Burmese economy tanking, fewer South Asians migrated and many of those already in the country left for home. Wartime disruptions and dislocations lessened Burma's appeal even more, and when the British, their nominal protectors, were ousted in 1948, South Asians' interest in Burma further waned.

There were, of course, still South Asians, many of them Muslims, in Burma after independence. Although such communities included groups that had participated in the anti-colonial coalition, with independence the country became more and more dominated by the Buddhist Bamar majority. Anti–South Asian and anti-Muslim activities accelerated sharply in Burma after Ne Win's coup in 1962, which led many of the remaining

South Asians to leave the country and reduced the status, rights, and privileges of the Muslims who remained, South Asian or otherwise.

So what does the Muslim community—or, more accurately, the various Muslim communities—in Burma look like today? It is not easy to answer this question because of the information gap caused by Burma's stubborn isolation. The last official government census was taken in 1983 and that one was incomplete because no population counts were taken in the parts of the country in states of insurgency at the time. The best estimates place the Muslim minority today at somewhere between four and eight percent of the total population, in a country of roughly fifty-five to sixty million. The Muslim population is widely dispersed. For example, so-called Panthays (Chinese Muslims) are located in various parts of northern Burma, including Mandalay; numerous Muslims of Malay ancestry live in the far southeast of the country; and thousands of Indian Muslims still dwell in Rangoon, particularly downtown in the area to the west of the Sule Pagoda.

The largest concentration of Muslims, however, resides in western Burma, in Rakhine State, much in the news of late because of reports of intermittent acts of Buddhist terror against Muslims in the region. Muslims constitute a large minority of the population, perhaps as much as a quarter, in this state of roughly four million. Muslims have lived in Rakhine since the eighth or ninth century. Most of the early Muslim migrants arrived in the region by sea as part of one or another circuit in the voluminous Bay of Bengal trade. However, Rakhine was lightly populated in comparison to neighboring Bengal, and some Bengalis had always migrated eastward over land. After Bengal became Islamicized in the early thirteenth century, migration eastward continued. Over time, Bengali Muslims came to constitute a sizable minority of Rakhine's population, especially in the far west. Rakhine was conquered and annexed by Burma in 1784, after which time some Burmese Muslims also settled down in the area. The British acquired Rakhine as a result of the First Anglo-Burmese War (1824–26), and once in control, they encouraged South Asian migration into the region, most of which consisted of Bengali Muslims from the area around

Chittagong. Over time, Muslims from Bengal overwhelmed in numbers other Muslim communities in Rakhine. As a result, some scholars and journalists refer to all Muslims in Rakhine as *Rohingya*—from *Rohang*, which in the Rohingya language is the word for Rakhine. Others believe that the Rohingya constitute but one discrete part of Burma's Muslim population: Chittagonian Bengalis. This Muslim subgroup, concentrated mainly in the far west of Rakhine, is allegedly comprised largely of people who have migrated relatively recently—and illegally—into Burma. In some ways, this is all definitional parsing: Whatever the case, it is clear that large elements of the Bamar population support a spectrum of "actions" against Muslims in Rakhine ranging from discrimination to persecution to paramilitary or military assaults to expulsion. Indeed, actors ranging from 969 to the military to the government and at times even to democracy advocate and Nobel Prize–winner Aung San Suu Kyi have proven willing to countenance, if not explicitly to endorse, varying levels of anti-Rohingya activity in Rakhine, with some willing to apply this same repression to Muslims in Burma more generally.

On the other hand, human rights groups, NGOs, and international organizations, including Human Rights Watch, Doctors Without Borders, and the UN, view the Rohingya not as "stateless" people but as rightful members of Burmese society who have been subjected, for decades if not centuries, to illegal and immoral actions stretching all the way to attempts at ethnic cleansing by elements of the Buddhist Bamar majority.

Although I think it is possible to distinguish, even in Rakhine, between Rohingya specifically and Muslims generally, both groups (and other minorities in Burma) have legitimate grievances regarding their treatment at the hands of the Bamar-controlled state. This is not to suggest that Muslims have been blameless in cases where anti-Muslim violence has occurred, but, by and large, extremist elements in the Bamar community, taking advantage of the political opening that began in 2011, have found reasons to settle old scores, emphatically reassert ethno-cultural solidarity and dominance in the country, and maybe even redraw the economic, demographic, and political maps.

To much of the world, news emanating from far-off Burma about "Buddhist terrorism" seems puzzling because it cuts so deeply against the stereotype of a peaceful, tolerant, and serene religion. In fact, Burma isn't the only Buddhist-majority country where extremist Buddhist elements are engaging in violence against other groups for political ends. (Sri Lanka and Thailand are two others.) Moreover, historically, there have been numerous terrorist groups with Buddhist backgrounds in Burma, as well as in other Buddhist countries and regions such as Bhutan, Nepal, Japan, and Tibet.

Burma has witnessed many dramatic developments in recent years, most of them positive but some troubling and even dangerous. Buddhist terrorism must be seen in this hazy light. Flurries of anti-Muslim activity, including terrorism, have occurred periodically during Burmese history, but Buddhists and Muslims have also lived together in the country in peace for long stretches. The Bamar are not (and have never been) universally anti-Muslim, much less universally involved in or even supportive of terrorism. Indeed, contacts in Yangon have recently told me of many Buddhists willing to harbor, in some cases even to stand with and protect, Muslim friends in the city when dangers arise.

Buddhist terrorism is clearly useful to elements in Burma, including politicos of various stripes who hope to unify the Bamar politically on an ethno-cultural basis as the country democratizes. It is hard to know how far they will go, in large part because we don't know how far they are currently going. One thing we can say for sure, though: The answer to the question of Buddhist terrorism in Burma has to do with the difference between 969 and 786.

CHATTING WITH MYANMAR'S BUDDHIST "TERRORIST"

The monk, Ashin Wirathu, had been portrayed on the cover of *Time* magazine's international edition over the caption, "the face of Buddhist terror." He was credited with inciting angry Buddhists in Myanmar to riot against the Muslim minority, burning mosques and Muslim-owned shops and houses, and attacking Muslims who dared to challenge them. In 2013 and 2014, scores were killed and thousands were displaced from their homes. In the town of Meiktila, a Buddhist mob surrounded a Muslim man and set him on fire.

Wirathu, who was blamed for fanning the flames of ethnic hatred, is the most well-known spokesman for the "969 Movement"—named after the nine special attributes of the Buddha, the six distinctive features of his teachings, and the nine characteristics of monks—which was formed to defend the purity of Burmese Buddhist culture against its adulteration from outside influences, primarily Muslim. Hence it was widely regarded as an anti-Islamic hate movement.

When I talked with Wirathu recently in his comfortable office in the Ma Soe Yein monastery in the central Burmese city of Mandalay he was prepared to defend himself against the terrorism label.

Buddhism is all about peace, he told me. "If we support Buddhism we are creating peace in the world," he said repeatedly. So far, nothing terrorist about that.

His monastic office radiated spiritual authority. Though Wirathu is only one of 14 senior monks on the governing body of the 2500-man monastic complex, he clearly occupied a leading position within it. Only the framed pictures on his wall—mostly newspaper clippings and pictures of himself—were indications of his charismatic, rabble-rousing reputation.

Though our conversation began cheerfully, Wirathu's demeanor darkened when the conversation shifted to the vulnerability of Myanmar's Buddhist culture to attacks from outside. "We have to protect our people," he said, frowning.

When asked, he implied that there were a host of people out to destroy Buddhism, and I kept pressing him to tell me whom they were.

"Muslims," he said, finally. Or more precisely, "Islamic extremists," as he called them, people who denigrated Buddhism. Not all Muslims were extremists, he said, though most were under their influence, so virtually all Muslims in Myanmar were suspect.

I asked him for examples of how the tiny Muslim minority in Myanmar—some four percent of the population—could possibly threaten the Buddhist majority. The first thing that came to his mind was the case of Muslim men wanting to marry Buddhist women. After marrying them, he said, the Muslim men would force their wives to convert to Islam and step on statues of the Buddha. It was not clear how frequently he thought this sort of thing happened. When I asked others in Mandalay they could only think of a handful of cases of ethnic intermarriage.

Wirathu also thought that Muslims were secretive, since their mosques were not open to everyone. (When I mentioned this to a local Muslim leader, he said that the mosques were closed solely to prevent people from coming inside with their shoes on and desecrating the worship space.)

Then Wirathu warmed up to his main concern, which was the penchant of "Islamic extremists" for violence, and their desire to rule the world. He cited the atrocities of groups such as al Qaeda and ISIS as examples. He also thought that their numbers were greatly expanding in Myanmar through immigration and having relatively larger families, and that this was a purposeful design to dilute the purity of Buddhist culture in the country and eventually take control.

"They are trying to transform Myanmar into a Muslim state," Wirathu said. He claimed that this was the reason that he and the 969 movement are trying to protect Burmese Buddhism from what he regards as a kind of cultural annihilation.

Wirathu insisted that his only role was to preach the truth. Though his fiery sermons have been reported as inciting violence, Wirathu disassociated himself from such acts, saying that his own followers were not under his control. He told me that Buddhists had the right "to defend themselves" and if at that time they "inflict injury," then that can be excused. Thus violence could be justified in a context of defense. But Buddhist ethics, he said, would not allow the faithful to intend to be violent, since, he again reminded me, Buddhism is all about peace.

Representatives of the United Nations' Commission on Human Rights, however, have identified Wirathu as one of the main figures in Myanmar's pattern of human rights abuse against Muslims, particularly the Rohingya who live in the northern portion of Rakhine province adjacent to Bangladesh. Though the Rohingya people claim to have lived in the region for centuries, many Burmese regard them as aliens, and the most recent government census refused to let them identify themselves on the rolls as Rohingya rather than Bengalis. Wirathu has been outspoken in his insistence that the Rohingya are not legitimately native to the country, but are interlopers.

According to Wirathu, rich Muslim countries have bought off the UN, and its human rights accusations were part of a Muslim plot. "It is not the United Nations," Wirathu told me, "but the United Muslim Nations." Wirathu claimed that President Obama was also duped by these influences, and this is the reason why he spoke about the rights of Rohingya people in his recent visit to the country.

The conspiracy was even broader, Wirathu said, since the world's news media were also under control of Islamic extremists. In fact, he claimed, it was the media that was in league with terrorists by branding him and other outspoken Buddhist leaders as the foe, as *Time* had done.

The other well-known Buddhist activist in the region was Galagoda Aththe Gnanasara, the leader of the Bodu Bala Sena movement in Sri Lanka, which *Time, Economist,* and other international news media have also criticized. Much like Wirathu, he has railed against the imagined threat of a small Muslim minority in his country, and like Wirathu was accused of inciting riots against it.

I asked Wirathu if he and the BBS were working together, and he admitted that he had met with Gnanasara, but insisted that their agendas were separate. Nonetheless, a number of news reports claim that Wirathu's 969 and Gnanasaara's BBS movements are in league, and there are reports that Wirathu has been in contact with Buddhist monks from Thailand's southern border with Malaysia, where pitched battles have been taking place between Buddhists and the Muslim majority in that locale.

Wirathu said it wasn't just Buddhists who were concerned about Islamic extremists. He said that his fears were shared by some Muslims, and gave the name of a leader of the Muslim community in Mandalay who he said was in agreement with him. Later that day I talked with the Muslim leader, and he said that of course he was concerned about al Qaeda and ISIS worldwide, but that the Muslims in Myanmar were of no threat to anyone. He implied that Wirathu was playing into the hands of politicians who wanted to use the Muslim scare for political purposes.

This was an analysis that I had heard from others in Myanmar, including journalists and political leaders. The ruling party had undertaken a great risk to their power by opening the government to a greater degree of democratic rule. Even though the military-backed Union Solidarity and Development Party swept the 2012 elections, its leaders were apprehensive about the 2015 elections and the likely candidacy of Nobel Prize-winning Burmese leader, Aung San Suu Kyi. Some thought that by creating an artificial threat the military's party would be seen as strong defenders of the nation, and they would gain in the upcoming elections as a result.

Wirathu has been ranting against Muslims for some time and in 2003 was put in prison for inciting violence against them. He was released in 2010, about the time of the democratic reforms, so some have speculated that his release was motivated by political considerations, like unleashing a tiger. But whether or not Wirathu was a pawn in this political calculation—and whether he was aware of it, if so—is unclear.

What is apparent is that he has convinced himself, and perhaps his angry following, that there has been a great but hidden struggle going on behind the quiet Buddhist civility and lush tropical landscape of the ancient Burma that is now the rapidly economically developing Myanmar. It is a battle between good and evil, between Buddhist morality and the Muslim hordes he imagines to be poised to conquer Burma's soul. And Wirathu would like to be its savior.

8

Buddhist Violence in Burma

In the West, Buddhism is frequently comprehended as a religion of sympathy and peace, with gauzy pictures of tranquil reflection, the murmur of droned petitions, a typical lotus blossom. So what are we to make of an as of now coursing video of a robed Burmese friar employing a durable shaft as he joins an executioner crowd beating a helpless Muslim man to the ground? Out of sight, mosques and houses are smoldering and Muslim youngsters are running for their lives.

Buddhism, a confidence honed everywhere throughout the world, is set apart by independence, balance and sympathy toward the welfare of the earth and every single "aware" animal. Be that as it may, when it is outfit to ethnic bigotry and amazing patriotism, it can turn carelessly vicious, as it has been and keeps on being apparent in Burma, now otherwise called Myanmar.

Buddhist viciousness, including deadly fierceness against non-Buddhist minorities, is not a marvel bound to Burma. In late decades, Sri Lanka's ethnic pressures have been lighted and reignited by Buddhist extremists. As in Burma, they discover sympathizers in Buddhist-overwhelmed governments and the military. Just weeks prior, Sri Lankan friars were taped driving a stone-tossing band toward a Muslim-possessed garments stockroom in rural Colombo, the capital.

In the Himalayan country of Bhutan two decades back, feelings of trepidation that a centuries-old Tibetan society and Buddhist government were under risk from a flood of ethnic Nepalis prompted expansive scale ejections of individuals who, authorities said, couldn't demonstrate they were natives. In Cambodia, the Khmer Rouge rose up out of an altogether Buddhist country.

In Burma, missing from the response to the grisly scenes of alarmed Muslims slaughtered and dislodged are an unambiguous judgment and good authority by Aung San Suu Kyi, whose father, Aung San, established the Burmese armed force, with which she now works in changing her nation. While referred to the world over as a candid champion of popular government, she has now turned into a Burmese legislator, cautious not to go up against the ethnic Burman Buddhist larger part, the capable friars or the military.

Ministers were likewise bold shields of majority rule government, however the inquiry that now emerges is, Democracy for whom? Since the political move started in Burma, friars have participated in assaults on Muslims first on the western Arakan coast, where stateless ethnic Bengali Muslims have settled for two centuries, and after that all the more as of late in other Burmese districts where Buddhists and Muslims lived respectively in peace.

After hostile to Muslim viciousness softened out a year back up the Arakan area (now likewise called Rakhine state) on the Bay of Bengal, Aung San Suu Kyi, an ethnic Burman and a Buddhist, called for adherence to the guideline of law, yet she demonstrated no open shock over the undeniably all around reported attacks by Buddhist town hordes and friars against the Muslim populace known as Rohingyas, a significant number of whom were compelled to escape in unseaworthy water crafts. An obscure number have died adrift and numerous thousands, their homes and belonging gone, live in outcast camps.

Assaults against Muslim have ejected sporadically from that point forward, spreading all the more generally crosswise over Burma, and starting to influence the stateless Rohingya Muslins as well as groups of Burmese Muslims whose citizenship is not being referred to. Human Rights Watch reported that in October of a year ago, in a blended Burmese and Rohingya Muslim territory of Arakan that had already gotten away demolition, satellite pictures demonstrated that 633 structures and 178 houseboats had been crushed. In mid-April of this year, the BBC and other media in Britain showed images from what was described as police video of Buddhist mobs attacking Muslims in Meikhtila, in central Burma, in March. Shops were looted, buildings burned and more than forty people killed. Again, monks were part of the mob and, again, the Buddhist-dominant police stood by and watched.

The Christian ethnic minorities in Burma have not been victims of targeted attacks so far, by most accounts, though a variety of ethnic groups waging war against the Burmese state for decades include many Christians. Most of them, a large number of them Baptists, were converted during the British colonial era, which ended with Burmese independence in 1948. Though most (but not all) non-Burman ethnic separatists have reached at least tentative cease-fire accords with the central government, their situations could become more precarious if Buddhist violence continues.

In Sri Lanka, paradoxically the most advanced country in the region in human development terms, British colonialism left a legacy of tension and division between the predominantly Sinhalese Buddhist people of central and southern Ceylon, as it was then known, and the long-established Tamil population of the north, with its cultural heart on the Jaffna Peninsula. Another, separate group of Tamils were brought from India later by the British to the central highlands of Sri Lanka as "tea-pluckers" in the sprawling plantations established by British and Sri Lankan companies.

These Tamils, like the Rohingyas in Burma, were denied citizenship for many years, but they did not join the Tamil rebellion in the north. Sri Lanka also has a Muslim population, classified as an ethnic group, and significant Christian communities after centuries of Portuguese, Dutch and British occupation. In a thirty-year civil war that ended in 2009, Muslims were caught in the middle of Sinhala-Tamil pressures.

Under British rule, the northern Tamils, many educated by American missionaries in the Jaffna area, became favored civil servants for the colonial government because of their high level of competence in English and well developed professional skills. After independence in 1948, the Sinhalese majority turned on them and demanded that the government replace them with Sinhala speakers (also abolishing English usage at the same time). When hostilities led to war in the mid-1980s, the conflict was defined, rightly or wrongly, in ethnic and religious terms, with most Tamils being Hindus and the Sinhalese Buddhists.

For a period in the late 1980s and early 1990s, there were in fact two simultaneous civil wars in Sri Lanka, when an extremist Sinhala Marxist-Leninist-Buddhist movement, the People's Liberation Front, argued that the Sinhalese-led government had given away too much to the Tamils in a short-lived truce and peace agreement in 1987, brokered by India. The JVP, as it was known by its initials in Sinhala, terrorized areas of the Sri Lankan south and interior hill country, with Buddhist monks' support. The violent movement fed on a sense of having been betrayed to "Hindu New Delhi," because of India's military intervention to end the Tamil war. During a ceremony in Colombo, a Sri Lankan Sinhalese sailor stepped out of an honor guard and hit the then Indian Prime Minister Rajiv Gandhi with his rifle.

Succeeding central governments in Sri Lanka, played the Buddhist card with increasing regularity and ferocity, running up a multicolored Buddhist banner rather than the national flag at one point in Jaffna and elsewhere in Tamil-majority areas. Atrocities were committed by both sides during the war between the central government and Tamil militants, though with greater indiscriminate brutality on the side of the Liberation Tigers of Tamil Eelam, which first annihilated virtually all more moderate rival groups and unarmed Tamil politicians early in the war, and assassinated not only a series of Sri Lankan national political leaders but also the country's leading human rights lawyer, Neelan Tiruchelvam, also a Tamil.

Sri Lankan analysts of intense Buddhist antipathy to Tamils and their culture have suggested that the Sinhalese majority has nurtured a sense of being a threatened minority in South Asia, partly because of the dominant presence of India, with its huge Hindu population, and the political power of the state of Tamil Nadu, whose support governments in New Delhi often need. Sri Lankans see Buddhism pushed to the margins in India, where even some of the most holy Buddhist sites are managed by Hindu organizations. Many Indian Buddhists are poor converts trying to escape the Indian caste system.

The spectacle of Buddhism-as-politics—except for the Tibetan situation, which has more to do with China than India—is largely missed or ignored by most Western Buddhists, who accept some of the practices as more lifestyle choices than religion, with many of these practices heavily influenced by Hinduism or Indian yoga gurus and ashrams.

In Sri Lanka, Buddhism is a faith that defines society for the Sinhalese, and it becomes the identifying characteristic when they feel threatened. That still doesn't entirely explain how it became the rallying call of the modern Sri Lankan military, or large segments of it, and how its nonviolent, introspective teachings were so easily abandoned not only in time of conflict—perhaps understandable given the brutality of the Tamil Tigers—but also when time came to make a just peace with the civilian population of the Tamil north.

The Tamil Tigers were not defeated until 2009 under a determined army assault. In putting down the long rebellion, the Sinhalese Buddhist side incurred universal opprobrium for its human rights abuses, and now triumphantly dominant in the central government, it remains unwilling to heal the Hindu Tamils' cultural wounds.

UNDERSTANDING BUDDHIST-MUSLIM RELATIONS IN BURMA (MYANMAR)

This post is part of the Interfaith Ramadan: Shared Vision of Inclusion & Co-Existence series, cross-posted there at Interfaith Ramadan here. As our series host Sara Ager writes:

Ramadan is a time when Muslim communities traditionally come together – to fast, to pray, to reflect, and to encourage one another. In that spirit, the Interfaith Ramadan blog series aims to extend that sense of community to people of all faiths and none. The series provides an inclusive platform where people from around the world share their experiences and offer their perspectives on interfaith issues...

Is Myanmar approaching genocide?

This was the question, and in fact the headline haunting my google news feed for much of the month of May. Today the plight of the Rohingya in Myanmar (or Burma as many still call it)* is far from certain, and the history which has brought us here is even more clouded. Over 60 years of military rule, numerous ethnic civil wars, fear and distrust of foreigners, and extraordinary poverty have all led to country today which would be in many ways socially unrecognizable to those who had visited in the 1940s or early 50s. As the long-time Myanmar expert David Steinberg has written:

Studying Burma/Myanmar is often neither science nor social science, but more akin to art, where truth is in the eye of the beholder. Consequently, different interpretations abound. – Steinberg *Burma/Myanmar: What Everyone Needs to Know (2009)*, p.10

As such, I offer this interpretation as an academic student of Buddhism for 15 years, writing here and elsewhere about Burma for a little over 10 years, and as a global citizen struck by wonderful and ongoing friendships with Muslims for going on 8 years. So, taken in turn, I'll try to briefly describe the Buddhism of Burma, the country as I know it today, and some of the roots of the violence toward Muslims there.

Burmese Buddhism

When and how Buddhism arrived in Burma is disputed. Epigraphic and archaeological evidence points to the 4th century C.E., while later chronicles claim that it arrived with Ashokan missionaries in the 3rd century B.C.E, and yet further claims suggest that a disciple of the historical Buddha brought the teachings to the area.

From there various forms of Buddhism ebbed and flowed, before Theravada was "decisively established following the conversion of King Anawrahtâ" (1040-1077)". And it is Theravadin Buddhism that dominates the country today, accounting for around 80-90% of the nation's population with nearly 60,000 monasteries in the country filled with nearly 500,000 monks and nuns, based on a 2008 estimate by Steinberg. A central tenant of Theravadin Buddhism – for both monastics and the laity – is the Five Precepts, abstaining from: harming living beings, taking the not-given, engaging in sensual/sexual misconduct, false or malicious speech, and intoxication. The first of these obviously comes to mind when we think of the harm done to Muslims in the country in recent years.

Burma the Country

It's with a heavy sigh that I think of Burma as a nation today. When I visited in 2011 there were some signs of hope for the country and I witnessed much of what makes people project romantic notions of an exotic, peaceful kingdom lost in time as some tourists did recently and Rudyard Kipling did years ago.

To be there is to be transported into the past in countless ways, from the ox-carts to poor infrastructure and subsistence farming, much of Burma has remained static for decades, if not longer. However, it is true also that nowhere in the country has time literally stood still.

Lives have come and gone, attempts to bring change arose and fell, and while some sought the slow-steady "Burmese Way" of social and economic progress, others have openly rebelled against the government. This has the turned country that could have been the great economic and social success of the nation into one of the poorest and socially isolated in the world.

Modern Burma, like so many post-colonial states, is a result of a foreign power -the British- asserting unity over often fractious and internally independent peoples. They, however, simply conquered other conquerers and there is no idyllic peaceful or static past to point to. To look at a map of the country today, the bulky center can be seen as a horse-shoe of*Bamar,* or ethnic Burmese, in the middle low-lands coming down to the fanning Irrawaddy delta and surrounded on three sides and down the narrow southern coastal strip by smaller ethnic groups. To maintain power, put simply butexplained in more detail elsewhere, the central *Bamar* majority has used military rule to force unity on the country. The burgeoning democracy there is fragile and may failas it has before.

Buddhist Violence against Muslims

This brings us to yet another incredibly complex and sad topic: the recent outbursts of violence against Muslims in Burma. These have been predominantly in the western Rakhine state bordering Bangladesh, but have not been limited to that area. There, the Muslims mostly identify as Rohingyas, "a group that originated in part of Bengal, now called Bangladesh" (BBC). This is where things get dicey, as despite the presence of Rohingya in Burma for decades and even centuries, Burmese nationalists or ethnocentrists accuse the Rohingya of being foreigners with no right to exist in the country. They accuse other Muslims of seeking to displace Buddhism through higher birth rates and stories of forced conversions to Islam.

However, what I hope to make clear is that this isn't a simple case of "Buddhist" aggression toward Islam. As the recent East-West Center report *Contesting Buddhist Narratives: Democratization, Nationalism, and Communal Violence in Myanmar* states:

Although nationalist movements such as 969 and MaBaTha express themselves in religious terms, they are not seeking to defend a doctrinal stance as such. Instead, they refer more to notions of Burmese national identity and traditional ideas about the fragility of Buddhism and its teachings that have circulated within Theravada Buddhist societies for centuries. (p.x; with thanks to Dr. Paul Fuller, whose blog pointed me to this and numerous other great resources and discussions of Buddhism in general and contemporary Burmese issues in particular.)

The report also speaks of this as a "reflexive defense against what is perceived by some to be the threat of a globally spreading Islam..." (ibid). However, just as anti-Muslim bigoted Christians in Western nations do not speak for Christianity, these groups - who represent a minority even in Burma- do not speak for Buddhism or Buddhists in general. In fact:

Within the vast Theravada Buddhist corpus and Myanmar Buddhists' particular understandings of these teachings, there are numerous values and historical examples that can promote religious pluralism, discourage hate speech, and encourage a more critical approach to rumors and misinformation. Indeed, some of these Buddhist counterarguments are already being advanced on the ground in Myanmar... (East-West, p.xi)

One example in action can be found in the Western monk living in Burma, Bhikkhu Subhuti, who has actively reached out to the local Muslim community, bringing them into the Buddhist monastery and fostering greater understanding in his monastic brothers and lay supporters. Another is Sitagu Sayadaw, who recently at a conference in Tehran unconditionally condemned violence against Muslims in Myanmar:

And going back to 2013, in the midst of attacks by Buddhists on Muslims around the country, in the town of Lashio Buddhist monks quickly sheltered and fed Muslims until violence subsided:

Other monks who sheltered Muslims in Burma during attacks were recently recognized by the Parliament of the World's Religions with World Harmony Awards. In reflecting on his actions, one monk, Rev. Seindita, is quoted saying, "they will have to kill me first," before allowing aggressors to harm the Rohingya masses.

From outside the country Buddhist leaders have likewise issued appeals, both to their own officials and to those inside Burma, to address the plight of the Rohingya. These include the recent joint letter signed by Jack Kornfield, Ven. Bhikkhu Bodhi, William Aiken, Tara Brach, Lama Surya Das, Alan Senauke, Taigen Dan Leighton, Larry Yang, Rev. angel Kyodo williams, and Rev. Dr. T. Kenjitsu Nakagaki; a statement by the Dalai Lama, and lastly, an Open Letter to Buddhists on Islamophobia by Joshua Eaton and Rev. Danny Fisher (and co-signed by nearly 300 others including myself), inspired by events in Burma in 2012 ahead of the holy month of Ramadan.

The existence of these positive, pluralist, and caring voices within the Burmese Buddhist community and beyond should eliminate any sense that Islamophobia is ubiquitous among Buddhists in Myanmar. Returning once more to the East-West Center's report:

However, the construction of a Buddhist counterargument that appeals to Buddhist ethics is unlikely to bring an end to communal violence by itself. In order to advance sustainable peace and coexistence in the country, these Myanmar Buddhist arguments for religious pluralism must be complemented by a series of political, economic, and legal reforms to address underlying insecurities and long-standing inequalities between communities.

As a country that has been so isolated for over 60 years though, it is likely that there are great deficits in inter-ethnic and inter-religious understanding that need to be addressed alongside other problems. Just as the issue at hand is complex, its solution too will be a complex one. None of this, unfortunately, brings us closer to answering the question: Is Myanmar approaching genocide?

But it does, I hope, bring some needed clarity about Buddhism's role there. It also should bring hope that through the better angels of our nature and the highest values of our religions, we can work together to begin addressing the very acute needs of the thousands of Rohingya living in terrible conditions in Burma as well as the more long-term reforms needed to establish a safe and stable society for all in the country and the region. As Imam Malik Mujahid, Chair of the Parliament of the World's Religions, said during the ceremony recognizing the three Burmese monks earlier this month:

"The Buddha proclaimed that we must love and care for all creatures. The Prophet Mohammad, peace be upon him, said that none of you are truly believers unless you wish for another what you wish for yourself. These teachings are at the heart of all our faiths, where the beauty of religion is rooted... While fear, anger and hate rises in America and communities around the world, people of compassion are rising to demonstrate neighborly loving relationships. We must become our brother's keeper."

* The name was changed by the current military dictatorship in 1989. To retain the previous name may be seen as throwing allegiance to a colonialist past, as Burma is the name for the nation first designated by the British who ruled over the country from 1824 to 1948. However, 'Burma' is also widely used by dissidents who do not recognize the legitimacy of the current regime and its choice to change the name.

9

Reasons for Buddhism's Attitude to Violence

Before looking all the more carefully at what is said in regards to the underlying foundations of viciousness, it merits drawing out reasons given in the writings for the shirking, addressing or non-embrace of brutality. Interconnected structures develop: nibbana as the objective of the otherworldly life; the requests of metta and karuna (adoring generosity and empathy); the requirement for peace, accord and amicability inside society.

Since a definitive objective of the profound way for the Buddhist is nibbana, demeanors towards savagery should first be found in connection to it. Nibbana is a definitive destruction of dukkha. It is a conceivable objective inside this life and, in addition to other things, includes a complete de-toxification of the brain from ravenousness, scorn and fancy, an upheaval in the way the world is seen, opportunity from desiring and freedom from the dream of sense of self. The Therigatha or Songs of the Sisters contain the absolute most moving declarations to this reality; they are paeans of happiness about freedom:

Mine is the rapture of opportunity won
As Path converges in Fruit and Fruit in Path.
Holding to nothing, I in Nibbana live,
This five-assembled being have I caught on.
Cut from its root, all ahead development is sat tight,

I too am stayed, victor on premise beyond any doubt

Undaunted. Resurrection comes never more.

Nibbana and samsara are contradictory. One is the stopping of the other. With regards to the objective of nibbana, activities, considerations and words can be assessed concerning whether they fabricate samsara or lead to nibbana: whether they are incompetent (akusala) or skilled(kusala). Liberality in brutality is regularly esteemed akusala. As such, it can't prompt the objective of nibbana. In the Ambalatthika-Rahulovada Sutta, the Buddha says to the Venerable Rahula:

On the off chance that you, Rahula, are covetous of doing a deed with the body, you ought to think about the deed with the body, in this way: "That deed which I am burning of doing with the body is a deed of the body that may conduce to the damage of self and that may conduce to the mischief of others and that may conduce to the damage of both; this deed of body is untalented (akusala), its yield is anguish, its outcome is anguish."

Damage to others is key to what is untalented. In the Sallekha Sutta guidance is given to friars about the purging of the brain as the premise of profound advancement. First among the musings which must be scrubbed are those associated with hurting and brutality; both speak to untalented states which lead downwards:

Cunda, as each incompetent state leads downwards, as each talented state leads upwards, even thus, Cunda, does non-hurting (avihimsa) come to be a higher state for a person who is unsafe, does limitation from assault on animals come to be a higher state for the person who makes surge on animals.

When the Buddha is in conversation with Bhaddiya, *sarambha* is added to *lobha, dosa*and *moha* (lust, hatred and delusion) as a defilement which flows from them. *Sarambha*can be translated as "accompanied by violence." As the mind filled with *lobha, dosa* and*moha* is led to actions which are *akusala,* so is the mind filled with the violence which accompanies the triad. All lead to a person's loss:

"Now what think you, Bhaddiya? When freedom from malice *(adosa)*... from delusion *(amoha)*... from violence *(asarambha)* that goes with these arises within oneself, does it arise to one's profit or to one's loss?" — "To one's profit, sir."

The point of the above suttas is that violent action and violent thought, actions which harm and debase others and thoughts which contemplate the same, stand in the way of spiritual growth and the self-conquest which leads to the goal of existence. In this respect, indulging in violence is doing to oneself what an enemy would wish. It is a form of self-harming:

> He who is exceedingly corrupt
>
> like a *maluva* creeper strangling a *sal* tree
>
> does to himself what an enemy would wish. —Dhp. v. 162

In contrast, abstaining from violence has personal benefit in the present and in the future. It is part of the training of mind and body which lays the foundation for spiritual progress.

The accusation has been made that the application of the terms *kusala* and *akusala* are oriented only towards an individualistic goal, making the motivation for abstention from violence a selfish one. But it can be argued that the distinction between altruism and egoism breaks down for anyone truly following the Noble Eightfold Path. There are also many textual references to the inherent importance of harmony, justice and compassion in society to balance those passages which seem to be solely individualistic. Harmony and justice are recognized as worthwhile in themselves as well as a prerequisite for the spiritual progress of society's members. Hence, in society, violence is to be eschewed because it brings pain to beings with similar feelings to oneself:

> All tremble at violence,
>
> Life is dear to all.
>
> Comparing others with oneself
>
> One should neither kill nor cause others to kill.

On the level of personal analogy, men and women are to condemn violence. It is an analogy which demands *metta* (loving kindness) and *karuna* (compassion) of the human being. They call on a frame of mind which cannot remain insensitive to suffering in others or untouched by the agony produced by violence. Non-violence, therefore, arises through the urge to prevent anguish in others:

Comparing oneself with others in such terms as "Just as I am so are they, just as they are so am I" *(yatha aham tatha ete yatha ete tatha aham),* one should neither kill nor cause others to kill.

The Buddha, however, did not credit all people with this level of awareness. He is recorded as saying that shame and fear of blame protect the world, and if there were not these forces, the world would come to confusion and promiscuity. Not all beings rally to the call for compassion on the grounds that others have like feelings to themselves or that harmony in society is necessary. Therefore, some texts invoke the concepts of heaven and hell, rewards and punishments, to control violence. Vivid pictures are drawn of the agonies of hell:

Brahman youth, here some woman or man is one who makes onslaught on creatures, is cruel, bloody-handed, intent on injuring and killing, and without mercy to living creatures. Because of that deed, accomplished thus, firmly held thus, he, at breaking up of the body after dying, arises in the sorrowful way, the bad bourn, the Downfall, the Niraya.

Even so, monks, that anguish and dejection that man experiences while he is being stabbed with three hundred spears, compared with the anguish of Niraya Hell does not count, it does not amount even to an infinitesimal fraction of it, it cannot even be compared to it. Monks, the guardians of Niraya Hell subject him to what is called the fivefold pinion. They drive a red-hot iron stake through each hand and each foot and a red-hot iron stake through his breast. Thereat, he feels feelings that are painful, sharp and severe. But he does not do his time until he makes an end of that evil deed.

Here, self-interest in terms of avoidance of future pain is appealed to as a reason to desist from violence. This emphasis can also be seen in the Petavatthu in which those fallen to the realm of the *petas* speak to those on the human level about the reasons for their suffering. Falsehood, failing in the duties of wife or husband, stinginess and fraud are some of the actions mentioned.

Story No. 32, however, speaks of a deerhunter who explains that he was "a ruthless man of bloody hands": "Among harmless creatures, I, with wicked mind, walked about, very ruthless, ever finding delight in slaying others unrestrained," he declares in verse three. His punishment is to be devoured by dogs during the daytime, the hours when he used to be involved in slaughter. He is able to teach the living that the First Precept should be kept and that it applies not only to the killing of human beings but also to animals. The deerhunter, therefore, is held up as an authoritative witness to what happens to violent individuals. His story is useful as a deterrent to socially disruptive elements and is confirmation of the importance Buddhism places on non-violence within the social fabric. The threat of future punishment is used to control potentially violent elements.

Two broad, interconnected areas, therefore, emerge in the reasons for the condemnation of violence within the Early Buddhist texts. Firstly, thoughts of violence and violent action are defilements and must be eradicated if *nibbana* is to be reached. In this light,*nibbana* is the highest ethical good. This stress alone, however, can lead to distortion if*nibbana* is seen as a metaphysical state above the empirical world and the path to it as divorced from society. Early Buddhism was rooted in the empirical. Violence was to be repudiated because it caused anguish to men and women and disruption in society. The human person was seen as precious. Harming a being who desired happiness and felt pain could rarely be right. If a society was to be established in which people could live without fear and with the freedom of mind to follow the Eightfold Path, violence had to be eschewed.

The question of political, defensive violence, however, must be mentioned here. Can violence be justified in a situation where the state needs to defend its citizens against external and internal threats? Is this a situation in which violence is not condemned? The texts suggest Buddhism would here insist on discrimination. The Cakkavatti Sihanada Sutta gives this advice to the righteous king:

This, dear son, that you, leaning on the Dhamma, honoring, respecting and revering it, doing homage to it, hallowing it, being yourself a Dhamma-banner, a Dhamma-signal, having the Dhamma as your master, should provide the right watch, ward and protection for your own folk, for the army, for the nobles, for vassals and brahmans and householders, for town and country dwellers, for the religious world and for beasts and birds.

This passage implies that the need for an army and consequently for the use of force in defense is accepted as a worldly necessity. But the picture which emerges is not glorification of the "just" war but an appeal for war and violence to be seen against a higher set of values.

Relevant perspectives on these political realities are seen in the Buddha's advice to the Vajjians and to King Pasenadi. The Vajjians are faced with vicious aggression from King Ajatasattu, King of Magadha, who is bent on destroying them. The latter sends a brahman to the Buddha for advice and a prediction about how successful he will be in war. The very fact that he does so shows that he does not consider the Buddha either ill-informed or dismissive of such political conflicts. The reply he receives is significant. The Buddha does not refer directly to Ajatasattu but implies that the use of arms against a people who are morally pure and in concord would be fruitless. His words to Ajatasattu become words of advice to the Vajjians that they should meet together in concord and give respect to their elders, their ancient institutions, their traditions and their women. No mention is made of the Vajjian military strength; only of their moral strength. Moral strength is held up as defense against violence. Yet it is not denied but implicitly understood that the Vajjians would have to use force to repulse aggression, and also present is an implicit condemnation of Ajatasattu's intentions.

King Pasenadi is also seen in conflict with Ajatasattu, meeting force with force. At first, Ajatasattu is the aggressor and the victor. The reported response of the Buddha is significant:

Monks, the King of Magadha, Ajatasattu, son of the Vedehi Princess, is a friend to, an intimate of, mixed up with, whatever is evil. The Kosalan King Pasenadi is a friend to, an intimate of, mixed up with, whatever is good.

Thus Pasenadi's role as defender of the nation against aggression is accepted as necessary and praiseworthy. In the next battle, Pasenadi is the victor. Ajatasattu's army is confiscated but Pasenadi is merciful enough to grant Ajatasattu his life. It is still Ajatasattu who is condemned. His fate is seen in kammic terms:

A man may spoil another just so far
As it may serve his ends, but when he's spoiled
By others he, despoiled, spoils yet again.
So long as evil's fruit is not matured
The fool does fancy: "Now's the hour, the chance!"
But when the deed bears fruit, he fareth ill.
The slayer gets a slayer in his turn,
The conqueror gets one who conquers him,
The abuser wins abuse, the annoyer frets:
Thus by the evolution of the deed
A man who spoils is spoiled in his turn.

In one respect, Pasenadi becomes an instrument of kamma for Ajatasattu. At another level, acceptance of political realities emerges. The king has a duty to protect his citizens from external threats of violence. Therefore, the advice given to a king or those with responsibility for government about reacting to the violence of others is fitted to the situation, a situation in which the use of violence may become a political necessity in a world governed by craving *(tanha).* Yet, even with affairs of state, war is placed in the perspective of a more important set of values. To Pasenadi, burdened by responsibility, the Buddha says:

Noble and brahman, commoner and serf,
None can evade and play the truant here:
The impending doom overwhelms one and all.
Here is no place for strife with elephants
Or chariots of war or infantry,
Nay, nor for war or woven spell or curse
Nor may finance avail to win the day.

War is not presented as worthy of praise in itself. It is recognized that battle cannot take place without hatred and the wish to kill, in both the mind of aggressor and victim. A Samyutta Nikaya passage illustrates this. A fighting man comes to the Buddha and explains his belief that the warrior who is killed whilst fighting energetically in battle is reborn in the company of the Devas of Passionate Delight. The Buddha's answer condemns this idea as perverted. A warrior is always led by the idea, "Let those beings be exterminated so that they may be never thought to have existed." Such a view can only lead downwards rather than to any heavenly world. The Buddha thus rejects any glorification of war, since there can be no glory when the mind is dominated by hate.

Another duty of the state is to punish. Punishment, although a harming of creatures and a cause of pain to them, is nevertheless seen as a social necessity because of the need to protect society from the greater violence which would flow from undeterred greed. Fear of punishment *(dandabhaya)* is described in vivid terms, with the mention of specific punishments. A man sees them and thinks: "If I were to do such deeds as those for which the rajahs seize a bandit, a miscreant, and so treat him... they would surely treat me in like manner." Important here is the fact that Early Buddhism would make discriminations about the question of punishment. As a deterrent, punishment has value. Meted out as an expression of hate, it is to be rejected. Inflicted where social justice is the requisite, it is also condemned, as seen in the Kutadanta Sutta, referred to in the next part.

The Roots of Violence

The Attadanda Sutta of the Sutta Nipata is the voice of someone overcome by despair because of the violence he sees:

Fear results from resorting to violence — just look at how people quarrel and fight. But let me tell you now of the kind of dismay and terror that I have felt.

Seeing people struggling like fish, writhing in shallow water, with enmity against one another, I became afraid.

At one time, I had wanted to find some place where I could take shelter, but I never saw such a place. There is nothing in this world that is solid at base and not a part of it that is changeless. I had seen them all trapped in mutual conflict and that is why I had felt so repelled. But then I noticed something buried deep in their hearts. It was — I could just make it out — a dart.

The above is from a translation of the Sutta Nipata which attempts to preserve the spirit of the text rather than the letter. Here it is the spirit of dismay and fear leading to discovery which is of prime importance. The speaker detects a common root — the dart of craving *(tanha)* and greed *(lobha)* — a view directly in line with the Four Noble Truths. Violence arises because the right nourishment is present.

However, it has been pointed out earlier that differences may exist in the way in which*tanha* conditions situations of violence. On analysis, two broad and mutually interdependent areas emerge: (1) violence arising from an individual's maladjustment, and (2) craving and violence arising from unsatisfactory social and environmental conditions, caused by the craving of others.

The latter can be taken first with reference to the following texts: The Kutadanta Sutta; the Cakkavatti Sihanada Sutta; and certain Anguttara Nikaya passages. The first weaves a myth within a myth. The inner myth tells the story of a king, King Wide-Realm, whose land is wracked with discontent and crime such that people are afraid to walk in the streets for fear of violence.

The king's solution is to hold a sacrifice for the nation and he goes to a holy man for advice. But the king is not given what he expects. The sage tells the king that fines, bonds and death for the wrongdoers would be self-defeating. Punishment is not the right path. On the contrary, it would increase the malady because the root causes remained untouched, in this instance, economic injustice and poverty. King Wide-Realm is advised to give food and seed corn to farmers, capital to traders and food to those in government service:

But perchance his majesty might think: "I'll soon put a stop to these scoundrels' game by degradation and banishment and fines and bonds and death." But their license cannot be satisfactorily put a stop to so. The remnant left unpunished would still go on harassing the realm. Now there is one method to adopt to put a thorough end to this disorder. Whosoever there be in the king's realm who devote themselves to keeping cattle and the farm, to them let his majesty give food and seed corn. Whosoever there be in the king's realm who devote themselves to trade, to them let his majesty give capital. Whosoever there be in the king's realm who devote themselves to government service, to them let his majesty give wages and food. Then those men, following each his own business, will no longer harass the realm; the king's revenue will go up; the country will be quiet and at peace; and the populace pleased with one another and happy, dancing their children in their arms, will dwell with open doors.

The above analysis recognizes that men and women can be pushed to violence if the prevailing conditions do not enable them to preserve their own lives without it. The instinct to survive is credited with enough strength to push people to struggle before they will sink into need. In such a situation, it follows that to press down the hand of the law will not be effective. In fact, it could encourage a growth in serious crime.

This is what happens in the Cakkavatti Sihanada Sutta, another mythological story dealing with disruption in society. It has already been mentioned with reference to the duty of kingship. But there is one clause concerning his duty that has not yet been mentioned: "Throughout your kingdom let no wrongdoing prevail. And whosoever in your kingdom is poor, to him let wealth be given." The kings of the story who keep to this are blessed with peace. Yet a king eventually arises who neglects the giving of wealth to the poor. He is soon faced with a situation beyond his control. Poverty becomes rampant and this leads to theft, since people would rather steal than die. When the king realizes the cause, he starts by being lenient on the wrongdoer, by giving him the means to live. Such kindness too late leads others to see the only way to survive is turning to theft and receiving a royal handout in return. The king has given charity, not justice, and crime increases leading to a return to brutal punishments. The brutality of the punishments encourages the people to be more extreme in their own crime as they try to survive. Punishment here fails to deter because of the desperation of the people. The sutta presents a disturbing picture of how a society can fall into utter confusion because of a lack of economic justice. The extremes reached are far greater than anything envisaged in the Kutadanta Sutta and they stem from the state's blindness to the realities of poverty. Thus the sutta states in refrain after every deterioration:

Thus from goods not being bestowed on the destitute, poverty... stealing... violence... murder... lying... evil-speaking... immorality grew rife.

Theft and killing lead to false speech, jealousy, adultery, incest and perverted lust until:

Among such humans, brethren, there will arise a sword-period *(satthantarakappa)*of seven days during which they will look on each other as wild beasts; sharp swords will appear ready to their hands, and they thinking, "This is a wild beast, this is a wild beast," will with their swords deprive each other of life.

In the Cakkavatti Sihanada Sutta, the nourishment of the violence is the state's neglect of the poor. The whole myth illustrates the principle of *paticca samuppada.* Each state of degeneration is dependent on the state before it. An evolutionary process is seen. An inevitability seems to emerge, an inevitable movement towards bestiality. It is significant that the sutta does not concentrate on the psychological state of the people. The obsessive cravings which overtake them are traced back to the failure of the state rather than to failings in their own adjustment to reality. The root is the defilement in the state — the *raga, dosa* and *moha* in the king which afflict his perception of his duty.

An Anguttara Nikaya passage states this principle in simple and direct terms. If the king is righteous, his ministers will be righteous, the country will be righteous and the natural world will be a friend rather than an enemy. The opposite, of course, is also true and is placed first in the sutta:

At such time, monks, as rulers are unrighteous *(adhammika),* their ministers are unrighteous, brahmans and householders are also unrighteous... The above passages show that a change of heart is needed where violence exists but this change is needed in those who wield power in society. When a state is corrupt, the citizens become victims of the state and their own wish to survive and they are then led to actions they would never consider if they were free from want. There is an understanding that, besides those who do evil, there exists a category of people to whom wrong is done and whose reactions are conditioned by the original wrongdoing.

To pass now to the psychological roots of violence, another myth can be cited, the Aggañña Sutta. Like the Cakkavatti Sihanada Sutta, it describes an evolutionary process which takes on its own momentum. The root of the process is significant — the craving of beings. The sutta explains, in myth form, the process by which undifferentiated beings come to earth from a World of Radiance to eat the earth's savory crust, to the point where there is private property and the division of labor. One of its purposes is to challenge the static, non-evolutionary theory of a divinely ordained caste system but it is significant also because evolution is guided by the growth of craving and individualism. The whole sutta turns on the individual and his craving as the root of violence. It depicts a situation before state power is established. Craving first enters when the beings taste the crust of the earth:

> Then, Vasettha, some being of greedy disposition said, "Lo now, what will this be?" and tasted the savory earth with his finger. He thus, tasting, became suffused with the savor, and craving *(tanha)* entered into him.

The craving develops. The natural world evolves to accommodate the beings, becoming ever less easy to manage. The bodies of the beings become gross and individually differentiated into male and female, comely and unlovely. Jealousy and competition enter. The savory crust disappears. Vegetables and plant life evolve. An important point is reached when the beings establish boundaries around their individually owned rice plots. Individualism is therefore institutionally consolidated and the consequence is violence:

> Now some being, Vasettha, of greedy disposition, watching over his plot, stole another plot and made use of it. They took him and, holding him fast, said, "Truly, good being, you have done evil in that, while watching your own plot, you have stolen another

plot and made use of it. See, good being, that you do no such thing again." "Aye, sirs," he replied. And a second time he did so. And yet a third. And again they took him and admonished him. Some smote him with the hand, some with clods, some with sticks. With such a beginning, Vasettha, did stealing appear and censure and lying and punishment became known.

The sutta illustrates that *tanha* coupled with individualism nourishes violence and conditions the necessity for state power to curb excesses. As such, its teaching is directly in the mainstream of Buddhist thought: craving and grasping lie at the root of negative and unwholesome states in society. However, more needs to be said about the causes and consequences of individualism.

The term *"puthujjana"* is used to describe the ordinary, average person:

Herein, monks, an uninstructed ordinary person, taking no account of the pure ones *(ariyanam),* unskilled in the Dhamma of the pure ones, untrained in the Dhamma of the pure ones, taking no account of the true men, unskilled in the Dhamma of the true men, untrained in the Dhamma of the true men, does not comprehend the things that should be wisely attended to, does not comprehend the things that should not be wisely attended to.

The term *"puthu"* has two main meanings: "several, many, numerous," on one hand, and "separate, individual," on the other. The usual definition of *puthujjana* is "one of the many folk," linking it with the first of the above-mentioned meanings. However, a case can be made for the second meaning also. In this analysis, the *puthujjana* is one who believes himself to be separate from the rest of humankind; one who believes he has a self to be protected, promoted and pampered. It is this assumption which leads to so much that is disruptive in society.

Violent tendencies link, at this point, with the defilement of *moha* (delusion): delusion in terms of a misunderstanding of *anicca* and *anatta.* The latter states that there is no abiding, unchanging substance within the human being. Men and women are verbs rather than nouns, causal processes rather than unchanging souls. Buddhism does not deny that there is a person, but it reformulates the definition of what constitutes a person to embrace continuity rather than static entity. As the sound of the lute cannot be found within the lute as it is taken apart, so the "I am" cannot be found in the human personality when it is dissected into the five *khandhas.*

Much anger and violence stem from the felt need to defend what is seen to be one's own or to grasp personal gain. It is a need which sees the gain of others as a threat to personal power and the rights of others as an attack on personal prestige. This is none other than the fault of the *puthujjana,* a failure to see the truth of *anatta* and the interdependence of all phenomena. It is this failure which leads to the self becoming the touchstone and measuring rule for every perception and judgment. It is the failure which leads to the urge to be violent in defense of needs and seeming rights. The Aggañña Sutta shows this ego illusion manifesting itself in the form of competitive individualism. That the ego illusion and *tanha* feed on one another is a theme found in many texts:

Monks, I will teach you the craving that ensnares, that floats along, that is far flung, that clings to one, by which this world is smothered, enveloped, tangled like a ball of thread, covered as with blight, twisted up like a grass rope, so that it does not pass beyond the Constant Round, the Downfall, the Way of Woe, the Ruin...

Monks, when there is the thought: "I am" — there come to be the thoughts: "I am in this world; I am thus; I am otherwise; I am not eternal; I am eternal; Should I be? Should I be in this world? Should I be thus? Should I be otherwise? May I become. May I become in this world. May I become thus. May I become otherwise. I shall become. I shall become otherwise." These are the eighteen thoughts which are haunted by craving *(tanhavicaritani)* concerning the inner self *(ajjhattikassa).*

One result of this interdependent feeding, the Buddhist texts assert, is disruption in society.

Another important area of study is the mechanism through which the "I" notion helps to generate unwholesome states. Buddhism sees a danger in the view of some schools of psychology that there is a creative use of the concept of self. In this respect, the Pali term *"papañca,"* commonly translated as proliferation, is important. The Madhupindika Sutta declares *papañca* to be the root of taking up weapons, and the defeat of *papañca*is the way to end such violence:

This is itself an end to the propensity to ignorance, this is itself an end of taking a weapon, of quarreling, contending, disputing, accusation, slander, lying speech.

As the previous analysis in this chapter points out, discrimination is central to the Buddhist approach and therefore generalizations such as the above need to be studied carefully. There is no doubt, however, that *papañca* is central to a Buddhist psychology of violence and to an understanding of the danger in the "I am" notion.

A study by Bhikkhu Nanananda, *Concept and Reality,* gives extensive coverage to the term *"papañca"*. He puts forward the view that it is linked with the final stage of sense cognition and that it signifies a "a spreading out, a proliferation" in the realm of concepts, a tendency for the conceptual process to run riot and obscure the true reality of things. He makes much use of the above-quoted Madhupindika Sutta and quotes the following:

Visual consciousness, brethren, arises because of eye and visible forms; the meeting of the three is sensory impingement; because of sensory impingement arises feeling *(vedana);* what one feels, one perceives *(sanjanati);* what one perceives, one reasons about *(vitakketi);* what one reasons about, one turns into*papañca (papañceti);* what one turns into *papañca,* due to that *papañca-sañña-sankha* assail him in regard to visible forms cognizable by the eye belonging to the past, the future and the present.

The same is said of the other senses.

Nanananda points out that a grammatical analysis of the above reveals that the process of perception involves deliberate activity up until *papañceti.* After this, deliberation vanishes. The subject becomes the object. The person who reasons conceptually becomes the victim of his own perceptions and thought constructions. So Nanananda writes:

Like the legendary resurrected tiger which devoured the magician who restored it to life out of its skeletal bones, the concepts and linguistic conventions overwhelm the worldling who evolved them. At the final and crucial stage of sense-perception, the concepts are, as it were, invested with an objective character.

His analysis is of immense significance to the study of how certain negative and destructive tendencies can grow in society; how objective perception and reason can seem to fade before the force of what might be irrational and obsessive. He roots the cause in the nature of language in the minds of persons governed by *tanha, mana* and*ditthi* — craving, conceit (the tendency to measure oneself against others), and views — which in themselves flow from ego-consciousness. *Papañca,* according to this analysis, manifests itself through *tanha, mana* and *ditthi.* It underlies each of these qualities and breeds conflict in society.

To look at the process in more detail: The conventions of language enter near the beginning of the process of sense perception, at the point where feeling gives rise to mental activity and concepts. The mind, if unchecked, will attempt to place order on its feelings through language. This language immediately introduces the duality of subject and object, subject and feeling. The "I" enters with "I feel aversion" or "I feel attraction" or "I like this" or" I don't like this." This emphasis on the "I" is predetermined by the very nature of language and reinforces the strength of the feeling and the tendency for the person to identify completely with what is felt. What seems to happen after that is that language takes on a dynamism of its own. Concepts proliferate and leave the empirical behind, under the driving force of *tanha, mana* and *ditthi.* For instance, the observation, "I feel aversion" might lead to further thoughts such as:

> I am right to feel aversion... Therefore, the object is inherently worthy of aversion... So, the object must threaten me and others... Therefore the objects must be got rid of... I cannot survive unless the object is annihilated from my sphere of vision and feeling... It is my duty to annihilate this for my sake and the sake of others.

Thus the entrance of "I" leads to the urge to protect the wishes of the ego and what is ego-based becomes a seemingly rational decision about duty. The above is a purely hypothetical progression, yet it is not an implausible one. It illustrates the way in which thought progresses further and further away from what is empirically observed. Speculation enters as the mind attempts to reason. Eventually, as the thought process develops further, what might appear to be reason cloaks obsession which, in turn, can make the person a victim of the apparent logic of language.

Kant in his *Critique of Pure Reason* seems to adopt a similar point of view. He challenged the view that speculative metaphysics using the categories of pure reason could extend our knowledge of reality. He attacked particularly those theologians who believed that the existence of God could be proved through logic alone. There was, he claimed, an irresistible impulse of the mind towards seeking unification and synthesis which led to the illegitimate use of language. It is this which is particularly relevant to this study. For instance, he posited that the mind assumed an unconditional personal ego just because all representations were unified by the "I think" construction. It also assumed a concept of God because of the drive to find an unconditioned unity. Such concepts, Kant felt, arose through the impulse of the mind and passed beyond the legitimate purview of language. It passed beyond the perceptions which could add knowledge and were not based on truly empirical data. Therefore, they could not give statements with any factual reality.

Kant grasped that there was an irresistible impulse which led to concepts taking on an unwarranted life of their own. Buddhism says that these concepts can generate obsessions, victimize the person who believes he or she is thinking logically, and lead to disruption in society. What is lost in the process is the ability to see objectively and value the empirical through senses unclouded by craving, conceit and views, or by greed, hatred and delusion.

Papañca, fed and generated by *tanha,* is therefore central to the theme of violence in the thoughts and actions of human beings. Buddhism suggests that the human person can become the victim of obsessive actions, thoughts and inclinations. It holds that the drift towards violence within one person or within society, especially if a communal or cultural obsession has arisen, may become an inevitable causal process unless the inner mechanism is discovered. Related to this is the danger and motivating force of dogmatic and speculative views as one of the roots of violence

— the *ditthi,* connected in the above analysis with *papañca.* In his advice to the Kalamas and to Bhaddiya, the Buddha said:

Be not mislead by report or tradition or hearsay. Be not misled by proficiency in the Collections, nor by mere logic or inference, nor after considering reasons, nor after reflection on or approval of some theory, nor because it fits becoming, nor by the thought: the recluse is revered by us.

Here, logic and inference are deemed to be as dangerous as what is passed on by doubtful report and tradition. The same approach is seen in the Brahmajala Sutta where a number of mistaken views, according to Buddhist analysis, are discussed. *Tanha*is seen as the root of these but logic and inference are also mentioned.

In the following, the question of conflict in relation to dogmatic views is more clearly expressed. The Buddha points out the danger of saying, "This is indeed the truth, all else is falsehood" *(idam-eva saccam, mogham-aññam).* For dispute is the result and: "If there is dispute, there is contention; if there is contention, there is trouble; if there is trouble there is vexation." Adhering dogmatically to views is a form of *papañca,* a particularly dangerous form. Several suttas in the Sutta Nipata take up this theme: the Pasura Sutta and the Kalahavivada Sutta, for instance. The former speaks of the person who goes forth roaring, looking for a rival to contest with, filled with pride and arrogance over his theories. A battle-like situation is implied, an attitude closely allied to that which actually results in warfare and armed struggle. Contemporary struggles in the world give ample evidence to prove that war and struggle are caused by the conflict of ideas, ideologies and concepts. They show how powerful and charismatic a force ideas can be. Whether it is nationalism, ethnicity or religion, groups can be pushed towards violence in defense of them. Buddhist analysis points out that some ideologies which might appear logical could, in fact, be the fruit of *papañca.* Adherents may be convinced of their truth but they might have progressed far from analysis based on empirical data.

In the above analysis of the roots of violence, two broad areas have been studied: the external and the internal, the environmental and psychological. Yet the two are not separate. They interconnect and feed one another, just as external sense objects interconnect with the senses, giving rise to consciousness and psychological processes. If a people's environment is unhealthy, corrupt or unjust, the seeds are sown for violent resistance, through the growth of motivating ideologies which take on a life of their own as they grip the minds of those who are being oppressed. If the environment is excessively competitive, consumer-oriented and materialistic, *tanha* will quickly arise, develop and expand into obsessive patterns of greed, taking over and dominating the perception of people who find themselves victims of craving rather than masters of their own perceptual processes. The step to violence is then small. If other elements are present, such as a group without access to the wealth visible in others, discrimination against minorities or racism, then the drive towards violence will be more rapid.

THE BUDDHA IS THE GREATEST EXPONENT OF NON-VIOLENCE

The Buddha, when He converted a non-Buddhist, got the convert to promise five things, These five promises are called ' Panca Sila ' (The Five Precepts).

The first promise of these five is that ' I promise not to kill any living being. ' This indicates that the primary quality a Buddhist should possess is non-violence. The Buddha denounced all forms of violence. The Buddha asked loving-kindness to be extended not only to men, but even to all animals.

All are frightened of punishment. All dread death. Therefore, since one is frightened of punishment and death, taking one's own self as the example, refrain from killing others. You must not destroy.

All are frightened of punishment. All love life. Therefore, since one is frightened of punishment and death, taking one's own self as the example, refrain from killing others. You must not destroy. Only the Buddha and Mahavira showed kindness to animals. Other religious leaders did not. Those other religious leaders encouraged the killing and eating of animals. In consequence, those other religious teachers will not receive the respect of animals.

Mahavira went beyond the extremes of non-violence. His main Doctrine is non-violence. He thought even water had life. He considers the sailing of ships and canoes suppressing water, as a sin. Since minor insects get killed when we breathe in and breathe out, he suggested that we should cover our nose and mouth with a piece of cloth. He does not even approve of ' tikotiparisuddha mamsa ' (flesh that is harmless in three ways) which has been allowed by the Budhha.

As a result of this, no follower of Jainism take meat or fish. Due to this extreme non-violence, Jainism became a difficult religion to practise. Jainism never spread outside India. Since insects get killed even in the cultivation process, the Jains do not indulge in any other industries or crafts, than trade.

10

Philosophy of Buddhist

The Four Noble Truths are one of the most fundamental Buddhist teachings, they appear many times throughout the most ancient Buddhist texts, the Pali Canon. They are among the truths the Buddha realised during his enlightenment experience. Why the Buddha taught in this way is illuminated by the social context of the time in which he lived. The Buddha was a Sramaa, a wandering ascetic whose "aim was to discover the truth and attain happiness". The Buddha claimed to have achieved this aim while under a bodhi tree near the Ganges River; the Four Noble Truths are a formulation of his understanding of "suffering", the fundamental cause of all suffering, the escape from suffering and what effort a person can go to so that they themselves can "attain happiness."

These truths are not expressed as a theory or tentative idea, rather the Buddha says:

"These Four Noble Truths, monks, are actual, unerring, not otherwise. Therefore, they are called noble truths."

The Buddha said that he taught them...

"...because it is beneficial, it belongs to the fundamentals of the holy life, it leads to disenchantment, to dispassion, to cessation, to peace, to direct knowledge, to enlightenment, to Nirvana. That is why I have declared it."

This teaching was the basis of the Buddha's first discourse after his enlightenment.

Mahayana Buddhism contains within itself an alternative version of the Four Noble Truths, in which the immortality of the Buddha occupies a central position.

Four Noble Truths

1. *Suffering (Dukkha)*: Now this, monks, is the noble truth of suffering: Birth is suffering, aging is suffering, sickness is suffering, death is suffering; union with what is displeasing is suffering; separation from what is pleasing is suffering; not to get what one wants is suffering; in brief, the five aggregates subject to clinging are suffering.
2. *Source of Suffering (Samudaya)*: Now this, monks, is the noble truth of the origin of suffering: It is this craving which leads to renewed existence, accompanied by delight and lust, seeking delight here and there; that is, craving for sensual pleasures, craving for existence, craving for extermination.
3. *The Cessation of Suffering (Nirodha)*: Now this, monks, is the noble truth of the cessation of suffering: It is the remainder less fading away and cessation of that same craving, the giving up and relinquishing of it, freedom from it and non-reliance on it.
4. *The Way Leading to the Cessation of Suffering (Magga)*: Now this, monks, is the noble truth of the way leading to the cessation of suffering: It is this Noble Eightfold Path; that is, right view, right intention, right speech, right action, right livelihood, right effort, right mindfulness, right concentration."

VARIANT FOUR NOBLE TRUTHS IN MAHAYANA BUDDHISM

Certain major Mahayana sutras, including the Mahaparinirvana Sutra and the Angulimaliya Sutra, present variant versions of the Four Noble Truths in line with their own metaphysics and soteriology. In the Mahaparinirvana Sutra, the Buddha declares that:

the Truth of Suffering relates to the failure to recognise the eternity of the Buddha;

the Truth of the Cause of Suffering concerns the perversion and distortion of the True Dharma;

The Truth of the Cessation of Suffering relates to the correct meditative cultivation of the tathagatagarbha (indwelling Buddha Essence in all beings) and not erroneously viewing it as non-Self and empty; cessation of suffering also arises with the elimination of inner defilements, when one can then enter into the Buddhic Essence within oneself: "When the afflictions have been eradicated, then one will perceive entry into the tathagata-garbha"; the Truth of the Path to the Cessation of Suffering entails envisioning the Buddha, Dharma and Sangha as eternal, immovable and indestructible.

The Angulimaliya Sutra similarly emphasises the seeing and knowing of the Buddha's eternality, immutability and peace as the key factors in liberation from suffering; failure to see this eternal nature of ultimate reality is said to constitute the primary cause of beings' continued entrapment in the sufferings of samsara.

THE FIVE PRECEPTS

The five precepts constitute the basic Buddhist code of ethics, undertaken by lay followers of the Buddha Gautama in the Theravadin tradition.

The laity undertake to follow these training rules at the same time as they become Buddhists, taking refuge in the Triple Gem: In the Buddha (teacher), in the Dharma (teaching) and thirdly in the Sangha (community of monks and nuns). A lay practitioner who has undertaken the precepts is called an Upasaka.

The Buddha is said to have taught the five precepts out of compassion, not out of any desire to control his followers and so they are to be undertaken voluntarily rather than as commandments from a god. They are to be seen as guidelines to how one who is awakened lives, not as mere moral injunctions imposed from outside and to be obeyed literally at all times.

The Buddha said that undertaking the precepts is a gift to oneself and others. He also described the rewards of following the precepts and the bad consequences of breaking the precepts.

The following are the five precepts rendered in English and then Pali.

1. I undertake the precept to refrain from taking the life (killing) of living beings.
   Panatipata veramani sikkhapadam samadiyami
2. I undertake the precept to refrain from stealing.
   Adinnadana veramani sikkhapadam samadiyami
3. I undertake the precept to refrain from sexual misconduct (adultery, rape, etc.).
   Kamesu micchacara veramani sikkhapadam samadiyami
4. I undertake the precept to refrain from false speech (lying).
   Musavada veramani sikkhapadam samadiyami
5. I undertake the precept to refrain from intoxicants which lead to heedlessness.
   Sura meraya majja pamadatthana veramani sikkhapadam samadiyami

Chinese Version of Five Precepts

The Chinese version as found in the Supplement to the Canon hardly differs:

1. As the Buddha refrained from killing until the end of his life, so I too will refrain from killing until the end of my life.
2. As the Buddha refrained from stealing until the end of his life, so I too will refrain from stealing until the end of my life.
3. As the Buddha refrained from sexual misconduct until the end of his life, so I too will refrain from sexual misconduct until the end of my life.
4. As the Buddha refrained from false speech until the end of his life, so I too will refrain from false speech until the end of my life.

5. As the Buddha refrained from alcohol until the end of his life, so I too will refrain from alcohol until the end of my life.

NOBLE EIGHTFOLD PATH

The Noble Eightfold Path is, in the Buddhist tradition as taught by the Buddha Sakyamuni, considered to be the way that leads to the end of suffering. It forms the fourth part of the Four Noble Truths, which are the most fundamental Buddhist teachings. The Noble Eightfold Path is essentially a practical guide of ethics, mental rehabilitation and mind deconditioning and is believed, by Buddhists, to result in an end to dukkha, or suffering, which is a goal that has informed and driven the entire Buddhist tradition since its inception 2500 years ago. As the name indicates, there are eight elements in the Noble Eightfold Path and these are further subdivided into three basic categories as follows:

- Wisdom (Sanskrit: prajna, Pali: panna)
  1. Right understanding
  2. Right intention
- Ethical conduct (Sanskrit: sila, Pali: sila)
  3. Right speech
  4. Right action
  5. Right livelihood
- Mental discipline (Sanskrit and Pali: samadhi)
  6. Right effort
  7. Right mindfulness
  8. Right concentration

In all of the elements of the Noble Eightfold Path, the word "right" is a translation of the word samyanc (Sanskrit) or samma (Pali), which denotes completion, togetherness and coherence and which can also carry the sense of "perfect" or "ideal".

Though the path is numbered one through eight, it is generally not considered to be a series of linear steps through which one must progress; rather, as the Buddhist monk and scholar Walpola Rahula points out, the eight elements of the Noble Eightfold Path "are to be developed more or less simultaneously, as far as possible according to the capacity of each individual. They are all linked together and each helps the cultivation of the others".

In Buddhist symbology, the Noble Eightfold Path is often represented by means of the Dharma wheel (Sanskrit: dharmacakra, Pali: dhammacakka), whose eight spokes represent the eight elements of the path.

Wisdom (Prajna-Panna)

The "wisdom" subdivision of the Noble Eightfold Path is constituted by those elements that refer primarily to the mental or cognitive aspect of a Buddhist practitioner's practice.

Right understanding

Right understanding can also be translated as "right view" or "right perspective". This element of the Noble Eightfold Path refers explicitly to the Four Noble Truths of Buddhism, stating that these must be fully understood by the Buddhist practitioner. In the Mahasatipathana Sutta, one of the Buddha Sakyamuni's discourses, right understanding is explained directly in terms of the Four Noble Truths:

> *And what, O bhikkhus, is right understanding? To understand suffering, to understand the origination of suffering, to understand extinction of suffering, to understand the path leading to the extinction of suffering; this is called right understanding.*

Additionally, right understanding is sometimes considered to encompass an understanding of the Buddhist idea of the non-permanence, or even nonexistence, of the self, an idea known as anatman in Sanskrit and anatta in Pali.

There are two stages for every stage of the eightfold path, a preliminary stage and the higher stages gradually obtained through the journey towards enlightenment. The preliminary stage of Right Views or right understanding is the knowledge of the Four Noble Truths. The higher stage require more than the comprehension of the Four Noble Truths, it also includes the knowledge and understanding of the not-self doctorine, imperminence, dependent origination, the five aggregates, kamma and rebirth and so on.

Right Thought

Right thought can also be translated as "right intention", "right resolve", or "right aspiration". This element of the Noble Eightfold Path deals, fundamentally, with the Buddhist practitioner's reasons for practising Buddhism and with his or her outlook towards the world. It enjoins renunciation of worldly things and an accordant greater commitment to spiritual matters; good will; and a commitment to non-violence, or ahimsa, towards other living beings. In the Magga-vibhanga Sutta, it is simply explained as follows:

> *And what is right thought? Being resolved on renunciation, on freedom from ill will, on harmlessness: This is called right thought.*

Ethical Conduct (Sila-Sila)

The "ethical conduct" (Sila) subdivision of the Noble Eightfold Path is constituted by those elements that are driven by and ultimately conducive to the Buddhist idea of karuga, which is generally translated as compassion and somewhat akin to the Christian notion of agape, or "unconditional love". This aspect of the Noble Eightfold Path is the most outward-oriented aspect of the Noble Eightfold Path insofar as it deals directly with a Buddhist practitioner's relationship with other members of his or her society.

Right Speech

Right speech (samyag-vac, samma-vaca), as the name implies, deals with the way in which a Buddhist practitioner would best make use of his or her words. In the Magga-vibhanga Sutta, this aspect of the Noble Eightfold Path is explained as follows:

> *And what is right speech? Abstaining from lying, abstaining from divisive speech, abstaining from abusive speech, abstaining from idle chatter: This, monks, is called right speech.*

Walpola Rahula glosses this by stating that not engaging in such "forms of wrong and harmful speech" ultimately means that "one naturally has to speak the truth, has to use words that are friendly and benevolent, pleasant and gentle, meaningful and useful".

Right Action

Right action (samyak-karmanta, samma-kammanta) can also be translated as "right conduct" and, as the name implies, deals with the proper way in which a Buddhist practitioner would act in his or her daily life. In the Magga-vibhanga Sutta, this aspect of the Noble Eightfold Path is explained as follows:

> *And what, monks, is right action? Abstaining from taking life, abstaining from stealing, abstaining from unchastity: This, monks, is called right action.*

Together with the idea of ahimsa and right speech, right action constitutes the Five Precepts (Sanskrit: pancasila, Pali: pancasila), which form the fundamental ethical code undertaken by lay followers of Buddhism and which are as follows:

1. To refrain from destroying living beings.
2. To refrain from stealing.
3. To refrain from sexual misconduct (adultery, rape, etc.).
4. To refrain from false speech (lying).
5. To refrain from intoxicants which lead to heedlessness.

Right Livelihood

Right livelihood (samyag-ajiva, samma-ajiva) is based around the concept of ahimsa, or harmlessness and essentially states that Buddhist practitioners ought not to engage in trades or occupations which, either directly or indirectly, result in harm to other living beings. Such occupations include "trading in arms and lethal weapons, intoxicating drinks, poisons, killing animals, [and] cheating", among others. "Business in human beings"-such as slave trading and prostitution-is also forbidden, as are several other dishonest means of gaining wealth, such as "scheming, persuading, hinting, belittling, [and] pursuing gain with gain".

Mental Development (Samadhi)

The "mental development" subdivision of the Noble Eightfold Path is constituted by those elements that deal with how a Buddhist practitioner can best go about shaping his or her outlook towards the world.

Right Effort

Right effort (samyag-vyayama, samma-vayama) can also be translated as "right endeavour" and involves the Buddhist practitioner's continuous effort to, essentially, keep his or her mind free of thoughts that might impair his or her ability to realize or put into practice the other elements of the Noble Eightfold Path; for example, wishing ill towards another living being would contradict the injunction-contained in the "Right thought" element-to have good will towards others and the "Right effort" element refers to the process of attempting to root out such an ill wish and replace it with a good wish. The Buddhist monk Ajahn Chah, of the Thai forest tradition of Theravada Buddhism, described right effort as follows:

> *Proper effort is not the effort to make something particular happen. It is the effort to be aware and awake in each moment, the effort to overcome laziness and defilement, the effort to make each activity of our day meditation.*

By making right effort, a Buddhist practitioner is considered to be engaging in an effort that is wholesome in terms of karma; that is, in terms of that effort's ultimate consequences to the practitioner.

Right Mindfulness

Right mindfulness, also translated as "right memory", together with right concentration, is concerned broadly with the practice of Buddhist meditation. Roughly speaking, "mindfulness" refers to the practice of keeping the mind alert to phenomena as they are affecting the body and mind. In the Magga-vibhanga Sutta, this aspect of the Noble Eightfold Path is explained as follows:

And what, monks, is right mindfulness?

(i) There is the case where a monk remains focused on (his/her) body in and of itself... ardent, aware and mindful... having already put aside worldly desire and aversion.

(ii) (He/she) remains focused on feelings in and of themselves... ardent, aware and mindful... having already put aside worldly desire and aversion.

(iii) (He/she) remains focused on the mind in and of itself... ardent, aware and mindful... having already put aside worldly desire and aversion.

(iv) (He/she) remains focused on mental qualities in and of themselves... ardent, aware and mindful... having already put aside worldly desire and aversion.

This, monks, is called right mindfulness.

Bhikkhu Bodhi, a monk of the Theravadin tradition, further glosses the concept of mindfulness as follows:

The mind is deliberately kept at the level of bare attention, a detached observation of what is happening within us and around us in the present moment. In the practice of right mindfulness the mind is trained to remain in the present, open, quiet and alert, contemplating the present event. All judgments and interpretations have to be suspended, or if they occur, just registered and dropped.

Right Concentration

Right concentration (samyak-samadhi, samma-samadhi), together with right mindfulness, is concerned broadly with the practice of Buddhist meditation.

And what, monks, is right concentration?

(i) Quite withdrawn from sensuality, withdrawn from unwholesome states, a monk enters in the first jhana: rapture and pleasure born from detachment, accompanied by movement of the mind onto the object and retention of the mind on the object.

(ii) With the stilling of directed thought and evaluation, (he/she) enters and remains in the second jhana: rapture and pleasure born of concentration; fixed single-pointed awareness free from movement of the mind onto the object and retention of the mind on the object; assurance.

(iii) With the fading of rapture, (he/she) remains in equanimity, mindful and fully aware and physically sensitive of pleasure. (He/She) enters and remains in the third jhana which the Noble Ones declare to be "Equanimous and mindful, (he/she) has a pleasurable abiding."

(iv) With the abandoning of pleasure and pain...as with the earlier disappearance of elation and distress...(he/she) enters and remains in the fourth jhana: purity of equanimity and mindfulness, neither in pleasure nor in pain.

This, monks, is called right concentration.

The Ninth and Tenth Elements

In the Great Forty Sutra (Mahacattarisaka Sutta), which appears in the Pali Canon, the Buddha explains that cultivation of the Eightfold Path leads to the development of two further stages once enlightenment has been reached. These also fall under the category of panna and are Right Knowledge (sammanana) and Right Liberation (or Right Release; sammavimutti). Some consider Right Association as an implicit ninth aspect of the Path.

The Noble Eightfold Path and Cognitive Psychology

From the standpoint of modern cognitive psychology, the Noble Eightfold Path can be seen as rooted in what is called cognitive dissonance, which is the perception of incompatibility between two cognitions. In the essay "Buddhism Meets Western Science", Gay Watson explains this dissonance as it relates to Buddhist teaching:

> *Buddhism has always been concerned with feelings, emotions, sensations and cognition. The Buddha points both to cognitive and emotional causes of suffering. The emotional cause is desire and its negative opposite, aversion. The cognitive cause is ignorance of the way things truly occur, or of three marks of existence: that all things are unsatisfactory, impermanent and without essential self.*

The Noble Eightfold Path is, from this psychological viewpoint, an attempt to resolve this dissonance by changing patterns of thought and behaviour. It is for this reason that the first element of the path is right understanding, which is how one's mind views the world. Under the wisdom (panna) subdivision of the Noble Eightfold Path, this worldview is intimately connected with the second element, right thought, which concerns the patterns of thought and intention that controls one's actions. These elements can be seen at work, for example, in the opening verses of the Dhammapada:

Preceded by perception are mental states,
For them is perception supreme,
From perception have they sprung.
If, with perception polluted, one speaks or acts,
Thence suffering follows
As a wheel the draught ox's foot.
Preceded by perception are mental states,
For them is perception supreme,
From perception have they sprung.
If, with tranquil perception, one speaks or acts,
Thence ease follows
As a shadow that never departs.

Thus, by wilfully altering one's distorted worldview-as well as the behaviours stemming from that worldview-and bringing out "tranquil perception" in the place of "perception polluted", one is enabled to potentially escape from suffering and develop one's mind. Watson points this out from a psychological standpoint:

THREE JEWELS

The Three Jewels, also rendered as Three Treasures, Three Refuges or Triple Gem are the three things that Buddhists give themselves to and in return look toward for guidance, in the process known as taking refuge.

Taking refuge in the Three Jewels is central to Buddhist lay and monastic ordination ceremonies, as originated by Gautama Buddha.

Taking refuge in the Triple Gem is generally considered to make one officially a Buddhist. Thus, in many Theravada Buddhist communities, the following Pali chant, the Vandana Ti-sarana is often recited by both monks and lay people:

- Buddham saranam gacchami

I go for refuge in the Buddha

- Dhammam saranam gacchami
  I go for refuge in the Dharma
- Sangham saranam gacchami
  I go for refuge in the Sangha

The Mahayana Chinese/Japanese version differs only slightly from the Theravada:

I take refuge in the Buddha, wishing for all sentient beings to understand the great way and make the greatest vow.

I take refuge in the Dharma, wishing for all sentient beings to deeply delve into the Sutra Pitaka, gaining an ocean of knowledge.

I take refuge in the Sangha, wishing all sentient beings to lead the congregation in harmony, entirely without obstruction.

Importance of the Triple Gem

The Triple Gem is important and is one of the major practices of mental "reflection" in Buddhism, we reflect on the true qualities of the Buddha, Dharma and Sangha. These qualities are called the Mirror of the Dharma in the Mahaparinibbana Sutta and help us attain the true "mind like a mirror".

Reflection in the Mirror of the Dharma

The qualities of the Buddha, Dharma and Sangha are frequently repeated in the ancient texts. It is a Buddhist practise to reflect upon them.

- *The Buddha:* "The Blessed One is an Arahant, perfectly enlightened, accomplished in true knowledge and conduct, fortunate, knower of the world, unsurpassed leader of persons to be tamed, teacher of devas and humans, the Enlightened One, the Blessed One."

  In some traditions, the Buddha as refuge, is known as the historical Buddha and also 'the full development of mind', in other words, the full development of one's highest potential *i.e.* recognition of mind and the completion or full development of one's inherent qualities and activities.
- *The Dharma:* "The Dhamma is well expounded by the

Blessed One, directly visible, immediate, inviting one to come and see, applicable, to be personally experienced by the wise."

Refuge in the Dharma in the Vajrayana tradition includes reference not only to the words of the Buddha, but to the living experience of realization and teachings of fully realized practitioners. In Tibetan Buddhism, it includes both the Kangyur (the teaching of the Buddha) and the Tengyur (the commentaries by realized practioners) and in an intangible way also includes the living transmission of those masters, which can also be very inspiring.

- *The Sangha:* "The Sangha of the Blessed One's disciples is practising the good way, practising the straight way, practising the true way, practising the proper way; that is, the four pairs of persons, the eight types of individuals-This Sangha of the Blessed One's disciples is worthy of gifts, worthy of hospitality, worthy of offerings, worthy of reverential salutation, the unsurpassed field of merit for the world."

In the Vajrayana, a more liberal definition of Sangha can include all practitioners who are actively using the Buddhas teachings to benefit themselves and/or others. It can be more strictly defined as the 'Realized Sangha' or 'Arya-Sangha', in other words, practitioners and historical students of the Buddha who have fully realized the nature of their mind, also known as realized Boddhisatvas; and 'Ordinary Sangha', which can loosely mean practitioners and students of the Buddha who are using the same methods and working towards the same goal.

In the Vajrayana traditions, there is another very important and expanded aspect of the Refuge, the refuge in the teacher. This can be understood on many levels including what is called the Three Roots-the Root of Blessing, Root of Methods and Root of Protection. Another way to understand this is as the Body (Sangha), Speech (Dharma) and Mind (Buddha) of the Buddha. The teacher has a prominent place in the Vajrayana, as without his personal permission and guidance, a practitioner cannot achieve proper spiritual progress.

Why is it called the Triple Gem?

In Buddhism, the following three are called Gems (Ratna) as they are invaluable:

- Buddha, who, depending on one's interpretation, can mean the Historical Buddha, Shakyamuni, or the Buddha nature or ideal within all beings;
- Dharma, which is the Teachings of the Buddha.
- Sangha, The Community of those great people who have attained Enlightenment. So that those people (Sangha) will help you to attain Enlightenment.

The three gems are so called since amongst all gems, the Buddha gem and Dharma gem are considered incomparable in value as they are not material, so cannot be created, destroyed or changed in any way. Buddha's mind in his earth body or sambhogakaya is frequently associated with the greatest gem of all, the diamond. In the Anguttara Nikaya (3:25), Buddha talks about the diamond mind:

These three types of persons are found in the world: One with a mind like an open sore; one with a mind like a flash of lightning; one with a mind like a diamond.

- One who is irascible and very irritable, displaying anger, hatred and sulkiness; such a one is said to be a person with a mind like an open sore.
- One who understands the Four Noble Truths correctly is said to have a mind like a flash of lightning.
- One who has destroyed the mind-intoxicating defilements and realized the liberation of mind and the liberation by knowledge is said to have a mind like a diamond

With this we understand that to take refuge in the Buddha is to take refuge in the mind like a diamond, the hardest natural substance that can cut through all delusion.

The Three Gems when used in the process of taking refuge, become the Three Refuges.

The expression Three Gems are found in the earliest Buddhist literature of the Pali Canon, besides other works there is one sutta in the Sutta-nipata, called the Ratana-sutta which contains a series of verses on the Jewels in the Buddha, Dharma and Sangha. In the Ratana-sutta, all the qualities of the Sangha mentioned are attributes of the Buddha's enlightened disciples.

The Three Refuges occur very frequently in the ancient Buddhist Texts and here the Sangha is used more broadly to refer to either the Sangha of Bhikkhus, or the Sangha of Bhikkhunis. "I go to Master Gautama for refuge and to the Dhamma and to the Sangha of Bhikkhus."

THREE MARKS OF EXISTENCE

After much meditation, the Buddha concluded that everything in the physical world (plus everything in the phenomenology of psychology) is marked by three characteristics, known as the three characteristics of existence, three signs of being or Dharma Seals. Together the three characteristics of existence are called ti-lakkhana, in Pali; or tri-laksana, in Sanskrit.

- Dukkha (Sanskrit duhkha) or unsatisfactoriness. Nothing found in the physical world or even the psychological realm can bring lasting deep satisfaction.
- Anicca (Sanskrit anitya) or impermanence. This refers not only to the fact that all conditioned things eventually cease to exist, but also that all conditioned things are in a constant state of flux. (Visualize a leaf growing on a tree. It dies and falls off the tree but is soon replaced by a new leaf.)
- Anatta (Sanskrit anatman) impersonality, or non-Self. The human personality, "soul", or Self, is a conventional appellation applied to the assembly of physical and psychological components, each individually subject to constant flux; there is no central core (or essence); this is somewhat similar to a bundle theory of mind or soul.

There is often a fourth Dharma Seal mentioned:

- Nirvana is peace. Nirvana is the 'other shore' from Samsara.

By bringing the three (or four) seals into moment-to-moment experience through concentrated awareness, we are said to achieve Wisdom-the third of the three higher trainings-the way out of

Samsara. In this way we can identify that, according to Sutra, the recipe (or formula) for leaving Samsara is achieved by a deep-rooted change to our Weltanschauung.

According to the Buddhist tradition, all phenomena (dharmas) are marked by three characteristics, sometimes referred to as the Dharma seals, that is dukkha (suffering), anicca (impermanence) and anatta (non-Self).

Dukkha

> *Whatever is impermanent is subject to change. Whatever is subject to change is subject to suffering.*
> *—The Buddha*

Striving for what we desire, we may experience stress and suffering-dukkha. Getting what we desired, we may find delight and happiness. Soon after, the novelty may wear out and we may get bored with it. Boredom is a form of dissatisfaction (or suffering) and to escape from it, we divert ourselves from such boredom by indulging in a pursuit of new forms of pleasure. Sometimes not willing to relinquish objects that we are already disinterested in, we start to collect and amass possessions instead of sharing with others who may have better use in it than we do. Boredom is a result of change. Change of our interest in that object of desire that so captivated us in the first place.

If we do not get bored already, then change may instead occur in the object of desire. Silverware may become tarnished, a new dress worn thin or a gadget gone obsolete. Or it may become broken, causing us to grieve. In some cases it may get lost or stolen. In some cases, we may worry about such losses even before they happen. Husbands and wives worry about losing their spouses even though their partners are faithful. Unfortunately, sometimes our very worry and fear drives us to act irrationally, resulting in distrust and breaking up of the very relationship that we cherished so much.

While we like changes such as becoming an adult when we are in our teens, we dislike the change called aging. While we strive for change to become rich, we fear the change of retrenchment. We are selective in our attitude towards the transient nature of our very existence. Unfortunately, this transient nature is unselective. We can try to fight it, just as many have tried since beginningless time, only to have our efforts washed away through the passages of time. As a result, we continually experience dissatisfaction or suffering due to the very impermanence of compounded phenomena.

Only in the realm of Nirvana-so Mahayana Buddhism insists-can true and lasting happiness be found. Nirvana is the opposite of the conditional, the transitory and the painful (dukkha), so it does not result in disappointment or deterioration of the state of bliss. Nirvana is the refuge from the otherwise universal tyranny of change and suffering. In other schools of Buddhism, nirvana is not viewed as the goal, but merely as a projection from the state of samsara. According to these schools samsara (confusion) and nirvana (perfection) are two sides of the same coin that must be transcended through diligent practice of meditation.

Anicca

All compounded phenomena (things and experiences) are inconstant, unsteady and impermanent. (Practically) everything is made up of parts and is dependent on the right conditions for its existence. Everything is in constant flux and so conditions and the thing itself is constantly changing. Things are constantly coming into being and ceasing to be. Nothing lasts.

The important point here is that phenomena arise and cease according to (complex) conditions and not according to our whims and fancy. While we have limited ability to effect change to our possessions and surroundings, experience tells us that our feeble attempts are no guarantee that the results of our efforts will be to our likings. More often than not, the results fall short of our expectations.

In Mahayana Buddhism, a caveat is added: one should indeed always meditate on the impermanence and changefulness of compounded structures and phenomena, but one must guard against extending this to the realm of Nirvana, where impermanence holds no sway and eternity alone obtains. To see Nirvana or the Buddha (in his ultimate Dharmakaya nature) as impermanent would be to indulge in "perverted Dharma" and would be seriously to go astray, according to the Buddha's final Mahayana doctrines. Other schools of Buddhism, however, feel uneasy with such a teaching.

Anatta

In Indian philosophy, the concept of a Self is called atman (that is, "soul" or metaphysical Self), which refers to an unchanging, permanent essence conceived by virtue of existence. This concept and the related concept of Brahman, the Vedantic monistic ideal, which was regarded as an ultimate atman for all beings, were indispensable for mainstream Indian metaphysics, logic and science; for all apparent things there had to be an underlying and persistent reality, akin to a Platonic form. The Buddha rejected all concepts of atman, emphasizing not permanence, but changeability. He taught that all concepts of a substantial personal Self were incorrect and formed in the realm of ignorance.

However, in a number of major Mahayana sutras (*e.g.* the Mahaparinirvana Sutra, the Tathagatagarbha Sutra, the Srimala Sutra, among others), the Buddha is presented as clarifying this teaching by saying that, while the skandhas (constituents of the ordinary body and mind) are not the Self, there does truly exist an eternal, unchanging, blissful Buddha-essence in all sentient beings, which is the uncreated and deathless Buddha-nature ("Buddha-dhatu") or "True Self" of the Buddha himself. This immaculate Buddhic Self (atman) is in no way to be construed as a mundane, impermanent, suffering "ego", of which it is the diametrical opposite. On the other hand, this Buddha-essence or Buddha-nature is also often explained as the potential for achieving Buddhahood, rather than an existing phenomenon one can grasp onto as being me or Self.

It is the opposite of a personalised, samsaric "I" or "mine". The paradox is that as soon as the Buddhist practitioner tries to grasp at this inner Buddha potency and cling to it as though it were his or her ego writ large, it proves elusive. It does not "exist" in the time-space conditioned and finite mode in which mundane things are bodied forth. It is presented by the Buddha in the relevant sutras as ultimately inexplicable, primordially present Reality itself-the living potency for Buddhahood inside all beings. It is finally revealed (in the last of the Buddha's Mahayana sutras, the Nirvana Sutra) not as the circumscribed "non-Self", the clinging ego (which is indeed anatta/anatman), but as the ever-enduring, egoless Great Self or Dharmakaya of the Buddha.

The scriptural evidence of the Nikayas and Agamas is ambivalent with regard to the Buddha's reported views on the existence or otherwise of a permanent Self (atman/atta). Though he is clearly reported to have criticized many of the heterodox concepts concerning an eternal personal Self and to have denied the existence of an eternal Self with regards to any of the constituent elements (skandha) of a being, he is nevertheless not reported to have explicitly denied the existence of a non-personal, permanent Self, contrary to the popular, orthodox view of the Buddha's teachings. Moreover, when the Buddha predicates "anatman" (anatta) with regards to the constituents of a being, there is a grammatical ambivalence in the use of the term.

The most natural interpretation is that he is simply stating that "the constituents are not the Self" rather than "the constituents are devoid of Self". This ambivalence was to prove troublesome to Buddhists after the Buddha's passing. Some of the major schools of Buddhism that developed subsequently maintained the former interpretation, but other influential schools adopted the latter interpretation and took measures to establish their view as the orthodox Buddhist position.

One such proponent of this hard-line "non-Self" position was the monk Nagasena, who appears in the Questions of King Milinda, composed during the period of the Hellenistic Indo-Greek kingdom of the 2nd and 1st centuries BC. In this text, Nagasena demonstrates the concept of absolute 'non-Self' by likening human beings to a chariot and challenges the Greek king "Milinda" (Menander) to find the essence of the chariot. Nagasena states that just as a chariot is made up of a number of things, none of which are the essence of the chariot in isolation, without the other pieces, similarly no one part of a person is a permanent entity; we can be broken up into five constituents-body, sensations, ideation, mental formations and consciousness-the consciousness being closest to the permanent idea of 'Self', but is ever-changing with each new thought according to this viewpoint.

According to some thinkers both in the East and the West, the doctrine of "non-Self", may imply that Buddhism is a form of nihilism or something similar. However, as thinkers like Nagarjuna have clearly pointed out, Buddhism is not simply a rejection of the concept of existence (or of meaning, etc.) but of the hard and fast distinction between existence and non-existence, or rather between being and no-thingness.

Phenomena are not independent from causes and conditions and do not exist as isolated things as we perceive them to be. Philosophers such as Nagarjuna stress that the lack of a permanent, unchanging, substantial Self in beings and things does not mean that they do not experience growth and decay on the relative level. But on the ultimate level of analysis, one cannot distinguish an object from its causes and conditions, or even object and subject. (This is an idea appearing relatively recently in Western science.) Buddhism thus has much more in common with Western empiricism, pragmatism, anti-foundationalism and even poststructuralism than with nihilism.

In the Nikayas, the Buddha and his disciples are commonly found to ask in question or declare "Is that which is impermanent, subject to change, subject to suffering fit to be considered thus: 'This I am, this is mine, this is my self'?" The question which the Buddha posts to his audience is whether compounded phenomena is fit to be considered as self, in which the audience agrees that it is unworthy to be considered so. And in relinquishing such an attachment to compounded phenomena, such a person gives up delight, desire and craving for compounded phenomena and is unbounded by its change. When completely free from attachments, craving or desire to the five aggregates, such a person experiences then transcends the very causes of suffering.

In this way, the insight wisdom or prajna of non-Self gives rise to cessation of suffering and not an intellectual debate over whether a self exists or not.

It is by realizing (not merely understanding intellectually, but making real in one's experience) the three marks of conditioned existence that one develops prajna, which is the antidote to the ignorance that lies at the root of all suffering. From the "tathagatagarbha-Mahayana" perspective (which diverges from the Theravadin understanding of Buddhism), however, a further step is required if full Buddhahood is to be attained: not only seeing what is impermanent, suffering and non-Self in the samsaric sphere, but equally recognising that which is truly Eternal, Blissful, Self and Pure in the transcendental realm-the realm of Mahaparinirvana.

Interpretations of the Three Marks by Various Schools

Some Buddhist traditions assert that Anatta pervades everything and is not limited to personality, or soul. These traditions assert that Nirvana also has the quality of Anatta, but that Nirvana (by definition) is the cessation of Dukkha and Anicca.

In Nagarjuna's MMK XXV:19, he says

There is not the slightest difference

Between Samsara and Nirvana

This verse points us to an interesting stress between dukkha and nirvana, through an argument based in anatta. This specific stress can be seen to be the key to (and possibly source for the development of) the deity yogas of vajrayana.

The sutra path enjoins us to identify the entire world (internally and externally) as samsara-a continual churning of suffering that nobody wants to be part of. Our practice is that of leaving the shores of samsara. On the other hand, we are told that unconditioned, enlightened activity is not actually different from samsara. Whereas the deity yoga of vajrayana enjoins us to identify the entire world as nirvana-a continual play of enlightening activity that everyone wishes to be a part of. Our practice here is that of arriving at the shores of nirvana.

At this level, the distinction between Sutra and Vajrayana remain that of view (departing vs. arriving), but basically the practitioner remains involved in undergoing a transformative development to his or her Weltanschauung and in this context, these practices remain rooted in psychological change, grounded in the development of Samatha, or training in concentration.

However, there are certain practices in Tantra which are not solely concerned with psychological change; these revolve around the basic idea that it is possible to induce deep levels of concentration through psycho-physical methods as a result of special exercises. The purpose remains the same (to achieve liberating view), but the method involves a 'short cut' for the training in Samatha.

DHARMA

Dharma or Dhamma in Buddhism has two primary meanings:

- the teachings of the Buddha which lead to enlightenment
- the constituent factors of the experienced world

In East Asia, the character for Dharma is pronounced fa in Mandarin and ho in Japanese. The Tibetan translation of this term is chos (cho).

Buddha's Teachings

What is called Buddhism in the west has been referred to in India (the teachings' place of origin) and the east generally for many centuries as buddha-dharma. This term has no sectarian connotations but simply means "Path of Awakening" and thus conforms to a universal understanding of dharma.

The status of dharma is regarded variably by different traditions. Some regard it as an ultimate and transcendent truth which is utterly beyond worldly things, somewhat like the Christian logos. Others, who regard the Buddha as simply an enlightened human being, see dharma as the 84,000 different teachings that the Buddha gave to various types of people based on their needs. The teachings are expedient means of raising doubt in the hearer's own cherished beliefs and view of life; when doubt has opened the door to the truth, the teaching can be put aside.

"Dharma" usually refers inclusively not just to the sayings of the Buddha but to the later traditions of interpretation and addition that the various schools of Buddhism have developed to help explain and expand upon the Buddha's teachings. For others still, they see the dharma as referring to the "truth" or ultimate reality or "the way things are".

The dharma is one of the Three Jewels of Buddhism of which practitioners of Buddhism seek refuge in (what one relies on for his/her lasting happiness). The three jewels of Buddhism are the Buddha (mind's perfection of enlightenment), the dharma (teachings and methods) and the Sangha (awakened beings who provide guidance and support).

Buddha's Dharma Body

The qualities of the Dharma (Law, truth) is the same as the qualities of the Buddha and forms his "truth body" or "Dhamma Kaya": In the Samyutta Nikaya, Vakkali Sutta, Buddha said to his disciple Vakkali that,

"Yo kho Vakkali dhammam passati so mam passati"

Vakkali, whoever sees Dhamma, sees me [the Buddha]

Another reference from the Agganna Sutta of the Digha Nikaya, says to his disciple Vasettha:

"Tathagatassa h'etam Vasettha adivacanam Dhamma-kayo iti pi...":

O Vasettha! The Word of Dhammakaya is indeed the name of the Tathagata

Qualities of Buddha Dharma

The Teaching of the Buddha also has six supreme qualities:

1. *Svakkhato:* The Dhamma is not a speculative philosophy, but is the Universal Law found through enlightenment and is preached precisely. Therefore it is excellent in the beginning (sila-Sanskrit sila-moral principles), excellent in the middle (samadhi-concentration) and excellent in the end (panna-Sanskrit prajna... Wisdom),
2. *Sanditthiko*: The Dhamma can be tested by practice and therefore he who follows it will see the result by himself through his own experience.

3. *Akaliko:* The Dhamma is able to bestow timeless and immediate results here and now, for which there is no need to wait until the future or next existence.
4. *Ehipassiko*: The Dhamma welcomes all beings to put it to the test and come see for themselves.
5. *Opanayiko*: The Dhamma is capable of being entered upon and therefore it is worthy to be followed as a part of one's life.
6. *Paccattam Veditabbo Vinnuhi*: The Dhamma can be perfectly realized only by the noble disciples (Ariyas) who have matured and enlightened enough in supreme wisdom.

Knowing these attributes, Buddhists believe that they will attain the greatest peace and happiness through the practice of the Dhamma. Each person is therefore fully responsible for himself to put it in the real practice.

Here the Buddha is compared to an experienced and skilful doctor and the Dhamma to proper medicine. However efficient the doctor or wonderful the medicine may be, the patients cannot be cured unless they take the medicine properly. So the practice of the Dhamma is the only way to attain the final deliverance of Nibbana.

These teachings ranged from understanding karma (Pali: kamma) (cause and effect) and developing good impressions in one's mind, to reach full enlightenment by recognizing the nature of mind.

Dharmas in Buddhist Phenomenology

Other uses include dharma, normally spelled with a small "d" (to differentiate), which refers to a phenomenon or constituent factor of human experience. This was gradually expanded into a classification of constituents of the entire material and mental world. Rejecting the substantial existence of permanent entities which are qualified by possibly changing qualities, Buddhist Abhidharma philosophy, which enumerated seventy-five dharmas, came to propound that these "constituent factors" are the only type of entity that truly exists. This notion is of particular importance for the analysis of human experience: Rather than assuming that mental states inhere in a cognizing subject, or a soul-substance, Buddhist philosophers largely propose that mental states alone exist as "momentary elements of consciousness" and that a subjective perceiver is assumed.

One of the central tenets of Buddhism, is the denial of a separate permanent "I" and is outlined in the three marks of existence. The three signs: 1. Dukkha (Pali: Dukkha)-Suffering, 2. Anitya (Pali: Anicca)-Change/Impermanence, 3. Anatman (Pali: Anatta)-Non-self. At the heart of Buddhism, is the denial of a "self" or "I" (and hence the delusion) as a separate self-existing entity.

Later, Buddhist philosophers like Nagarjuna would question whether the dharmas (momentary elements of consciousness) truly have a separate existence of their own. (*i.e.* Do they exist apart from anything else?) Rejecting any inherent reality to the dharmas, he asked (rhetorically):

When all dharmas are empty, what is endless? What has an end?

What is endless and with an end? What is not endless and not with an end?

What is it? What is other? What is permanent? What is impermanent?

What is impermanent and permanent? What is neither?

Auspicious is the pacification of phenomenal metastasis, the pacification of all apprehending;

There is no dharma whatsoever taught by the Buddha to whomever, whenever, wherever.--Mulamadhyamakakarika, nirvanaparikna, 25:22-24

Dharma as Righteousness

According to S. N. Goenka, teacher of Vipassana Meditation, the original meaning of dhamma is "dhareti ti dhamma', or "that which is contained". Dharma in the Buddhist scriptures has a variety of meanings, including "phenomenon" and "nature" or "characteristic". Dharma also means 'mental contents' and is paired with citta, which means heart/mind. The pairing is paralleled with the pairing of kaya (body) and vedana (feelings or sensations, that which arise within the body but experienced through the mind), in major sutras such as the Mahasatipatthana sutra. Dharma is also used to refer to the teachings of the Buddha, not in the context of the words of one man, even an enlightened man, but as a reflection of natural law which was re-discovered by this man and shared with the world. A person who lives their life with an understanding of this natural law, is a "dhammic" person, which is often translated as "righteous".

BUDDHIST COSMOLOGY

Buddhist cosmology is the description of the shape and evolution of the universe according to the canonical Buddhist scriptures and commentaries.

Introduction

The self-consistent Buddhist cosmology which is presented in commentaries and works of Abhidharma in both Theravada and Mahayana traditions, is the end-product of an analysis and reconciliation of cosmological comments found in the Buddhist sutra and vinaya traditions. No single sutra sets out the entire structure of the universe. However, in several sutras the Buddha describes other worlds and states of being and other sutras describe the origin and destruction of the universe. The synthesis of these data into a single comprehensive system must have taken place early in the history of Buddhism, as the system described in the Pali Vibhajyavada tradition (represented by today's Theravadins) agrees, despite some trivial inconsistencies of nomenclature, with the Sarvastivada tradition which is preserved by Mahayana Buddhists.

The picture of the world presented in Buddhist cosmological descriptions cannot be taken as a literal description of the shape of the universe. It is inconsistent and cannot be made consistent, with astronomical data that were already known in ancient India. However, it is not intended to be a description of how humans perceive their world; rather, it is the universe as seen through the divyacakrus, the "divine eye" by which a Buddha or an arhat who has cultivated this faculty can perceive all of the other worlds and the beings arising (being born) and passing away (dying) within them and can tell from what state they have been reborn and into what state they will be reborn.

Buddhist cosmology can accordingly be divided into two related kinds: spatial cosmology, which describes the arrangement of the various worlds within the universe and temporal cosmology, which describes how those worlds come into existence and how they pass away.

Spatial Cosmology

Spatial cosmology can also be divided into two branches. The vertical cosmology describes the arrangement of worlds in a vertical pattern, some being higher and some lower. The sahasra cosmology describes the grouping of these vertical worlds into sets of thousands, millions or billions.

Vertical Cosmology

In the vertical cosmology, the universe exists of many worlds-one might say "planes"-stacked one upon the next in layers. Each world corresponds to a mental state or a state of being. A world is not, however, a location so much as it is the beings which compose it; it is sustained by their karma and if the beings in a world all die or disappear, the world disappears too. Likewise, a world comes into existence when the first being is born into it. The physical separation is not so important as the difference in mental state; humans and animals, though they partially share the same physical environments, still belong to different worlds because their minds perceive and react to those environments differently.

The vertical cosmology is divided into three realms, or dhatus, each corresponding to a different type of mentality. These three (Tridhatu) are the Arupyadhatu, the Rupadhatu and the Kamadhatu. This technical division does not correspond to the more informal categorization of the "six realms". In the latter scheme, all of the beings born in the Arupyadhatu and the Rupadhatu may be classified as "gods" or "deities" (deva), as can a considerable fraction of the beings born in the Kamadhatu, even though the deities of the Kamadhatu differ more from those of the Arupyadhatu than they do from humans. It is to be understood that deva is an imprecise term referring to any being living in a longer-lived and generally more blissful state than humans. Most of them are not "gods" in the common sense of the term, having little or no concern with the human world and rarely if ever interacting with it; only the lowest deities of the Kamadhatu correspond to the gods described in many polytheistic religions.

The term "brahma" is used both as a name and as a generic term for one of the higher devas. In its broadest sense, it can refer to any of the inhabitants of the Arupyadhatu and the Rupadhatu. In more restricted senses, it can refer to an inhabitant of one of the nine lower worlds of the Rupadhatu, or in its narrowest sense, to the three lowest worlds of the Rupadhatu. A large number of devas use the name "Brahma", *e.g.* Brahma Sahampati, Brahma Sanatkumara, Baka Brahma, etc. It is not always clear which world they belong to, although it must always be one of the worlds of the Rupadhatu below the Suddhavasa worlds.

Arupyadhatu

The Arupyadhatu (Sanskrit) or Arupaloka (Pali) or "Formless realm" would have no place in a purely physical cosmology, as none of the beings inhabiting it has either shape or location; and correspondingly, the realm has no location either. This realm belongs to those devas who attained and remained in the Four Formless Absorptions of the arupadhyanas in a previous life and now enjoys the fruits (vipaka) of the good karma of that accomplishment. Bodhisattvas, however, are never born in the Arupyadhatu even when they have attained the arupadhyanas.

There are four types of Arupyadhatu devas, corresponding to the four types of arupadhyanas:

- Naivasamjnanasamjnayatana or Nevasannanasannayatana "Sphere of neither perception nor non-perception". In this sphere the formless beings have gone beyond a mere negation of perception and have attained a liminal state where they do not engage in "perception" (samjna, recognition of particulars by their marks) but are not wholly unconscious. This was the sphere reached by Udraka Ramaputra (Pali: Uddaka Ramaputta), the second of the Buddha's two teachers, who considered it equivalent to enlightenment.

- Akimcanyayatana or Akincannayatana "Sphere of Nothingness" (literally "lacking anything"). In this sphere formless beings dwell contemplating upon the thought that "there is no thing". This is considered a form of perception, though a very subtle one. This was the sphere reached by Arara Kalama, the first of the Buddha's two teachers; he considered it to be equivalent to enlightenment.
- Vijnananantyayatana or Vinnananancayatana "Sphere of Infinite Consciousness". In this sphere formless beings dwell meditating on their consciousness (vijnana) as infinitely pervasive.
- Akasanantyayatana or Akasanancayatana "Sphere of Infinite Space". In this sphere formless beings dwell meditating upon space or extension (akasa) as infinitely pervasive.

Rupadhatu

The Rupadhatu or "Form realm" is, as the name implies, the first of the physical realms; its inhabitants all have a location and bodies of a sort, though those bodies are composed of a subtle substance which is of itself invisible to the inhabitants of the Kamadhatu. According to the Janavasabha Sutta, when a brahma (a being from the Brahma-world of the Rupadhatu) wishes to visit a deva of the Trayastrinsa heaven (in the Kamadhatu), he has to assume a "grosser form" in order to be visible to them.

The beings of the Form realm are not subject to the extremes of pleasure and pain, or governed by desires for things pleasing to the senses, as the beings of the Kamadhatu are. The bodies of Form realm beings do not have sexual distinctions.

Like the beings of the Arupyadhatu, the dwellers in the Rupadhatu have minds corresponding to the dhyanas (Pali: jhanas). In their case it is the four lower dhyanas or rupadhyanas. However, although the beings of the Rupadhatu can be divided into four broad grades corresponding to these four dhyanas, each of them is subdivided into further grades, three for each of the four dhyanas and five for the Suddhavasa devas, for a total of seventeen grades (the Theravada tradition counts one less grade in the highest dhyana for a total of sixteen). Physically, the Rupadhatu consists of a series of planes stacked on top of each other, each one in a series of steps half the size of the previous one as one descends. In part, this reflects the fact that the devas are also thought of as physically larger on the higher planes. The highest planes are also broader in extent than the ones lower down, as discussed in the section on Sahasra cosmology. The height of these planes is expressed in yojanas, a measurement of very uncertain length, but sometimes taken to be about 4,000 times the height of a man and so approximately 4.54 miles or 7.32 kilometers.

Suddhavasa Worlds

The Suddhavasa worlds, or "Pure Abodes", are distinct from the other worlds of the Rupadhatu in that they do not house beings who have been born there through ordinary merit or meditative attainments, but only those Anagamins ("Non-returners") who are already on the path to Arhat-hood and who will attain enlightenment directly from the Suddhavasa worlds without being reborn in a lower plane (Anagamins can also be born on lower planes). Every Suddhavasa deva is therefore a protector of Buddhism. Because a Suddhavasa deva will never be reborn outside the Suddhavasa worlds, no Bodhisattva is ever born in these worlds, as a Bodhisattva must ultimately be reborn as a human being.

Since these devas rise from lower planes only due to the teaching of a Buddha, they can remain empty for very long periods if no Buddha arises. However, unlike the lower worlds, the Suddhavasa worlds are never destroyed by natural catastrophe. The Suddhavasa devas predict the coming of a Buddha and, taking the guise of Brahmins, reveal to human beings the signs by which a Buddha can be recognized. They also ensure that a Bodhisattva in his last life will see the four signs that will lead to his renunciation.

The five Suddhavasa worlds are:

- *Akanistha or Akanittha:* World of devas "equal in rank" (literally: having no one as the youngest). The highest of all the Rupadhatu worlds, it is often used to refer to the highest extreme of the universe. The current Sakra will eventually be born there. The duration of life in Akanistha is 16,000 kalpas (Vibhajyavada tradition). The height of this world is 167,772,160 yojanas above the Earth.
- *Sudarsana or Sudassi:* The "clear-seeing" devas live in a world similar to and friendly with the Akanistha world. The height of this world is 83,886,080 yojanas above the Earth.
- *Sudrsa or Sudassa:* The world of the "beautiful" devas are said to be the place of rebirth for five kinds of anagamins. The height of this world is 41,943,040 yojanas above the Earth.
- *Atapa or Atappa:* The world of the "untroubled" devas, whose company those of lower realms wish for. The height of this world is 20,971,520 yojanas above the Earth.
- *Avrha or Aviha:* The world of the "not falling" devas, perhaps the most common destination for reborn Anagamins. Many achieve arhatship directly in this world, but some pass away and are reborn in sequentially higher worlds of the Pure Abodes until they are at last reborn in the Akanistha world. These are called in Pali uddhatsotas, "those whose stream goes upward". The duration of life in Avaha is 1,000 kalpas (Vibhajyavada tradition). The height of this world is 10,485,760 yojanas above the Earth.

Brhatphala Worlds

The mental state of the devas of the Brhatphala worlds corresponds to the fourth dhyana and is characterized by equanimity (upeksa). The Brhatphala worlds form the upper limit to the destruction of the universe by wind at the end of a mahakalpa, that is, they are spared such destruction.

- *Asannasatta:* "Unconscious beings", devas who have attained a high dhyana (similar to that of the Formless

Realm) and, wishing to avoid the perils of perception, have achieved a state of non-perception in which they endure for a time. After a while, however, perception arises again and they fall into a lower state.

- *Brhatphala or Vehapphala*: Devas "having great fruit". Their lifespan is 500 mahakalpas. (Vibhajyavada tradition). Some Anagamins are reborn here. The height of this world is 5,242,880 yojanas above the Earth.
- *Punyaprasava:* The world of the devas who are the "offspring of merit". The height of this world is 2,621,440 yojanas above the Earth.
- *Anabhraka:* The world of the "cloudless" devas. The height of this world is 1,310,720 yojanas above the Earth.

Subhakrtsna Worlds

The mental state of the devas of the Subhaktsna worlds corresponds to the third dhyana and is characterized by a quiet joy (sukha).

These devas have bodies that radiate a steady light. The Subhakatsna worlds form the upper limit to the destruction of the universe by water at the end of a mahakalpa, that is, the flood of water does not rise high enough to reach them.

- *Subhakrtsna:* The world of devas of "total beauty". Their lifespan is 64 mahakalpas (some sources: 4 mahakalpas) according to the Vibhajyavada tradition. 64 mahakalpas is the interval between destructions of the universe by wind, including the Subhakstsna worlds. The height of this world is 655,360 yojanas above the Earth.
- *Apramanasubha:* The world of devas of "limitless beauty". Their lifespan is 32 mahakalpas (Vibhajyavada tradition). They possess "faith, virtue, learning, munificence and wisdom". The height of this world is 327,680 yojanas above the Earth.
- *Parittasubha:* The world of devas of "limited beauty". Their lifespan is 16 mahakalpas. The height of this world is 163,840 yojanas above the Earth.

Abhasvara Worlds

The mental state of the devas of the Abhasvara worlds corresponds to the second dhyana and is characterized by delight (priti) as well as joy (sukha); the Abhasvara devas are said to shout aloud in their joy, crying aho sukham! ("Oh joy!"). These devas have bodies that emit flashing rays of light like lightning. They are said to have similar bodies (to each other) but diverse perceptions.

The Abhasvara worlds form the upper limit to the destruction of the universe by fire at the end of a mahakalpa, that is, the column of fire does not rise high enough to reach them. After the destruction of the world, at the beginning of the vivartakalpa, the worlds are first populated by beings reborn from the Abhasvara worlds.

- *Abhasvara or Abhassara:* The world of devas "possessing splendor". The lifespan of the Abhasvara devas is 8 mahakalpas (others: 2 mahakalpas). Eight mahakalpas is the interval between destructions of the universal by water, which includes the Abhasvara worlds. The height of this world is 81,920 yojanas above the Earth.
- *Apramanabha or Appamanabha:* The world of devas of "limitless light", a concept on which they meditate. Their lifespan is 4 mahakalpas. The height of this world is 40,960 yojanas above the Earth.
- *Parittabha or Parittabha:* The world of devas of "limited light". Their lifespan is 2 mahakalpas. The height of this world is 20,480 yojanas above the Earth.

Brahma Worlds

The mental state of the devas of the Brahma worlds corresponds to the first dhyana and is characterized by observation (vitarka) and reflection (vicara) as well as delight (priti) and joy (sukha). The Brahma worlds, together with the other lower worlds of the universe, are destroyed by fire at the end of a mahakalpa.

- Mahabrahma-the world of "Great Brahma", believed by many to be the creator of the world and having as his titles "Brahma, Great Brahma, the Conqueror, the Unconquered, the All-Seeing, All-Powerful, the Lord, the Maker and Creator, the Ruler, Appointer and Orderer, Father of All That Have Been and Shall Be." According to the Brahmajala Sutta (DN.1), a Mahabrahma is a being from the Abhasvara worlds who falls into a lower world through exhaustion of his merits and is reborn alone in the Brahma-world; forgetting his former existence, he imagines himself to have come into existence without cause. Note that even such a high-ranking deity has no intrinsic knowledge of the worlds above his own. Mahabrahma is 1 1/2 yojanas tall. His lifespan variously said to be 1 kalpa (Vibhajyavada tradition) or 1 1/2 kalpas long (Sarvastivada tradition), although it would seem that it could be no longer than 3/4 of a mahakalpa, *i.e.*, all of the mahakalpa except for the Sanvartasthayikalpa, because that is the total length of time between the rebuilding of the lower world and its destruction. It is unclear what period of time "kalpa" refers to in this case. The height of this world is 10,240 yojanas above the Earth.

- Brahmapurohita-the "Ministers of Brahma" are beings, also originally from the Abhasvara worlds, that are born as companions to Mahabrahma after he has spent some time alone. Since they arise subsequent to his thought of a desire for companions, he believes himself to be their creator and they likewise believe him to be their creator and lord. They are 1 yojana in height and their lifespan is variously said to be 1/2 of a kalpa (Vibhajyavada tradition) or a whole kalpa (Sarvastivada tradition). If they are later reborn in a lower world and come to recall some part of their last existence, they teach the doctrine of Brahma as creator as a revealed truth. The height of this world is 5,120 yojanas above the Earth.
- Brahmaparisadya-the "Councilors of Brahma" or the devas "belonging to the assembly of Brahma". They are also called Brahmakayika, but this name can be used for any of the inhabitants of the Brahma-worlds. They are half a yojana in height and their lifespan is variously said to be

1/3 of a kalpa (Vibhajyavada tradition) or 1/2 of a kalpa (Sarvastivada tradition). The height of this world is 2,560 yojanas above the Earth.

Kamadhatu

The beings born in the Kamadhatu differ in degree of happiness, but they are all, other than arhats and Buddhas, under the domination of Mara and are bound by desire, which causes them suffering.

Heavens

The following four worlds are bounded planes, each 80,000 yojanas square, which float in the air above the top of Mount Sumeru. Although all of the worlds inhabited by devas (that is, all the worlds down to the Caturmaharajikakayika world and sometimes including the Asuras) are sometimes called "heavens", in the western sense of the word the term best applies to the four worlds listed below:

- *Parinirmita-vasavartin*: The heaven of devas "with power over (others') creations". These devas do not create pleasing forms that they desire for themselves, but their desires are fulfilled by the acts of other devas who wish for their favor. The ruler of this world is called Vasavartin (Pali: Vasavatti), who has longer life, greater beauty, more power and happiness and more delightful sense-objects than the other devas of his world. This world is also the home of the devaputra (being of divine race) called Mara, who endeavors to keep all beings of the Kamadhatu in the grip of sensual pleasures. Mara is also sometimes called Vasavartin, but in general these two dwellers in this world are kept distinct. The beings of this world are 4,500 feet tall and live for 9,216,000,000 years (Sarvastivada tradition). The height of this world is 1,280 yojanas above the Earth.
- *Nirmanarati*: The world of devas "delighting in their creations". The devas of this world are capable of making any appearance to please themselves. The lord of this world is called Sunirmita (Pali Sunimmita); his wife is the

rebirth of Visakha, formerly the chief of the upasikas (female lay devotees) of the Buddha. The beings of this world are 3,750 feet tall and live for 2,304,000,000 years (Sarvastivada tradition). The height of this world is 640 yojanas above the Earth.

- *Tusita*: The world of the "joyful" devas. This world is best known for being the world in which a Bodhisattva lives before being reborn in the world of humans. Until a few thousand years ago, the Bodhisattva of this world was Svetaketu (Pali: Setaketu), who was reborn as Siddhartha, who would become the Buddha Sakyamuni; since then the Bodhisattva has been Natha (or Nathadeva) who will be reborn as Ajita and will become the Buddha Maitreya (Pali Metteyya). While this Bodhisattva is the foremost of the dwellers in Turita, the ruler of this world is another deva called Santusita. The beings of this world are 3,000 feet tall and live for 576,000,000 years (Sarvastivada tradition). The height of this world is 320 yojanas above the Earth.
- *Yama*: Sometimes called the "heaven without fighting", because it is the lowest of the heavens to be physically separated from the tumults of the earthly world. Its ruler is the deva Suyama; according to some, his wife is the rebirth of Sirima, a courtesan of Rajagrha in the Buddha's time who was generous to the monks. The beings of this world are 2,250 feet tall and live for 144,000,000 years (Sarvastivada tradition). The height of this world is 160 yojanas above the Earth.

Worlds of Sumeru

The world-mountain of Sumeru is an immense, strangely shaped peak which arises in the centre of the world and around which the Sun and Moon revolve. Its base rests in a vast ocean and it is surrounded by several rings of lesser mountain ranges and oceans. The three worlds listed below are all located on or around Sumeru: the Trayastrinsa devas live on its peak, the Caturmaharajikakayika devas live on its slopes and the Asuras live in the ocean at its base. Sumeru and its surrounding oceans and mountains are the home not just of these deities, but also vast assemblies of beings of popular mythology who only rarely intrude on the human world.

- *Trayastrimsa*: The world "of the Thirty-three (devas)" is a wide flat space on the top of Mount Sumeru, filled with the gardens and palaces of the devas. Its ruler is Sakra devanam indra, "lord of the devas". Besides the eponymous Thirty-three devas, many other devas and supernatural beings dwell here, including the attendants of the devas and many apsarases (nymphs). The beings of this world are 1,500 feet tall and live for 36,000,000 years (Sarvastivada tradition) or 3/4 of a yojana tall and live for 30,000,000 years (Vibhajyavada tradition). The height of this world is 80 yojanas above the Earth.
- *Caturmaharajikakayika*: The world "of the Four Great Kings" is found on the lower slopes of Mount Sumeru, though some of its inhabitants live in the air around the mountain. Its rulers are the four Great Kings of the name, Virushaka, Virupakna and their leader Vaisravasa. The devas who guide the Sun and Moon are also considered part of this world, as are the retinues of the four kings, composed of Kumbhashas (dwarfs), Gandharvas (fairies), Nagas (dragons) and Yakhas (goblins). The beings of this world are 750 feet tall and live for 9,000,000 years (Sarvastivada tradition) or 90,000 years (Vibhajyavada tradition). The height of this world is from sea level up to 40 yojanas above the Earth.
- *Asura*: The world of the Asuras is the space at the foot of Mount Sumeru, much of which is a deep ocean. It is not the Asuras' original home, but the place they found themselves after they were hurled, drunken, from Trayastrinsa where they had formerly lived. The Asuras are always fighting to regain their lost kingdom on the top of Mount Sumeru, but are unable to break the guard of the Four Great Kings. The Asuras are divided into many groups and have no single ruler, but among their leaders are Vemacitrin (Pali: Vepacitti) and Rahu.

Earthly Realms

- *Manusyaloka*: This is the world of humans and human-like beings who live on the surface of the earth. The mountain-rings that engird Sumeru are surrounded by a vast ocean, which fills most of the world. The ocean is in turn surrounded by a circular mountain wall called Cakravara which marks the horizontal limit of the world. In this ocean there are four continents which are, relatively speaking, small islands in it. Because of the immenseness of the ocean, they cannot be reached from each other by ordinary sailing vessels, although in the past, when the cakravartin kings ruled, communication between the continents was possible by means of the treasure called the cakraratna (Pali cakkaratana), which a cakravartin and his retinue could use to fly through the air between the continents. The four continents are:
    - Jambudvipa or Jambudipa is located in the south and is the dwelling of ordinary human beings. It is said to be shaped "like a cart", or rather a blunt-nosed triangle with the point facing south. (This description probably echoes the shape of the coastline of southern India.) It is 10,000 yojanas in extent (Vibhajyavada tradition) or has a perimeter of 6,000 yojanas (Sarvastivada tradition) to which can be added the southern coast of only 3 1/2 yojanas' length. The continent takes its name from a giant Jambu tree (Syzygium cumini), 100 yojanas tall, which grows in the middle of the continent. Every continent has one of these giant trees. All Buddhas appear in Jambudvipa. The people here are five to six feet tall and their length of life varies between 80,000 and 10 years.
    - Purvavideha or Pubbavideha is located in the east and is shaped like a semicircle with the flat side pointing westward (*i.e.*, towards Sumeru). It is 7,000 yojanas in extent (Vibhajyavada tradition) or has a perimeter of 6,350 yojanas of which the flat side is 2,000 yojanas long (Sarvastivada tradition). Its tree is the acacia. The

people here are about 12 feet tall and they live for 250 years.

- o Aparagodaniya or Aparagoyana is located in the west and is shaped like a circle with a circumference of about 7,500 yojanas (Sarvastivada tradition). The tree of this continent is a giant Kadambu tree. The human inhabitants of this continent do not live in houses but sleep on the ground. They are about 24 feet tall and they live for 500 years.
- o Uttarakuru is located in the north and is shaped like a square. It has a perimter of 8,000 yojanas, being 2,000 yojanas on each side. This continent's tree is called a kalpavkkha (Pali: kapparukkha) or kalpa-tree, because it lasts for the entire kalpa. The inhabitants of Uttarakuru are said to be extraordinarily wealthy. They do not need to labor for a living, as their food grows by itself and they have no private property. They have cities built in the air. They are about 48 feet tall and live for 1,000 years and they are under the protection of Vaisravana.

- *Tiryagyoni-loka*: This world comprises all members of the animal kingdom that are capable of feeling suffering, from the smallest insect to the elephant.
- *Pretaloka*: The pretas, or "hungry ghosts", are mostly dwellers on earth, though due to their mental state they perceive it very differently from humans. They live for the most part in desert and waste places.

Narakas

Naraka or Niraya is the name given to one of the worlds of greatest suffering, usually translated into English as "hell" or "purgatory". As with the other realms, a being is born into one of these worlds as a result of his karma and resides there for a finite length of time until his karma has achieved its full result, after which he will be reborn in one of the higher worlds as the result of an earlier karma that had not yet ripened. The mentality of a being in the hells corresponds to states of extreme fear and helpless anguish in humans. Physically, Naraka is thought of as a series of layers extending below Jambudvipa into the earth. There are several schemes for counting these Narakas and enumerating their torments. One of the more common is that of the Eight Cold Narakas and Eight Hot Narakas.

Cold Narakas

- Arbuda-the "blister" Naraka
- Nirarbuda-the "burst blister" Naraka
- Atata-the Naraka of shivering
- Hahava-the Naraka of lamentation
- Huhuva-the Naraka of chattering teeth
- Utpala-the "blue lotus" Naraka
- Padma-the "lotus" Naraka
- Mahapadma-the "great lotus" Naraka

Each lifetime in these Narakas is twenty times the length of the one before it.

Hot Narakas

- Sanjiva-the "reviving" Naraka. Life in this Naraka is 162×10^{10} years long.
- Kalasutra-the "black thread" Naraka. Life in this Naraka is 1296×10^{10} years long.
- Samghata-the "crushing" Naraka. Life in this Naraka is $10,368 \times 10^{10}$ years long.
- Raurava-the "screaming" Naraka. Life in this Naraka is $82,944 \times 10^{10}$ years long.
- Maharaurava-the "great screaming" Naraka. Life in this Naraka is $663,552 \times 10^{10}$ years long.
- Tapana-the "heating" Naraka. Life in this Naraka is $5,308,416 \times 10^{10}$ years long.
- Pratapana-the "great heating" Naraka. Life in this Naraka is $42,467,328 \times 10^{10}$ years long.
- Avici-the "uninterrupted" Naraka. Life in this Naraka is $339,738,624 \times 10^{10}$ years long.

The Foundations of the Earth

All of the structures of the earth, Sumeru and the rest, extend downward to a depth of 80,000 yojanas below sea level-the same as the height of Sumeru above sea level. Below this is a layer of "golden earth", a substance compact and firm enough to support the weight of Sumeru. It is 320,000 yojanas in depth and so extends to 400,000 yojanas below sea level. The layer of golden earth in turn rests upon a layer of water, which is 8,000,000 yojanas in depth, going down to 8,400,000 yojanas below sea level. Below the layer of water is a "circle of wind", which is 16,000,000 yojanas in depth and also much broader in extent, supporting 1,000 different worlds upon it.

Sahasra Cosmology

While the vertical cosmology describes the arrangement of the worlds vertically, the sahasra (Sanskrit: "thousand") cosmology describes how they are grouped horizontally. The four heavens of the Kamadhatu, as mentioned, occupy a limited space no bigger than the top of Mount Sumeru. The three Brahma-worlds, however, stretch out as far as the mountain-wall of Cakravana, filling the entire sky. This whole group of worlds, from Mahabrahma down to the foundations of water, constitutes a single world-system. It corresponds to the extent of the universe that is destroyed by fire at the end of one mahakalpa.

Above Mahabrahma are the Abhasvara worlds. These are not only higher but also wider in extent; they cover 1,000 separate world-systems, each with its own Sumeru, Cakravana, Sun, Moon and four continents. This system of 1,000 worlds is called a sahasra-cunika-lokadhatu, or "small chiliocosm". It corresponds to the extent of the universe that is destroyed by water at the end of 8 mahakalpas.

Above the Abhasvara worlds are the Subhakstsna worlds, which cover 1,000 chiliocosms, or 1,000,000 world-systems. This larger system is called a dvisahasra-madhyama-lokadhatu, or "medium dichiliocosm". It corresponds to the extent of the universe that is destroyed by wind at the end of 64 mahakalpas.

Likewise, above the Subhakhtsna worlds, the Suddhavasa and Brhatphala worlds cover 1,000 dichiliocosms, or 1,000,000,000 world-systems. This largest grouping is called a trisahasra-mahasahasra-lokadhatu or "great trichiliocosm".

Temporal Cosmology

Buddhist temporal cosmology describes how the universe comes into being and is dissolved. Like other Indian cosmologies, it assumes an infinite span of time and is cyclical. This does not mean that the same events occur in identical form with each cycle, but merely that, as with the cycles of day and night or summer and winter, certain natural events occur over and over to give some structure to time.

The basic unit of time measurement is the mahakalpa or "Great Eon". The exact length of this time in human years is never defined exactly, but it is meant to be very long, to be measured in billions of years if not longer.

A mahakalpa is divided into four kalpas or "eons", each distinguished from the others by the stage of evolution of the universe during that kalpa. The four kalpas are:

- Vivartakalpa "Eon of evolution"-during this kalpa the universe comes into existence.
- Vivartasthayikalpa "Eon of evolution-duration"-during this kalpa the universe remains in existence in a steady state.
- Samvartakalpa "Eon of dissolution"-during this kalpa the universe dissolves.
- Samvartasthayikalpa "Eon of dissolution-duration"-during this kalpa the universe remains in a state of emptiness.

Each one of these kalpas is divided into twenty antarakalpas (Pali antarakappa, "inside eons") each of about the same length. For the Sarvartasthayikalpa this division is merely nominal, as nothing changes from one antarakalpa to the next; but for the other three kalpas it marks an interior cycle within the kalpa.

Vivartakalpa

The Vivartakalpa begins with the arising of the primordial wind, which begins the process of building up the structures of the universe that had been destroyed at the end of the last mahakalpa. As the extent of the destruction can vary, the nature of this evolution can vary as well, but it always takes the form of beings from a higher world being born into a lower world.

The example of a Mahabrahma being the rebirth of a deceased Abhasvara deva is just one instance of this, which continues throughout the Vivartakalpa until all the worlds are filled from the Brahmaloka down to Naraka. During the Vivartakalpa the first humans appear; they are not like present-day humans, but are beings shining in their own light, capable of moving through the air without mechanical aid, living for a very long time and not requiring sustenance; they are more like a type of lower deity than present-day humans are.

Over time, they acquire a taste for physical nutriment and as they consume it, their bodies become heavier and more like human bodies; they lose their ability to shine and begin to acquire differences in their appearance and their length of life decreases. They differentiate into two sexes and begin to become sexually active. Then greed, theft and violence arise among them and they establish social distinctions and government and elect a king to rule them, called Mahasammata, "the great appointed one". Some of them begin to hunt and eat the flesh of animals, which have by now come into existence. These developments are described in the Agganna Sutta (DN.27).

Vivartasthayikalpa

First Antarakalpa: The Vivartasthayikalpa begins when the first being is born into Naraka, thus filling the entire universe with beings. During the first antarakalpa of this eon, human lives are declining from a vast but unspecified number of years (but at least several tens of thousands of years) toward the modern lifespan of less than 100 years. At the beginning of the antarakalpa, people are still generally happy. They live under the rule of a universal monarch or "wheel-turning king" (cakravartin), who conquer. The Mahasudassana-sutta (DN.17) tells of the life of a cakravartin king, Mahasudassana (Sanskrit: Mahasudarsana) who lived for 336,000 years.

The Cakkavatti-sihanada-sutta (DN.26) tells of a later dynasty of cakravartins, Darhanemi and five of his descendants, who had a lifespan of over 80,000 years.

The seventh of this line of cakravartins broke with the traditions of his forefathers, refusing to abdicate his position at a certain age, pass the throne on to his son and enter the life of a sramara. As a result of his subsequent misrule, poverty increased; as a result of poverty, theft began; as a result of theft, capital punishment was instituted; and as a result of this contempt for life, murders and other crimes became rampant.

The human lifespan now quickly decreased from 80,000 to 100 years, apparently decreasing by about half with each generation (this is perhaps not to be taken literally), while with each generation other crimes and evils increased: lying, adultery, evil speech, greed and hatred, wrong views, incest and other sorts of sexual abnormalities, disrespect for parents and elders.

During this period, according to the Mahapadana-sutta (DN.14) three of the four Buddhas of this antarakalpa lived: Krakucchanda Buddha (Pali: Kakusandha), at the time when the lifespan was 40,000 years; Kanakamuni Buddha (Pali: Konagamana) when the lifespan was 30,000 years; and Kasyapa Buddha (Pali: Kassapa) when the lifespan was 20,000 years.

Our present time is taken to be toward the end of the first antarakalpa of this Vivartasthayikalpa, when the lifespan is less than 100 years, after the life of Sakyamuni Buddha, who lived to the age of 80.

The remainder of the antarakalpa is prophesied to be miserable: lifespans will continue to decrease and all the evil tendencies of the past will reach their ultimate in destructiveness. People will live no longer than ten years and will marry at five; foods will be poor and tasteless; no form of morality will be acknowledged. The most contemptuous and hateful people will become the rulers. Incest will be rampant. Hatred between people, even members of the same family, will grow until people think of each other as hunters do of their prey.

Eventually a great war will ensue, in which the most hostile and aggressive will arm themselves and go out to kill each other. The less aggressive will hide in forests and other secret places while the war rages. This war marks the end of the first antarakalpa.

Second Antarakalpa: At the end of the war, the survivors will emerge from their hiding places and repent their evil habits. As they begin to do good, their lifespan increases and the health and welfare of the human race will also increase with it. After a long time, the descendants of those with a 10-year lifespan will live for 80,000 years and at that time there will be a cakravartin king named Sarkha. During his reign, the current bodhisattva in the Tunita heaven will descend and be reborn under the name of Ajita. He will enter the life of a sramara and will gain perfect enlightenment as a Buddha; and he will then be known by the name of Maitreya.

After Maitreya's time, the world will again worsen and the lifespan will gradually decrease from 80,000 years to 10 years again, each antarakalpa being separated from the next by devastating war, with peaks of high civilization and morality in the middle. After the 19th antarakalpa, the lifespan will increase to 80,000 and then not decrease, because the Vivartasthayikalpa will have come to an end.

Sarvartakalpa

The Sarvartakalpa begins when beings cease to be born in Naraka. This cessation of birth then proceeds in reverse order up the vertical cosmology, *i.e.* pretas then cease to be born, then animals, then humans and so on up to the realms of the deities. When these worlds as far as the Brahmaloka are devoid of inhabitants, a great fire consumes the entire physical structure of the world. It burns all the worlds below the Abhasvara worlds. When they are destroyed, the Sarvartasthayikalpa begins.

Sarvartasthayikalpa

There is nothing to say about the Sarvartasthayikalpa, since nothing happens in it below the Abhasvara worlds. It ends when the primordial wind begins to blow and build the structure of the worlds up again.

Other Destructions: The destruction by fire is the normal type of destruction that occurs at the end of the Sarvartakalpa. But every eighth mahakalpa, after seven destructions by fire, there is a destruction by water. This is more devastating, as it eliminates not just the Brahma worlds but also the Abhasvara worlds.

Every sixty-fourth mahakalpa, after 56 destructions by fire and 7 destructions by water, there is a destruction by wind. This is the most devastating of all, as it also destroys the Subhakhtsna worlds. The higher worlds are never destroyed.

11

Bhutanese Buddhist

It is believed that Buddhism was introduced to Bhutan in the late 8th century CE by Guru Padmasambhava (also known as Padmakara or Padma Raja; and earlier as Saroruha Vajra or simply Saroruha), a monk from the Swat Valley, (now in Pakistan). In Bhutan and Tibet, Guru Padmasambhava is also known as Guru Rinpoche ("Precious Master"), and followers of the Nyingma school regard him as the second Buddha. Bhutan is a country of Shabdrung, a follower of Buddhism. Buddhism flourished in Bhutan before Shabdrung, the religion had its stronghold from his time when he unified the country in the early 17th century. Folk tales remark that the country was under Buddhist influence for many centuries before, and retained its culture and religion identity for longer period. "There were several reasons why Bhutan has been able to retain its cultural identity while neighbouring areas to the south and north have been undergoing profound and fundamental changes". Historically, the diversity and heterogeneity that have characterized South Asian society and the tolerance of Hinduism for cultural diversity have had a strong influence on Bhutanese society.

Along with Buddhism, other religions have also played a significant role. Hinduism and Buddhism have distinct border though nowadays have interliving between them. Mostly, Buddhists are found in the north and Hindus in the south of the country. Being a Buddhist country, it has close relations with Japan, Nepal, China, India and other Buddhist countries. After 1960, some Christian families are also seen in the country. Father

William Machea (known as the Brother of Bhutan) is the source of the popularisation of Christianity in Bhutan. But then also, Christianity was not allowed to preach openly in the country. The government had restricted the preaching of religions other than Hinduism and Buddhism.

If Bhutan's religious history is to be traced back, the first religion flourished in the country was Bonism led by Lhase Shangma. But as the leader himself was exiled, the religion could not exist and set its footholds. The existence of Bonism ended in 1222 when Phajo Drugom Shigpo entered Bhutan. During the course of time, Bhutan was being stucked by Geluckpas and many other religious sects. When the Geluckpa drove other sect of Buddhism from Tibet, they entered Bhutan. This became the source that Bhutan pertains its distinct cultural heritage. Most of the primitive rules followed in Tibet were reformed and a new form of Buddhism flourished in Bhutan, though its principles didn't change. Buddhism flourished in the 3rd century, when Ashoka sent his followers including his own son Mahendra to preach Buddhism in neighbouring countries.

The other record indicates that the Buddhism was firstly preached by Lam Gyalwa Lhanangpa in the 12th century. Thinley Rabyang is other Lam who stretched his hands in preaching Buddhism in about 1522, in Bhutan, though he could not attain much success.

Buddhism was effectively flourished in Bhutan from the time of Guru Rinpochhe. Preaching of Guru Rinpochhe is the greatest in the Buddhist history of Bhutan. He is favoured fellow to preach of Buddhism in the Himalayan land-sheds. Some leaders had entered Bhutan as exiled or ordered by their elders. Instead, Guru Rinpochhe was invited officially by the Bhutanese in the initiation of the Bumthang king, Sendya Gyab in 784 CE.

This way Buddhuism was finally recognised in Bhutan. Though many sects cursed it, its supremacy never detained. A boy could become a novice monk between the age of five and ten. If found acceptable, the child was invested with a red cloak and a piece of cloth placed round his neck; and thereafter he no longer belonged to his parents. The gelongs fed him, taught him to pray and read holy books. He had to renounce all connection with women and with any form of cultivation but could engage in trade or serve the government. The gelongs were obliged to perform religious worship in public to read holy books for private individuals and to burn the dead. The gelongs are abstained from fish or flesh on 8th, 14th and 30th of each month and were for bidden to take wine, although some drank in secret.

PREACHING OF BUDDHISM

Drukpa Kagyukpa is the state religion of the country. "The advent of Buddhism into Mon Yul in early seventh century A.D not only brought about a religious transformation of the people but also set a process of historical evolution of the country.

When in first century China was under Buddhist influence, Tibet was a pagan country. However, when in the 7th century (before Tibet was influenced by Bonism doctrine), the Tibetan King Tshrongtshen Gampo (624-49 CE) was married with Chinese and Nepalese princesses, both Buddhist, its doctrine changed the spiritual and religious structure of Tibetan community. Those two queens ordered the construction of 108 monasteries in Nepal, Tibet, Sikkim, China and Bhutan. Kichu monastery of Paro and Jampe Lhakhang of Bumthang are the two located in Bhutan. In this way Buddhism was firstly introduced in Bhutan in the 7th century CE but did not come in concrete existence as in China and Tibet.

Later on many Buddhist leaders entered Bhutan for preaching Buddhism from Tibet and other neighboring countries. Though in earlier it was reluctantly dominated, it created a firm existence as state religion and now respected by all Bhutanese.

Ral Pachelan was the king of Tibet between 816 and 836 CE. His follower Lam Shangpa Gyarey entered Bhutan preaching Buddhism in 830. Buddhism was further strengthened by brother of Tibetan king Lang Dharma (836-842). His effort lasted for six years and was assassinated by a Buddhist monk Pal Dorji in 842 CE.

After the clash of Nabudara and Sendya Gyab in Bumthang, 12 monasteries including Takshang monastery, Bumthang Kurje,

Damar monastery, and Paro Chhumphu monastery were built in Bhutan.

During the time Tshrongtshen Gampo of Tibet, Buddhism flourished in South Asia. In this period, 108 monasteries were bulit under the active leadership of Nepalese princess, Bhrikuti, in Nepal, Sikkim, Bhutan, Tibet, China and other neighbouring places.

Buddhism was divided into two sects as Hinayana and Manayana during the Fourth Great Buddhist Council [FGBC] meeting at Jalandhara {date not mentioned}. Since the people from Hinayana {Theravada} had not attended there, the sect was declared as the lesser vehicle and the Mahayana as the greater vehicle.

But after the time of Garapsel, Atisa and Rinchhen of Tibet divided Buddhism into three sects as Nyingmapa {old sect}, Kadampa {reformed sect}, and Sakyapa. Kadampa existed in Tibet till Gelukpa {Yellow Hat Sect} dominated the country. Nyingmapas were exiled to Bhutan, Sikkim and Tibet during the 14th century.

Tibetan sages and lamas had stretched hands in preaching Buddhism in Bhutan whose activities are discussed below. During their preaching they were attacked from neighbouring countries and from within the country. Among the attackers, Gelukpas of Tibet and Lam Kha Nga from within Bhutan were the main. It happened such that Buddhism never ended though cursed by many feudal lords and sectorial religion.

THE NYINGMA SECT

The Nyingma Sect has the longest history among all the sects" of Tibetan Buddhism. "Nyingma" literally means "ancient" or "old", thus the "Nyingma Sect" means "the old sect". Its name traces back to the Indian master, Guru Padmasambhava, also known as Guru Rinpoche, who came to Tibet in 817 at the invitation of King Trisong Detsan. The Nyingma Sect was said to carry on tantric teachings as well as related practices and rituals, which were handed down from "the first dissemination period of Tibetan Buddhism". The sect is also known as the "Red Sect" or "Red Hat Sect", for the red hat that eminent monks used to wear, but it does not seem to be an appropriate title.

As an independent sect, Nyingma was formed in "the second dissemination period of Tibetan Buddhism", as no sects were formed in "the first dissemination period of Tibetan Buddhism". In its early days, tantric teachings were handed down orally from father to son or teacher to close disciple, so the Nyingma Sect did not form a unified systematic doctrine, as well as established and authoritative monasteries, thus leading to a relaxed monastic institution.

Although the teachings and lineage of the Nyingma Sect are comparatively complex, they fall into three transmission lineages: Kama, namely Oral Transmission Lineage; II. Terma, namely Concealed Treasures Transmission lineage; III. Daknang, Visionary Lineage.

In the early stage of "the second dissemination period of Tibetan Buddhism", three masters crucial to the formation of the Nyingma Sect deserve special mention. They are historically called the "Three Master Sois", namely Soipoqeb Sakyaqoinam, Soiqoi Xirabzhaba, Soi Sakyasanga. Master Soipoqeb Sakyaqoinam, from his childhood, followed many tantric masters at that time, and learned extensive texts of the Nyingma Sect, gradually grasping various tantric doctrines popular at that time. For instance, he followed Master Nang Yexe Qoinam and studied the Imaginary Tantra, and then Master Togar Namkala imparted to him the Collection of Tantras. As the result, Soipoqeb Sakyaqoinam basically learned all the tantric teachings handed down from the distant lineage of Buddhist scriptures.

Later, Soipoqeb Sakyaqoinam presented Great Master Chomi Sakyayeshe with 100 tael of gold, in return learning the Path to the Great Perfection. After various instructions of great masters of the Nyingma Sect and through his own hard work, Soipoqeb Sakyaqoinam rose to be a famous master with good command of the doctrines of the Nyingma Sect and one immersed in religious knowledge. What deserves mention is that he established the Wobalhung Monastery, setting up a unified centre of religious activities for the Nyingma Sect. From then on, Master Soipoqeb Sakyaqoinam set out to launch a series of religious activities to develop the doctrines of the Nyingma Sect. It was a new era for the sect, as the establishment of the Wobalhung Monastery allowed it to join the line of regular monasteries with complete teachings and rituals as well as a monastery institution, ending its former scattered structure and noninstitutional condition.

When Master Soipoqeb Sakyaqoinam passed away, Soiqoi Xirabzhaba succeeded him. He-in turn established and completed the regulations and institutions of the monasteries, as he took in charge of the Wobalhung and Chopo monasteries and the meditation place of Zhagyewo, ensuring their religious activities took on a regular form, For instance, he ordered that religious activities in the Wobalhung Monastery should be held in the morning, at noon in the Chopo Monastery, and in the evening at Zhagyewo.

At the same time, in order to expand the scale of religious activities, he presided over the construction of a grand temple, named the Air Flying Temple, which was supported by nine main pillars. Altogether, 42 statues of Buddha were housed there; on the walls were paintings of the Mandala. Other small temples were also built at that time. Master Soiqoi Xirabzhaba made great achievements in the theory of Buddhist Tantra, especially in Buddhist Logic.

Famous for his great debating ability, he came to be one of the main rivals of many Buddhist monks from the newly rising sects of Tibetan Buddhism when they debated the scriptures. As he was always victorious and gained great prestige, many his rivals in the end willingly became his disciples. Because a large number of Buddhist monks of the Nyingma Sect at that time were laymen, rather than ordained monks, they put more emphasis on the practice of Tantricism, instead of the study of Sutric theory. On the condition that there were quite limited talents in good command of debate in Buddhist Tantras in the Nyingma Sect, Master Soiqoi Xirabzhaba distinguished himself and made an important contribution to the good image of the Nyingma Sect among other Buddhist sects.

Soi Sakyasanga, also known as Lhagyiqinbo Chopoba, was born in 1074, when his father, Master Soiqoi Xirabzhaba died. Historical Tibetan records show that Master Soiqoi Xirabzhaba had three sons and several daughters, who were all Buddhist monks or nuns practicing the doctrines of the Nyingma Sect. Master Soi Sakyasanga, the last son, was the only one to make great achievements and continue his father's cause.

He was brought up by his mother and uncle to manage family affairs as he learned much knowledge at home before the age of fifteen. At that time, the family was well off so that someone needed to be in charge of family affairs. In the following four years from the age of fifteen, Soi Sakyasanga left home to follow one master or another, systematically learning Buddhist sutras and Tantras, especially all the tantric teachings of distant lineage of the Nyingma Sect. In the end, he became the successor of this lineage. Chopo Monastery, as his place of residence, was reconstructed and renovated on a large scale. It usually held largescale religious activities four times every year, namely spring, summer, autumn, and winter gatherings. In 1134, Soi Sakyasanga passed away at the age of 60. In his brief life, he contributed to furthering the formal monastery development of the Nyingma Sect, successfully completing the tasks and responsibilities of an occupational Buddhist master.

Due to the ceaseless efforts of the three masters, the Nyingma Sect had evolved into an independent sect with established monasteries, systematic Buddhist classics and fixed monastic institutions. It also won a certain prestige at that time. The lineage belonged to the distant Buddhist classics lineage, which is the most orthodox and authoritative lineage and is still being handed down.

Besides the three masters above, there is another figure that made a special contribution to the development of the Nyingma Sect., namely Lhungqin Rabgyamba, born in 1308 with the name of Zimei Aosei. At the age of twelve, he became a Buddhist monk and studied tantric teachings before many masters of the Nyingma Sect and other sects at that time. He also studied the Five Sutras by Maitreya, Seven Sutras of Buddhist Logic by Dharmak and other Tantras. Therefore, Lhungqin Rabgyamba came to be a famous master proficient in tantric and sutric teachings. He was a prolific master and his most important works are 35 Kinds of Nyingti Practices and Seven Tibetan Commentaries, which mainly expounded the teachings of Great Perfection, the highest stage of practice of the Nyingma Sect. In his later years, he lectured on another profound Tantra, the Flying Air Nyingti, and contributed much to its dissemination, before dying in 1363 at the age of 56.

In his short life, Master Lhungqin Rabgyamba not only completed and developed the teachings and doctrines of the Nyingma Sect, but also cultivated many famous Buddhist monks. He played a crucial role in the expansion of the sect's influence. He also visited Bhutan, where he built the Tarbalin Monastery, and that led to the eventual spread of the Nyingma Sect, to Nepal. Eventually, many Buddhist monks from Bhutan and Nepal came to Choqin Monastery to learn the teachings of the Nyingma Sect.

The Nyingma Sect further developed in the 17th century under the patronage of the 5th Dalai. He not only supported the sect's original monasteries, promoting the influence of Dorjezha Monastery and Minchulhin Monastery, but also built in person a new monastery called the Monastery of Longevity Continent for imparting the teachings of the Nyingma Sect. He also ordered the transformation of Lhalung Monastery in Lozha, in the Shannan area, built by Dusting Qenba, the founder of the Khanna Kargyu sect, into a monastery of the Nyingma Sect. Furthermore, the social position of the Nyingma Sect greatly improved at that time. Since the period of the 5th Dalai, the local government of Tibet used to invite Buddhist monks of the Nyingma Sect to practice divination and help them when they encountered war and other turmoil, natural disasters, plague and so on. Therefore, during the time of the 5th Dalai, the influence and development of the Nyingma Sect reached its zenith.

At present, there are altogether 753 Buddhist monasteries of the Nyingma Sect throughout the Tibetan areas of China, second only to the Gelug Sect among all the sects of Tibetan Buddhism. As a sect with the longest history, it has undergone a prolonged historical process of evolution. As we know, a batch of famous monasteries, including Samye monastery in the Tibet Autonomous Region, were built in the 8th century. But this was not enough for the Nyingma Sect, and there were also many other old monasteries in the Tibetan areas. For instance, Master Birocana, one of the fast batch of Buddhist monks in "the first dissemination period of Tibetan Buddhism", went to promote Buddhism to today's Arba Tibetan area of Sichuan province in the 8th century. He did much to propagate Buddhism there: He translated foreign Buddhist scriptures into Tibetan, practiced meditation, imparted Buddhist doctrines to local disciples, and made efforts to build monasteries. Due to his great efforts, the Arba Tibetan area saw a flourishing of Tibetan Buddhism of the Nyingma Sect, with more monasteries than any other sect, a unique phenomenon in areas influenced by Tibetan Buddhism. So, the Nyingma Sect not only has a long history in the Arba Tibetan area, but also great influence there.

In addition, Tubo Buddhism, predecessor of the Nyingma Sect, was introduced in succession into the Diqen Tibetan area of Yunnan province in the 8th century. Although at present the number of the Buddhist monasteries of the Nyingma Sect stands only the third there, it was the place where the sect was first introduced into Tibetan areas.

Tubo Buddhism was introduced into Qinghai Tibetan areas in the 9th century. In 841, when King Lhang Dharma launched a move to suppress Buddhism, three Tibetan Buddhist monks, namely Mar Shakya Yeshi, Yogejung and Tsang Rabsel, fled to the Tibetan areas in the eastern part of Qinghai Province, taking with them many Buddhist sutras on monastic disciplines. They made great contributions to preventing the Dharma from disappearing they lectured on Buddhism and cultivated Buddhist disciple in Gyanzha county of Hongnam Tibetan Autonomous Prefecture and in the Haiton areas, such as Shenho, Holhung. Huzhu, Lhedo, Xining and so on. Many monasteries were built at that time as centres of religious activities, including Dando Monastery and White Horse Monastery. At present, many monasteries of the Nyingma Sect are found throughout the Tibetan areas of Qinghai province, second in number to the Gelng Sect.

The monasteries of the Nyingma Sect mainly cover four provinces: the Tibetan Autonomous Region, with 344 monasteries; Ganzi and Arbe of Sichuan Province, with 262 monasteries; Tibetan areas of Gansu Province, with eight monasteries and Diqen Tibetan area of Yunnan Province, with four monasteries. In terms of time of construction, several monasteries such as Samye Monastery were built during "the first dissemination period of Tibetan Buddhism", while a large number were built dur-ing "the second dissemination period of Tibetan Buddhism". So other sects' monasteries in the course of construction influenced the monasteries of the Nyingma Sect. At present, many monasteries of the Nyingma Sect, whether in terms of construction scale or of monastic institution, can match those of other sects, even of the Gelug Sect – such as Karto, Choqin and White Jade monasteries of the Ganzi area of Sichuan Province, and Samye, Minchulhin and Doijezha monasteries of the Sharman area of the Tibet Autonomous Region.

Karto Monastery located 20 kilometres north of White Jade County of"the Ganzi Tibetan prefecture of Sichuan Province, was a monastery with a long history. It was built by Eminent Monk Gardampa Desheshiba, a disciple of Master Chopuba, one of three master Sois of the Nyingma Sect, in the middle of the 12th century. In its heyday, Karto Monastery occupied an area of 1,000,000 square meters, and had 48 sutra-reciting halls, 42 sutra-debating halls, and 513 residential houses for Buddhist monks. The monastery also had 11 sutra-printing halls; where over 900 Buddhist scriptures in Tibetan or Sanskrit were housed. The most famous buildings were its three Buddha temples'. The first temple housed a bronze stupa from India, with a height of 9.4 meters; the second temple housed a bronze statue of Buddha Sakyamuni, with a height of 8 meters; and the third temple was a tantric temple. In terms of succession of Buddhist teachings and rituals, Karto Monastery imparted what belonged to the Minchulhin School called "Southern Lineage", as well as "the Distant Lineage of Buddhist Scriptures" of the Nyingma Sect. The Abbot of the monastery succeeded under the system of "Reincarnation of the Living Buddha ". Generally speaking, Karto Monastery was an established monastery of the Nyingma Sect, with a large scale, complete equipment and structure. Before the peaceful liberation of 1959, under the patronage of Tusi Dege, Karto Monastery furthered its development and influence and gained higher prestige in the Tibetan areas, leading to ceaseless worshippers going to pay homage. Today, after large-scale reconstruction and renovation directed by the Chinese government, Karto Monastery has resumed its former splendid and is thriving.

In 1675, the White Jade Monastery was built by an eminent monk called Renzengungsam Xirab, near White Jade County of the Ganzi area in Sichuan Province and became another famous monastery of the Nyingma Sect. The monastery is characterized by its teachings and practices of Buddhist sutras and Tantras, which is different from other establishments of the Nyingma Sect. It has some relationship to the teachings and rituals of the Marcangpa subsect of the Pachu Kargyu Sect of Tibetan Buddhism. For instance, although the Abbot of the White Jade Monastery was chosen through the system of Reincarnation of the Living Buddha, they had to go to Dege Barbang Monastery of the Karma Kargyu Sect to receive ordination from Living Buddha Situ. Here it should be explained that Barbang Monastery, the ancestral temple of Tusi Dege, held a special position in the areas of Tusi Dege. So, there had been particular political and cultural background with regard to the phenomenon that the Buddhist teachings and rituals of the Nyingma Sect were merged with that of the Kargyu Sect. Nonetheless, White Jade Monastery has always been regarded as being of the Nyingma Sect, and has many sub-monasteries. Related materials have it that the White Jade Monastery owns over 100 sub-monasteries of the Nyingma Sect in many Tibetan areas, such as the Arba and Ganzi areas of Sichuan Province, Gyamda in the Qamdo area of the Tibet Autonomous Region, Golo of Qinghai Province and so on. So, it is clear that White Jade Monastery is of crucial importance throughout Tibetan areas.

In 1684, the fifth Dalai Lama Arwan Lobsang Gyacho ordered his disciple Baima Renzem, a great scholar and eminent Buddhist monk of the Nyingma Sect, to go to the area of Kam to spread Buddhism. With the support of Tusi Lhinchong and Tusi Dege, Master Baima Renzem constructed Choqin Monastery northeast of Dege. Master Baima Renzem, the abbot of the Choqin Monastery, was posthumously admitted as its first Living Buddha. Thanks to various degree of support from the central government of the Qing Dynasty, local forces and neighbouring countries, Choqin

Monastery rose to become a most famous monastery of the Nyingma Sect in the area of Shikam, with its scale and speed of development and other aspects exceeding that of Karto and White Jade monasteries. Sichuan Province Archives show that, "in the ninth year of King Yongzheng of-the Qing Dynasty (1731), Prince Go came to the area of Kam, and presented 100 statues of gilded Buddha. The third Renboqin, whose mother was Dala's aunt, established a sutra-preaching monastery financed by the forces of Tibet. Bhutan sent its Buddhist monks to study scriptures, and engaged with much money the first Lama of the monastery as its state master. The fifth Renboqin received the donation from Bhutan, and set up a senior sutra-preaching monastery and accommodated those who studied in the monastery without charge. Due to various support and assistance, Choqin Monastery developed with great speed and came to be the most important of the three monasteries of the Nyingma Sect in the Tibetan areas of Sichuan province." The words above show how Choqin Monastery flourished and, meanwhile, Choqin itself did much to contribute to the development of the Nyingma Sect. For instance, in the teachings of Buddhism, it took after what the Gelug Sect had achieved in systematic study of the theory of Buddhist sutras, offering 13 compulsory courses of Buddhist scriptures of the Open School of Tibetan Buddhism, which was equal to the five sutras of that learned in the Gelug Sect. In addition, it taught the works of Master Lhungqin Jamraba and other famous scholars of the Nyingma Sect.

Therefore, the Choqin Monastery came to be the central monastery where teachings of the Nyingma Sect were systematically imparted in the Ganzi, Arba areas, even throughout the Tibetan areas. It even turned into the highest institution for attaining advanced Buddhist knowledge and study Tibetan traditional culture. Before the peaceful liberation of 1959, it housed 500-600 resident monks, and "it seemed that its prestige had surpassed that of the Dorjezha Monastery and the Minchulhin Monastery in the Lhasa areas." "Buddhist monks of the Nyingma Sect from various places went here for study, and among of them included Buddhist monks from Bhutan and Nepal." Therefore, the Choqin Monastery has won high prestige not only throughout the Tibetan areas of the People's Republic of China, but also in neighbouring countries. As far as in the Tibetan areas of PRC is concerned, there are altogether over 100 sub-monasteries of the Nyingma Sect of Tibetan Buddhism, mainly covering the Arba and Ganzi areas of Sichuan Province, and the Yushu area of Qinghai Province.

As the place where Tibetan Buddhism originated and flourished, the Tibet Autonomous Region owned a large number of monasteries of various sects, which was unrivalled throughout the Tibetan areas. As far as the Nyingma Sect is concerned, the Dorjezha and Minchulhin monasteries have exerted great influence not only in the Tibet Autonomous Region, but also throughout the Tibetan areas.

The Dorjezha Monastery was located on the foot of a cliff on the northern bank of the Yarlung Tsangpo River, in Gonggar County of the Sharman area. Seen from a distance, the medium-scale monastery blends well with the cliff, constituting a grand landscape. Dorjezha Monastery was said to have been built by a noble called Zhaxi Dotje whose family had been in decline. Dorjezha, in Tibetan literally means Diamond Cliff, originated from a green stone called Varja naturally produced on the cliff at the back of the monastery, hence the monastery's name.

After its construction, especially owing to the strong support of the fifth Dalai Lama, Dorjezha Monastery developed with great speed. At its height, it housed over 2,000 resident monks, which was rare in the monasteries of the Nyingma Sect. The monastery was destroyed in the Cultural Revolution, and after the third plenary session of the eleventh Central Committee of Communist Party of China (CPC) in 1978, the central government earmarked much money to be used in its reconstruction and renovation. Living Buddha Dorjezha Jambeilobsung, deputy chairman of the Chinese People's Political Consultative Committee (CPPCC) of the Tibet Autonomous Region, and deputy director of Chinese Buddhism Committee, usually went to Dorjezha Monastery to preside over Buddhist activities. At present, the Dorjezha Monastery manages well, and most of its 29 monks are aged between 16 and

30, with only two old monks, respectively aged 71 and 77. All the monks, except one from Renbo County of Xigaze, are natives of Gonggar County. Dorjezha Monastery has a strict institution system. It set up the Democratic Management Commission of the Dorjezha Monastery in charge of its finances, religious activities, and daily affairs.

The commission is composed of one director, two deputy directors and three members, and every one has his responsibility. With regard to its teaching lineage, it calls itself the ancestral monastery of the Northern Lineage of the Nyingma Sect of Tibetan Buddhism, with many sub-monasteries all around the Tibetan areas, especially Sichuan Province.

Dorjezha Monastery has kept close relations with Choqin Monastery, which is in Dege County of the Ganzi area of Sichuan Province. As both of the monasteries belong to the Northern Lineage of the Nyingma Sect, Dorjezha and Choqin monasteries share similar Buddhist teachings, doctrines and religious rituals, and at the same time, they have learned from each other to offset their respective weakness.

At present, in practical use of the Buddhist teachings and rituals, especially grasp of Buddhist knowledge, Dorjezha Monastery lags far behind Choqin Monastery, so the former often engages many eminent monks from the latter as teachers to raise the general standard of religious and cultural knowledge of its monks.

Generally speaking, as one out of two monasteries of the Nyingma Sect with the highest prestige in the Tibet Autonomous Region (the other is the Mincholhing Monastery), Dorjezha Monastery not only has a high reputation among adherents in the Tibetan Autonomous Region, but has also exerted a certain influence throughout the Tibetan area. It is worth noting that the Abbot of Dorj ezha Monastery succeeded according to the system of Reincarnation of the Living Buddha, and the title of Dorjezha Monastery was respectfully called "Renchenginmo Dorjezha Jambeilobsam Gyinmeinamzogyacho". The present Living Buddha is the tenth Living Buddha Rechenqinmo Dorjezha Jambeilobsam, whose rank in the CPPCC of the Tibet Autonomous Region indicates the concern and hope of the Chinese Communist Party and central government towards Dorjezha Monastery.

Mincholhin Monastery, located in Zhache Village of Zhanam County in the Shannan area, was famous for the succession and propagation of teachings of the Southern Lineage of the Nyingma Sect in the Tibetan areas. In was built in 1676 by Master Dedalhiba, who once served as the fifth Dalai Lama's teacher imparting to him the terma (Concealed Treasure) of the Nyingma Sect. Apart from spreading the teachings and rituals of the Southern Lineage, Mincholhin Monastery was celebrated for its study of the "Ten Treatises of Buddhism Doctrines", which covers the whole system of Tibetan traditional culture, including Rhetoric, Worlds and Expressions, Syntax, Drama, Astrology, Technology, Medicine, Grammar, Logic and Philosophy.

It deserves mention that Mincholhin Monastery distinguishes itself from other monasteries of the Nyingma Sect, which tent to emphasize religious practices and meditations while belittling the importance of the study of Buddhist theory. Mincholhin Monastery, particularly, not only attaches great importance to the general grasp of theoretical knowledge of Tibetan Buddhism, but also makes efforts to probe Tibetan traditional culture systematically and has attained great achievements.

Thus, Mincholhin Monastery became a comprehensive university on Tibetan Buddhism, not only probing Tibetan traditional culture but also going beyond the sphere of religious culture. Before the peaceful liberation of Tibet in 1951, innumerable monks from other areas were attracted to Mincholhing Monastery to study because of its reputation, including many officials of local governments who were attracted to learn Tibetan traditional culture.

Therefore, it seems that its contribution to the prosperity and development of Tibetan traditional culture is far greater than the role it played in the development of the Nyingma Sect itself. For instance, the handwriting skill that Mincholhin Monastery achieved was well known. This influenced Tibetan calligraphers over many generations, and greatly furthered the development of the cause of Tibetan calligraphy. In addition, in the 18th to the 19th centuries, there arose many eminent Buddhist monks of the Nyingma Sect who were proficient in the "Ten Treatises of Buddhism Doctrines" and created high achievements in Tibetan traditional culture, which obviously advanced the good environment for studying Tibetan traditional culture that the Mincholhin Monastery had created and advocated.

At present, it has 53 resident monks, with five aged from 45 to 74; and the others ranging in age from 17 to 34. Among them, except for two who are respectively from Chomei and Samri counties, all are natives of Zhanam County. The monastery is managed democratically and composed of a chief director, deputy director and members. It still maintains its advantage in advocating and promoting the good tradition of studying Tibet traditional culture.

The Samye Monastery, as we know, is presided over by the Nyingma, Sagya, and Gelug sects. The guardian halls of the Nyingma and Sagya sects house respectively the sacred guardian deities of the two sects, showing they not only possess their own powers within the monastery, but also take responsibility to protect its dignity and authority. Within the sharing arrangement, there is no priority in terms of religious rituals, which means that each of the three sects has equal rights. Rituals are staged based mainly on a collective decision by followers of the three sects. Therefore, from the viewpoint of the monastery itself, the lines between the sects are definitely blurred.

As is well known, Jokhang is a celebrated monastery of Tibetan Buddhism at home and abroad. In the view of history, Jokhang was among the first batch of temples built during the reign of King Songtsan Gampo, so it can be regarded as of the Nyingma Sect. The Jokhang is listed as one of the national important culture relics under special protection, and it has been rebuilt and renovated many times by the local and central Chinese government. Among the mass followers of Tibetan Buddhism, the Samye Monastery, especially the Statues of Buddha Sakyamuni housed in the temple, has enjoyed a sacred and pre-eminent positions Hence, Jokhang has become a sacred temple dominating the various sects of Tibetan Buddhism, without distinct dividing lines between them. Here it is worth noting that in 1409, Master Tsongkapa, the founder of the Gelug Sect, successfully held in Jokhang the Grand Prayer Ceremony, the largest ever in terms of scale, content and significance, and thereafter, the Gelug Sect has continued the tradition to hold large-scale ceremonies until today. Although the Gelug Sect naturally became the sect managing the daily affairs of Jokhang, because of good timing, geographical convenience and harmonious human relations it developed, nevertheless there is no distinct idea of sects in the Jokhang. Not only are many principal Buddhas and guardian deities worshipped there, but it also has many statues of eminent monks of various sects of Tibetan Buddhism as well as paintings related to them. Around the temple are the halls of various sects of Tibetan Buddhism, packed with worshippers at every season. At any time, every influential sect can hold its religious rituals and activities there. Every year, millions of Buddhist adherents have come to Jokhang to pay homage, along with innumerable disciples and tourists. Although the Samye, Jokhang and Chamzhub monasteries are composite monasteries blending various sects of Tibetan Buddhism, among disciples of the Nyingma Sect, even eminent monks through the generations, share the unswerving view that the three monasteries mentioned above are their ancestral monasteries, which is of great importance to the Nyingma Sect.

Taking a panoramic view of the 700 Buddhist monasteries of the Nyingma Sect, it is not difficult to conclude that the Nyingma Sect has played a crucial role in the field of Tibetan Buddhism. It has a great influence among the mass adherents of Tibetan Buddhism in the Tibetan areas, especially among the common people, which is second only to the Gelug Sect.

THE KARGYU SECT

The Kargyu Sect, one of four most important sects of Tibetan Buddhism, has exerted great influence on it in the Tibetan areas. In Tibetan, "kar" means "statement of Buddha" and "gyu" means "carry forward", hence the name of "kargyu" means "handing Dharma down orally". The sect got its name as it stressed the practice of Tantricism, which was usually passed on orally from teacher to disciple. The Kargyu Sect is also known as the White Sect for the whitestripped robes that its monks always wore. This is seemingly inappropriate, just as History and Doctrines of Different Buddhist Sects states: "Later, some historical works from Bhutan called it 'White Sect Lineage', which came from the tradition that Master Marpa, Master Milarapa and Master Noropa, the three forefathers of the Kargyu Sect, usually wore white robes.

This style hence was handed down from generation to generation, becoming the sect's fashion. But the name of the Kargyu Sect, widely known among Tibetans, seemed to be more appropriate than that of the White Sect, because the former properly reflects its features of oral transmission of its teachings." As the book pointed out, in Tibetan "Kargyu" means "carry down orally", and it also indicates the importance of transmission of its knowledge from teacher to student, so the word "kargyu" is an apprppriate one to reflect its characteristics.

The Kargyu Sect was formed "in the second period of dissemination of Tibetan Buddhism", during which it was founded by Translator and Master Marpa, who was succeeded by the Great Yogi Milarapa and Master Tabo Lhagyi. It was not until the time of Master Tabo Lhagyi that the Kargyu Sect was formally established and attained greatness, however. As is well known, among various sects of Tibetan Buddhism, the Kargyu Sect has the most numerous and jumbled branches. In terms of teaching lineage, despite its numerous and jumbled branches, there is no discernible difference on doctrines and disciplines advocated by each branch, as all can trace their origins to the lineage of Translator and Master Marpa and Master Milarapa. Generally speaking, the sect falls into two lineage, one is called the Tabo Kargyu, founded by Translator Marpa and carried on by Master Milarapa; while the other is known as Shangpa Kargyu, created by Qoinbo Namjor. Later, the Shangpa Kargyu gradually declined and disappeared, while the Tabo Kargyu developed and flourished, developing Four Large Branches and Eight Minor Branches, as well as many other subbranches.

The Shangpa Kargyu was founded by Master Qoinbo Namjor, who was born in 1085. At the age of ten, he began to study Tibetan and Sanskrit. Three years later, he started to learn the Bon religion under a great master of the Bon religion, and then changed to study "the Great Perfection" of the Nyingma Sect. When he attained certain language ability and religious knowledge, Qoinbo Namjor went to Nepal to study Sanskrit and Tantricism, taking a quantity of gold with him. Later, he travelled to India, where he received teaching from many scholars and yogis, including Master Milepa, and mastered the Vajrayana teachings popular in India at that time. When he returned to Tibet, he received monastic ordination under Master Namri Tangba, the eminent monk of the Kardam Sect of Tibetan Buddhism. Thereafter, Master Qoinbo Namjor began to build Buddhist monasteries at Phengyul, north of Lhasa, and then travelled to Shang in the Xigaze area, where he spread the Vajrayana teachings he had mastered and built many Buddhist monasteries in three years. Consequently, Shang became the foundation and centre where Master Qoinbo Namjor spread his teachings and taught disciples.

What's more, his influence quickly expanded around the area. The lineage he founded came to be known as the Shangpa Kargyu. It was said Master Qoinbo Namjor travelled to India to study Tantricism seven times, which indicated he gained his knowledge directly from Indian masters rather than from the lineage of Translator Marpa. So, the disciples and followers of the Shangpa Kargyu maintained an independent lineage, even though it shared similar doctrines and rituals with the Tabo Kargyu handed down from Masters Marpa, Milarapa and Tabo Lhagyi. Anyway, the Shangpa Kargyu, compared with the Tabo Kargyu, the orthodox lineage of the Kargyu Sect, is still one of two important sects among the numerous and jumbled sects of the Kargyu Sect of Tibetan Buddhism.

Here it is worth mentioning that Master Tongdong Gyibo, who was famous for building chain bridges in Tibet in the 15th century, was still regarded as being an eminent monk of the Shangpa Kargyu. It was said that he had built altogether over 100 chain bridges in the region, collecting money mainly by organizing people to perform Tibetan opera. Hence, he enjoyed high prestige among Tibetan people and he was worshipped in forms of statues and Tangka in many Buddhist monasteries. What's more, Many Tibetan historical works agree that many eminent Buddhist monks, including Master Tsongkapa, founder of the Gelug Sect, and his close disciple, also regarded as the first Panchan Gandain Zhuba, once studied from great scholars and translators of the Shangpa Kargyu. Therefore, the Shangpa Kargyu played an important role in the history of Tibetan Buddhism. However, from the 15th to the 16th century, it gradually declined and eventually disappeared.

While the Tabo Kargyu was the only one that not only carried on the teachings of the Kargyu Sect but has also survived until today, it was also considered as the orthodox part of the Kargyu Sect. Therefore, to some degree, the establishment of the Tabo Kargyu marked that the Kargyu Sect had formally come into being.

Master Tabo Lhagyi was the founder of the Tabo Kargyu, which took his title. "Tabo" was a place in the south of the Tibet Autonomous Region, where Master Tabo Lhagyi had made great achievements in his religious cause; "Lhagyi" was a respectful title for a doctor, as Master Tabo Lhagyi started to practice medicine in his youth and gained a certain local reputation. Local people were willing to call him Tabo Lhagyi and this address spread and became his title. Master Tabo Lhagyi had many addresses, such as Mater Niwa Gonggar, his born name, but was also known as Master Soinam Renqen as well as Master Gangpo Par, from the Gangpo Monastery where in his later age he used to reside and spread his teachings.

At the age of 26, he was formally ordained as a Buddhist monk. At first, he studied under Kampus Nordain and other eminent monks from Maryu Bdemchogradorje Tantricism and Vinaya (Buddhist Monastic Disciplines); then, he went to Phengyur, where he studied under Master Gyiayuwa, from whom he systematically studied the teachings handed down from Master Artisa, namely the teachings of the Kardam Sect. At that time, he achieved much in the theory of sutras and Tantras. At the same time, as he felt the importance of meditation, he built a small room near Sarka Monastery to practice meditation under the patronage of his parents. It was said that Master Tabo Lhagyi could maintain his meditation for 13 days unbroken, so as to prevent and destroy any feelings of cupidity and vexation. When he practiced, he slept little, and even after he fell asleep, he could capture the bright light of the Bodhisattva of ten states mentioned in the Golden Bright Sutra. He also ate nothing for five days while meditating. Through this hard way of practice, he perceived the essence of Tantricism and succeeded in attaining the great pleasure stage of Tantricism. It was not until he was 32 years old that Tabo Lhagyi heard of Master Milarapa. Then, he went to the western regions of the Tibet Autonomous Regions to seek him. On his way, he visited several formal masters of the Kardam Sect, who admonished him not to throw away its teachings. After a hard trek, Tabo Lhagyi finally stood before Master Milarapa, the latter immediately perceived his marvelous ability and imparted to him all the secret teachings he owned. Master Milarapa offered Vajra initiation to Tabo Lhagyi, who practiced according to the teachings of his teacher and finally attained success. After this, he received Yoga of the Physic heat, one of six practices of Naropa. All in all, it took 'fabo Lhagyi only 13 month to grasp and digest all the profound Tantricism that Master Milarapa imparted.

Thereafter, in accordance to what Master Milarapa advised and arranged, Tabo Lhagyi went back to the Lhasa area to further the practice of meditation, and three years later, he withdrew from the people and dwelled in secluded places among deep mountains and great gorges. From then on, he began to hold strong belief in the teachings of Master Milarapa, and set about the sacred ways of creating the Tabo Kargyu School of the Kargyu Sect. In 1121, at Talha Gangpo, on the north bank of the Yarlung Zangbo River in today's Tabo area, the master built a monastery (Gangpo Monastery). This became the base from which Master Tabo Lhagyi set out to impart the teachings he had grasped and perceived, cultivating a large number of disciples. His famous work Gradual Ways to Deliverance, written on the basis of Gradual Ways to Enlightenment of the Kardam Sect and Great Scale Teachings by Milarapa, was one of the compulsory courses of Tabo Kargyu. So, it is reasonable that many scholars of later ages held that the Tabo Kargyu merged the teachings of the Kardam into Kargyu sects, one of its characteristics.

Master Tabo Lhagyi presided over the religious affairs of the Gangpo Monastery for over 30 years, until, in 1150, he resigned his position in favour of his niece, Gongba Cechen Nyingbo, who was also the main successor of the Tabo Kargyu. Thereafter, the Abbot of the Gangpo Monastery was always one of descendents of Master Tabo Lhagyi, whose family continued to live and reside there. It is known that after the demise of Gongba Cechen Nyingbo, the Abbot of the Gangpo Monastery succeeded according to the system of Reincarnation of the Living Buddha, so the Tabo Kargyu was regarded as one of several sects taking the lead in developing this system in the Tibetan areas.

Gangpo was famous for Master Tabo Lhagyi, but in the end it failed to form a large-scale monastery. However, the greatest contribution he made was that he cultivated four close disciples who then built monasteries and spread Buddhism in the Lhasa and Xigaze areas. Thus, there came into being four comparatively independent branches of the Tabo Kargyu namely, the Karma, Phachu, Bharong and Chaipa Branches ?C that marked that the Tabo Kargyu, or the Kargyu Sect in a widersense, beginning to enter its prime period of flourishing.

The Karma Branch of the Tabo Kargyu

The Karma Branch is the most influential sect of the Kargyu Sect of Tibetan Buddhism, and it was also the first sect to adopt the Reincarnation System of Living Buddha. What's more, the Karma Branch established in succession several reincarnation systems of Living Buddha, among of which the Black Cap lineage and the Red Cap lineage were the most famous. Thereafter, the Karma Branch was of great importance in Tibetan Buddhism.

It was founded by Master Dustin Qenba, one of four famous disciples of Master Tabo Lhagyi. He was born at Dorkangzhexuegang Gyirewa, and his family was of the clan of Tadong Garpo. His father, Gongba Dorjegongbo, was a' Tantric yogi. At the age of eleven, Dustin Qenba followed his father to learn Buddhist prayers and simple practices of Tantricism. Five years later, he was ordained as a Buddhist monk and was given the ordination name Qoigyi Zhaba by Kampus Cholha Chesengezha of Qoigo Monastery. At the age of 19, he left for the Lhasa area to study Buddhism. At first, he systematically studied under Master Duilhung Gyiamawa and Master Kaba Qoigyisengge Five Sutras by Maitreya, The Middle Way, Buddhist Logic and other basic Buddhist theories, then he went to Master Shiareba and other eminent monks, from whom he studied Gradual Ways to Enlightenment and other teachings of the Kardam Sect.

He also received ordination from Kampus Meiduseng, who taught him Buddhist monastic disciplines. Dusun Qenba moved from one master to another, and in this way he systematically studied comprehensive sutras and Tantras. When he was aged 30, he succeeded in paying a visit to Great Master Tabo Lhagyi, under whom he studied for about three years, and grasped the essence of Tantricism of the Kargyu Sect, especially learning the practice of meditation, in which he attained the best achievements. From then on, he rose to be-come an erudite master of Tibetan Buddhism and shouldered responsibility for promoting the Tabo Kargyu. After he returned home in 1157, at Karma near Dorkhang Changdu Leiwuqi, Master Dusun Qenba established the Karma Lhading Monastery, also known as the Karma Dansa Monastery.

From this base, he tried his best to propagate the teachings of the Kargyu Sect as well as his own teachings. Thus, there came into being the Karma Branch, named after the Karma Lhading Monastery, the first to divide from the Tabo Kargyu. At that time, at Dorkhang, there were altogether over one thousand disciples who followed Master Dusun Qenba, who controlled certain social powers in the area. He exerted great influence on the development of the Karma Branch of Tabo Kargyu, especially in the political and social situation of the Tibet Autonomous Region. For instance, he often mediated in large and important local conflicts, donated large quantities of treasures to the Gangpo Monastery and other monasteries in the Lhasa areas. In his later years, he went back the Lhasa area, and in 1189, he built Chubo Monastery at nearby Duilhung. Thereafter, the Karma Lhading and Duilhung monasteries became two ancestral monasteries of the Karma Branch of the Kargyu Sect of Tibetan Buddhism, while the Chubo Monastery was reconstructed many times and turned out to be the chief monastery of the Karma Branch of the Kargyu Sect.

Master Dusun Qenba died at the age of 83 at the Chubu Monastery he had established, but, before dying, he left an injunction that he would reincarnate, so his reincarnated soul boy should be searched for after his death. It was the great invention of Master Dusun Qenba, pioneering the "Reincarnation System of Living Buddhas" in the history of Tibetan Buddhism and even the whole of Buddhism.

The direct lineage of the Living Buddha system of the Karma Branch of Tabo Kargyu that Master Dusung Qenba created was the Living Buddha later called the "Black Cap Lineage" and also the Abbot of Chubo Monastery. With regard to the title of the Living Buddha of the Karma Kargyu and its origins", History and Doctrines of Different Buddhist Sects has the answer: "Although it was said that Master Dusun Qenba wore a black cap, so that the lineage he created was called 'the Black Cap Lineage', in fact it was from Master Karma Bashi that the lineage gained the title of 'Black Cap Lineage'. The emperor granted Master Karma Bashi a black cap symbolizing his official position." Con-ceming the accounts that Master Dusung Qenba wore the black cap, legend states: "At that time, hundreds of flying Taras weaved a special cap with their hairs and presented it to Master Dusung Qenba, had from then on [he] often wore this special and marvelous black cap." Actually, it is only an imaginary story and the historical record shows it was the second Living Buddha Karma Bashi who attained a black cap. The Black Cap Lineage was named after a black cap with gold edges that the Mongolian Khan Meng Ge bestowed on Master Dusung Qenba. Afterwards, it was handed down to the 17th lineage. Meanwhile, the Red Cap Lineage was named after a red cap with golden edges conferred by the Yuan government. When it was handed down to the 10th lineage, the Qing government banned the Red Cap Lineage because it was accused of involvement in a Gurkha invasion of the Xigaze area. From then on, the lineage of the Red Cap was ended.

Generally speaking, the history of the Karma Branch of the Tabo Kargyu was developed with the two main threads, the Black Cap Lineage and the Red Cap Lineage. So from the course of the two lineages' origination, development, and declination, we can acquire the whole history and current situation of the Karma Branch of the Tabo Kargyu.

BUDDHIST LEADERS

Guru Rinpochhe

Earlier Bhutan was divided into small states ruled by individual feudal lords fighting each other from time to time. Amongst these principalities, Bumthang was one. It was being governed by feudal king named Sendya Gyab. Saying his forefather's kingdom, Nabudara {Nauchhe} of southern Duar attacked the kingdom of Sendya Gyab. During war around an iron castle, the son of Sendya Gyab, Taglamebar was said to have been killed.

This loss brought in Sendya unsatisfaction. He ordered the destruction of all temple and idols. This itching made him seriously ill. When no sign of recovery was seen, messengers were sent to Maratika, Nepal {some say India} with cupful of gold dust. Thus Guru Rinpochhe was invited to Bhutan. He subdued, as Bhutanese records speak, the feudal deities and preached Buddhism reconstructing temples and monasteries. Then Sendya Gyab and his citizens were made the followers of Buddhism, the Nyinmagpa sect. So 'he is regarded as the second Buddha'.

Phajo Drugam Shigpo [1184-1251]

The other distinct Tibetan Lama who came to preach Buddhism in Bhutan was Phajo Drugom Shigpo. He came from Kham, eastern Tibet. He was instructed to preach Buddhisn in Bhutan by Sangye Oendrey, founder of Drukpa School in Tibet. Phajo was educated in Ralung. He entered Bhutan in 1222 AD. Namthars indicate that he had lot of visions of Guru Rinpochhe and was instructed by him as well. With Sonam Palden, he preached Buddhism in Bhutan mostly in northern part. He made the religion recognised in the country and brought the Bhutanese under unity and friendliness.

Kuenga Sengye [1314-1347]

Among the Abbots of Ralung, the seventh Abbot Kuenga Sengye was the first to come to Bhutan. He was said to be invited by great grandson of Phajo Drugom Shigpo. On his visit to Dechenphug in Thimphu valley, it is said that he had subdued the local deity Genyen Jagpa Melan, making him the protector of Buddhist faith. Now the statue of Jagpa can be seen in Dechenphug, regal looking, riding a red horse and holding a sword.

Drukpa Kuenley [1455-1525]

A favourite Drukpa Lam of Bhutan is Drukpa Kuenley, elder cousin of Ngawang Chhoegyal. His preaching in humour and compassion started in Bhutan by 1490. He was a special form of holiness, which has been called 'crazy wisdom' or "devine madness". He is said to be against the monasteries as the priests were in habit of asking everything from the people and the teaching was in slow process. He was with people teaching them through humour, poetry, song, love and dance and in the ways quoted in Namthars. Historians stressed, his teachings tried to show that the spiritual life of a person is tied and bound to his real and everyday life and that through all the different experiences, a person can achieve full enlightenment. Thus his teachings were direct to preach and made lot of people his followers in short period of time.

Ngawang Chhoegyal [1465-1540]

This Abbot of Ralung visited first in 1497 though he visited Bhutan many times. On his visits, he was accompanied by two of his sons and helped him in the construction of temples and monasteries mostly in western Bhutan such as Druk Chhoeding in Paro, Pangri Zampa and Hongtsho in Thimphu and Chhimey Lhakhang in Punakha. His son Ngagi Wangchuk constructed the first Trongsa, Jakar and Lhuntshi Dzongs. All these lamas preach the Drukpa Kagyugpa sect. Amongst the lamas of other sects, Nyingmapas were successful in establishing their influence in Bhutan.

Longchhen Rabjam Drimey Oezer [1308-1363]

Of the Tibetan lamas, most famous and respected Nyingmapa lama, Oezer was one. He was regarded as the Buddhist Scholar. He spent about ten years in Bhutan preaching Nyingmapa Buddhism. On his preaching process, he built a number of temples and monasteries including Tharpaling and Ugyen Chhoeling in Bumthang and Kuenzangling in Kurtoe. He strengthened the Nyingmapa in Bhutan, which was being dominated before.

Pema Lingpa [1450-1521]

The Bhutanese saint who further strengthened the Nyingmapa sect was Pema Lingpa. He was born in Chelwa Rithrang of Tang valley of Bumthang in Iron Horse year. As he had discovered many Ters {treasures} hidden by Guru Rinpocche, he was popularly known as Terton Pema Lingpa. Among his discoveries here is one produced:

Mebartsho lake is said to be in dense forest of Bumthang. There Guru Padmasambhawa (Lotus-born) had buried a casket and prophesied that it will be discovered by a predestined person in future at proper time. Pema Lingpa discovered the treasure.

He preached the Buddhist faith as was instructed in the Spiritual Wisdom. Now his fame as Terton (treasure discoverer) spread not only in Bhutan but also in Tibet. Today his text and secret dances, commissional art etc. are all important cultural treasure of the country. And the Rpyal family of the country is regarded to be the descendents of Pema Lingpa.

These lamas including their many other followers who accompanied them during their visit to Bhutan, have strengthened religious structure but but were not able to establish a fixed and bound administration under one power. Weaknesses of those lamas were that they were not able to establish a concrete network of centralised administration, but it is their toil that Buddhism exists today as the royal cult of Bhutan. Bhutanese Buddhist deities had their counterparts in the Hindu Pantheon. KK Bose saw many similarities between the two religions.

Tibetan Buddhism, with its large influenced areas, various internal sects, large quantity of monasteries and onks, nuns and followers, not only has exerted profound and extensive influence on the fields of politics, the economy, culture and so on, but also made its way into neighbouring nationalities.

Before the peaceful liberation of Tibet in 1951, and even before the Democratic Reform of 1959, Tibet had long been society of feudal serfdom under the despotic religious/political rule of monks and nobles. Tibetan Buddhism dominated the ideology of Tibetan people, and the upper class of Buddhist monks directly engaged in state affairs, which went entirely beyond the normal functions of religion. It was not until the Democratic Reform that Tibet was able to abolish eudal serfdom and launch the necessary religious reforms to achieve a separation of religion and state.

The Chinese government strictly implemented the policy of religious freedom, liberating the masses in the fields of ideology, culture, production and living. Statistics show that, before the Democratic Reform, in the Tibet autonomous region, there were altogether 2,711 Tibetan Buddhist monasteries of various sects, 114,103 Buddhist monks and nuns (including 4000 living Buddhas of the upper class), which accounted for the 10 percent of the entire population.

Other Tibetan areas showed a similar proportion. For instance, in Qinghai Province, there were 722 Buddhist monasteries, 57,647 Buddhist monks and nuns (among them 1,240 living Buddhas); in Sichuan Province, 747 monasteries, 93,700 monks and nuns; in Gansu Province, 369 monasteries, 16,900 monks and nuns (310 living Buddhas); in the Diqin Tibetan Autonomous Prefecture of Yunnan Province, 3,233 monks and nuns, with 34 living Buddhas. The number of monasteries and monks and nuns in the Inner Mongolian and Xinjiang autonomous regions were not included. Altogether, there were 285,583 monks and nuns residing in 4,573 monasteries. With so many people not taking part in production activities, undeniably, they added a heavy economic burden on the local people of the Tibetan areas.

Bibliography

Adikaram, E. W.: *Early History of Buddhism in Ceylon*, Buddhist Cultural Centre, Dehiwala, 1994.

Basham, A. L.: *History and Doctrines of the Ajivikas*, Luzac, London, 1951.

Beal, Samuel: *Buddhist Records of the Western World*, Paragon, London, 1885.

Bhattacharyya, Dipak Chandra: *Studies in Buddhist Iconography*, Manohar, New Delhi, 1978.

Charles S. Prebish: *Buddhism: A Modern Perspective*, Pennsylvania State University Press, University Park, 1975.

Chihara, D.: *Hindu-Buddhist Architecture in Southeast Asia*, E.J. Brill, Leiden, 1996.

Conze, Edward: *Buddhism: Its Essence and Development*, Harper Torchbooks, New York, 1965.

Dehejia, Vidya: *Discourse in Early Buddhist Art: Visual Narratives of India*, Munshiram Manoharlal, Delhi, 1997.

Evers, Hans-Dieter: *Monks, Priests and Peasants: A Study of Buddhism and Social Structure in Central Ceylon*, Brill, Leiden, 1972.

Frank E. Reynolds: *Guide to the Buddhist Religion*, G. K. Hall, Boston, 1981.

Gray, Basil: *Buddhist Cave Paintings at Tun-huang*, University of Chicago Press, Chicago, 1959.

Haldar, J. R.: *Early Buddhist Mythology*, Manohar, New Delhi, 1977.

Jacobson, Nolan Pliny: *Buddhism, the Religion of Analysis*, Feffer & Simons, London, 1974.

Karetsky, Patricia Eichenbaum: *The Life of the Buddha: Ancient Scriptural and Pictorial Traditions*, University Press of America, Lanham, 1992.

Knox, Robert: *Amaravati: Buddhist Sculpture from the Great Stupa*, British Museum Press, London, 1992.

Kvaerne, Per: *An Anthology of Buddhist Tantric Songs*, Universitetsforlaget, Oslo, 1977.

Lamotte, Etienne: *History of Indian Buddhism: From the Origins to the Saka Era*, Institute Orientaliste, Louvain-La-Neuve, 1988.

Law, B. C.: *The Buddhist Conception of Spirits,* Bharatiya Publishing House, Varanasi, 1974.

Michio Takeyama: *The Harp of Burma,* Charles Tuttle, Rutland, 1968.

Morgan, Kenneth W.: *The Path of the Buddha,* Ronald Press, New York, 1974.

Murcott, Susan: *The First Buddhist Women,* Parallax Press, Berkeley, 1991.

Nagao, Gadjin: *Madhyamika and Yogacara: A Study of Mahayana Philosophies,* SUNY Press, Albany, 1991.

Okazaki, Joji: *Pure Land Buddhist Painting,* Kodansha International, Tokyo, 1977.

Powers, John: *Wisdom of Buddha: The Samdhinirmocana Sutra,* Dharma Publishing, Berkeley, 1994.

Ram, Rajendra: *A History of Buddhism in Nepal A.D. 704-1396,* Motilal Banarsidass, Delhi, 1978.

Rawson, Philip: *The Art of Southeast Asia,* Praeger, New York, 1967.

Sarkisyanz, E.: *Buddhist Backgrounds of the Burmese Revolution,* Martinus Nijhoff, The Hague, 1965.

Snodgrass, Adrian: *The Symbolism of the Stupa,* Cornell University Southeast Asian Studies Program, Ithaca, 1985.

Soper, Alexander C.: *Arts of China: Buddhist Cave Temples, New Researches,* Kodansha, Tokyo, 1969.

Sprung, Mervyn: *The Problem of Two Truths in Buddhism and Vedanta,* Reidel, Boston, 1973.

Thanissaro Bhikkhu: *The Buddhist Monastic Code: The Patimokkha Training Rules Translated and Explained,* Metta Forest Monastery, Valley Centre, 1994.

Wagle, Narendra: *Society at the Time of Buddha,* Humanities Press, New York, 1967.

Warder, A. K.: *Outline of Indian Philosophy,* Motilal Banarsidass, Delhi, 1971.

Wijayaratna, Mohan: *Buddhist Monastic Life According to the Texts of the Theravada Tradition,* Cambridge University Press, Cambridge, 1990.

William LaFleur: *The Karma of Words: Buddhism and the Literary Arts in Medieval Japan,* University of California Press, Berkeley, 1983.

Yu, Chai Shin: *Early Buddhism and Christianity: A Comparative Study,* Motilal, Delhi, 1980.

Index

A

Anti-Muslim Laws, 122.
Anti-Muslim Riots, 31, 38, 69, 75, 89, 98, 169, 170.

B

Buddha, 1, 2, 3, 4, 6, 7, 8, 9, 10, 11, 12, 13, 15, 18, 21, 22, 23, 25, 33, 37, 41, 45, 46, 47, 51, 56, 60, 61, 62, 63, 64, 65, 83, 106, 108, 112, 129, 130, 131, 132, 133, 140, 141, 142, 143, 145, 154, 155, 156, 160, 162, 189, 191, 193, 195, 196, 212, 213, 214, 215, 220, 232, 233, 234, 235, 236, 262, 266, 267, 268, 269, 270, 272, 273, 278, 280.
Buddhist Cosmology, 138, 236, 237.
Buddhist Extremism, 115.
Buddhist Militancy, 35, 36.
Buddhist Monastic Groups, 88.
Buddhist Monks, 11, 12, 19, 20, 22, 26, 27, 28, 29, 30, 31, 32, 35, 38, 47, 49, 55, 58, 63, 67, 69, 85, 86, 87, 104, 105, 110, 111, 112, 113, 119, 122, 155, 161, 169, 178, 188, 262, 264, 265, 266, 268, 272, 276, 284.
Buddhist Violence, 20, 33, 36, 39, 72, 182.

C

Ceylonese Riots, 89.

D

Democracy, 20, 21, 49, 50, 80, 114, 121, 122, 123, 159, 160, 166, 167, 169, 174, 181, 186.
Development, 2, 4, 13, 14, 15, 19, 32, 44, 49, 62, 82, 165, 179, 182, 190, 217, 220, 222, 231, 232, 263, 264, 266, 268, 271, 279, 281.
Dharma, 3, 7, 33, 37, 62, 65, 125, 128, 129, 133, 134, 137, 154, 212, 215, 222, 223, 224, 225, 226, 228, 232, 233, 234, 235, 236, 259, 265, 273.

G

Government, 20, 26, 27, 28, 29, 30, 32, 34, 44, 49, 50, 52, 67, 68, 69, 78, 80, 86, 93, 95, 96, 97, 98, 99, 101, 102, 103, 104, 105, 106, 110, 111, 114, 116, 117, 119, 121, 123, 160, 162, 166, 168, 169, 170, 173, 174, 178, 179, 180, 181,

182, 183, 184, 186, 196, 198, 199, 253, 258, 259, 264, 267, 269, 271, 272, 280, 284.

H

Hinduism, 9, 14, 16, 17, 34, 44, 59, 125, 126, 127, 128, 129, 130, 131, 154, 184, 257, 258.

J

Jainism, 9, 21, 126, 127, 129, 132, 133, 134, 135, 209.

K

Kargyu Sect, 267, 273, 274, 275, 276, 277, 278, 279, 280.

M

Mahayana Buddhism, 5, 6, 7, 9, 14, 15, 16, 33, 85, 211, 227.

Mawanella Riots, 96.

Monasticism, 47, 62, 65, 155.

Myanmar Buddhist, 122, 189.

N

Nyingma Sect, 260, 261, 262, 263, 264, 265, 266, 267, 268, 269, 270, 271, 272, 273, 275.

O

Organization, 15.

P

Philosophy of Buddhist, 210.

Policy, 26, 34, 60, 124, 139, 142, 284.

Politics, 25, 29, 44, 49, 165, 168, 171, 184, 283.

Protection, 4, 27, 29, 74, 122, 123, 147, 158, 195, 223, 249, 272.

R

Religious Conflict, 74, 172.

S

Sectarian Violence, 118.

T

Terrorism, 31, 34, 35, 38, 77, 164, 170, 171, 175, 176.

Traditions, 1, 4, 10, 11, 44, 53, 54, 66, 72, 84, 85, 96, 129, 130, 132, 133, 138, 195, 222, 223, 231, 232, 236, 254.

V

Violence, 1, 2, 3, 19, 20, 21, 22, 23, 25, 27, 28, 29, 30, 31, 32, 33, 35, 36, 37, 39, 40, 69, 70, 71, 72, 73, 74, 75, 76, 77, 78, 79, 80, 81, 91, 99, 100, 101, 102, 103, 104, 105, 106, 111, 112, 113, 114, 117, 118, 119, 120, 121, 123, 124, 127, 130, 141, 157, 159, 161, 166, 170, 171, 174, 175, 177, 179, 180, 182, 185, 187, 188, 189, 190, 191, 192, 193, 194, 195, 196, 197, 198, 199, 200, 201, 202, 203, 204, 206, 207, 208, 209, 216, 253.

Violent Buddhists, 104.

❑❑❑